D1623871

OUT OF

THE BEST

BOOKS

OUT OF THE BEST BOOKS

AN ANTHOLOGY OF LITERATURE

VOLUME 4:
THE WORLD AROUND US

Bruce B. Clark and Robert K. Thomas

1968

Published by Deseret Book Company, Salt Lake City, Utah

Library of Congress No. 68-56386

Copyright 1968

by

DESERET BOOK COMPANY

Printed by

DESERET NEWS PRESS

in the United States of America

To the memory of our mothers
and all that they gave us:

Alice Budge Clark
Maud Rencher Thomas

PREFACE

The three volumes of *Out of the Best Books* which preceded this one were conscious attempts to present materials reflecting a wide variety of cultures and countries. In this way we hoped to emphasize the universal meaning of the principles which were being explored. Humility, for instance, has no boundaries, and love knows neither time nor place.

Volume four not only continues to select from world literature, but it also focuses on the smaller if no less overwhelming world of civic and social demand. For most of us, this is the world with which we must cope most directly. We need to understand those who live in different countries, but we must work effectively with those who surround us daily. The themes developed in each section of this text should strengthen Latter-day Saint women in their attempts to influence the circumstances in which they find themselves.

Some of the force of the selections which make up this volume will be lost, however, if they are viewed merely as illustrating a concept or decorating an idea. Great art impels as well as illustrates. Great poetry persuades as well as informs. In the words of a profound sixteenth century critic, Sir Philip Sidney, literature "doth not only show the way, but giveth so sweet a prospect into the way, as will entice any man to enter into it." Expressing truth is only part of the function of good writing, for truth must become operative in lives before it can prevail.

Some of the excitement of participating in cultural refinement lessons should come from noting each author's skill in arousing and directing our responses. While most of us may not develop comparable writing skills, our sensitivity to how the author makes his point can aid us in using the means which are at our disposal to modify situations which need changing.

More often than not a desired change in our circumstances begins with individual reform, for our relationship to the world around us reflects rather accurately our inner world. If our values are shallow or flawed, we will have little success in helping others to establish a sound moral base for their lives. If our personal discipline is at question, we will be ill-prepared to help find answers which bear on community or national problems.

Not only must our lives be exemplary; they must also be dynamic. We hope that we are all involved in the development of growing, maturing attitudes which will help supplant poor taste with good, eliminate vulgarity and grossness in our lives and teach us to discriminate between the momentary and the eternal.

The qualities which this volume examines—discovery, discipline, faith, growth, beauty, persistence, serenity—cut through the frivolous and the faddish to establish a foundation for individual development and social maturity. We *can* change both inner and outer worlds.

Robert K. Thomas
June, 1968

A Note about the Authors:

Bruce B. Clark, who has written sections 1, 3, 5, and 7 of this fourth volume, has been a teacher at Brigham Young University since 1950, where he currently is Professor of English and Dean of the College of Humanities. Widely known as a teacher and educational administrator, he has been listed since 1962 in *Who's Who in America*. After spending the summer of 1967 in Europe, he was invited to return for several weeks in the spring of 1968 to study European education in England, Russia, Czechoslovakia, East Germany, and Denmark under auspices of the Comparative Education Society of America. Within the L. D. S. Church he has held many positions, including service as a bishop twice and as a high councilor three times.

Robert K. Thomas, who has written the preface and sections 2, 4, and 6 of this volume, has been at Brigham Young University since 1951, where he too is a Professor of English and has had a distinguished career as a teacher and administrator. For several years he served as Director of the B. Y. U. Honors Program, then in 1967 became Assistant Academic Vice-President, and in 1968 was appointed Academic Vice-President at Brigham Young University. He too has been a bishop and high councilor in the L. D. S. Church and is currently serving as a counselor in the B. Y. U. Eighth Stake Presidency.

Acknowledgments

Selections under copyright are reprinted by permission and courtesy of publishers indicated below:

Bookcraft, Inc., Salt Lake City: for "The March of Zion's Camp" from *The Long Road* by S. Dilworth Young.

Brandt & Brandt, 101 Park Avenue, New York: for "Nancy Hanks" by Rosemary Carr Benet; and for excerpts from "Ordeal by Handcart" by Wallace Stegner.

Harper & Row Publishers and Norma Millay Ellis: for "On Hearing a Symphony of Beethoven" from *Collected Poems* by Edna St. Vincent Millay, copyright 1928 and 1955; and for the opening nine lines of "Conversations at Midnight," by Edna St. Vincent Millay, copyright 1937 and 1964.

Doris Holmes: for "Talk" by John Holmes.

Houghton Mifflin Company: for "Ars Poetica" by Archibald MacLeish: and for the opening 26 lines of "Lincoln" by John Gould Fletcher.

J. B. Lippincott Company: for excerpts from *Their Mother's Sons* by Edward Strecker, copyright 1946 and 1951 by Edward A. Strecker, M. D.

The Macmillan Company: for "Sight" by W. W. Gibson; for "Cargoes" by John Masefield, copyright 1912 by the Macmillan Company, renewed 1940 by John Masefield; for "Silence" by Marianne Moore; and for "The Balloon of the Mind" by William Butler Yeats.

William Morrow and Company, Inc.: for "Love Poem," from *The Iron Pastoral*, by John Frederick Nims, copyright 1947 by John Frederick Nims.

New Directions Publishing Corporation: for "The River Merchant's Wife: a Letter" from *Personae* by Ezra Pound, copyright 1926 and 1954.

Orbis Publishing House, Prague, Czechoslovakia: for "People and Ants" by Peter Balgha, translated by George Theiner, published in *Seven Short Stories* edited by Libuse Prokopova and Oldrich Benes, copyright 1967.

Oxford University Press: for "Pied Beauty" and "Moonrise" by Gerard Manley Hopkins.

Carol Lynn Pearson: for "Day-Old Child," "Guilt," "Of the Mysteries," "Prayer," "The Lord Speaks to a Literary Debauché Newly Arrived in Heaven," and "To a Beloved Skeptic" from *Beginnings* by Carol Lynn Pearson, published by Trilogy Arts, Box 843, Provo, Utah, copyright 1967.

Random House, Inc., and Alfred A. Knopf, Inc.: for the opening 19 lines of "Apology for Bad Dreams" from *Roan Stallion and Other Poems* by Robinson Jeffers; and for "Early Marriage" from *Early Americana* by Conrad Richter.

Joan Crawford, executrix of the Albert Wetjen estate, for permission to reprint "Command" by Albert Wetjen. Copyright renewed 1953.

TABLE OF CONTENTS

xiii

SECTION ONE

The Excitement of Discovery

by Bruce B. Clark

THE EXCITEMENT OF DISCOVERY

One truth discovered is a link with the immortal. —William Hazlitt

The world in which a person serves is limited only by one's desire to discover. Such a thought becomes even more challenging when we realize that the "world" in which we live is not one world but several—the vast physical world and all its wonders and beauty, the unseen spiritual world and all its powers, the world of people and all their complex types and relationships, the hidden world within each person and all its complexities of feeling and thought, and finally the world of eternal truths and principles that bind all these other worlds into a harmonious unity. Our goal is to discover all these worlds as fully and honestly as possible, to separate the trivial from the significant in what we discover, to direct our lives in harmony with eternal principles, and to give our energies towards making the world better and more beautiful. As someone once said, when we examine the world and all its problems, we should see to it that we are more a part of the solution than of the problem.

When anyone mentions the excitement of discovery, people usually think of looking with their eyes, for sight is the natural beginning of exploring the world. At least it is for most people. And the worth of our eyes as cameras with which to see the detailed wonders of the world is made especially dramatic and poignant whenever we meet one who is blind, as in the following simple poem by the English poet W(ilfrid) W(ilson) Gibson:

Sight

By the lamplit stall I loitered, feasting my eyes
On colors ripe and rich for the heart's desire—
Tomatoes, redder than Krakatoa's[1] fire,
Oranges like old sunsets over Tyre,
And apples golden-green as the glades of Paradise.

------

[1]Volcano on an Indonesian island between Sumatra and Java.

And as I lingered, lost in divine delight,
My heart thanked God for the goodly gift of sight
And all youth's lively senses keen and quick . . .
When suddenly, behind me in the night,
I heard the tapping of a blind man's stick.

Not many people are literally blind, but there is another kind of blindness that is widespread—the blindness that comes from looking without seeing. We are surrounded on all sides with the wonders of nature and people, but how many of us see what we look at? That most people are poor observers can be easily shown not only by almost any interrogation at a court trial but simply by asking someone to close his eyes abruptly and then report what he was looking at before his eyes closed. Arnold Bennett (1867-1931), major English novelist and author of *The Old Wives' Tale*, clearly pointed all of this out in an essay a half century ago:

From "Seeing Life"

Arnold Bennett

In the matter of looking without seeing we are all about equal. We all go to and fro in a state of the observing faculties which somewhat resembles coma. We are all content to look and not see.

And if and when, having comprehended that the role of observer is not passive but active, we determine by an effort to rouse ourselves from the coma and really to see the spectacle of the world . . . , we shall discover, slowly in the course of time, that the act of seeing, which seems so easy, is not so easy as it seems. Let a man resolve, "I will keep my eyes open on the way to the office of a morning," and the probability is that for many mornings he will see naught that is not trivial, and that his system of perspective will be absurdly distorted. The unusual, the unaccustomed, will infallibly attract him, to the exclusion of what is fundamental and universal. Travel makes observers of us all, but the things which as travelers we observe generally show how unskilled we are in the new activity.

A man went to Paris for the first time, and observed right off that the carriages of suburban trains had seats on the roof like a tram-car. He was so thrilled by the remarkable discovery that he observed almost nothing else. This enormous fact occupied the whole foreground of his perspective. He returned home and announced that Paris was a place where people rode on the tops of trains. A Frenchwoman came to London for the first time—and no English person would ever guess the phenomenon which vanquished all others in her mind on the opening day. She saw a cat walking across a street. The vision excited her. For in Paris cats do not roam in thoroughfares, because there are practically no houses with gardens or "areas"; the flat system is unfavourable to the enlargement of cats. I remember once, in the days when observation had first presented itself to me as a beautiful pastime, getting up very early and making the circuit of inner London before the summer dawn in quest of interesting material. And the one note I gathered was that the ground in front of the all-night coffee-stalls was white with eggshells! What I needed then was an operation for cataract. I also remember taking a man to the opera who had never seen an opera. The work was *Lohengrin*. When we came out he said: "That swan's neck was rather stiff." And it was all he did say. . . . He was not mistaken. His observation was most just; but his perspective was that of those literary critics who give ten lines to pointing out three slips of syntax, and three lines to an ungrammatical admission that the novel under survey is not wholly tedious.

But a man may acquire the ability to observe even a large number of facts, and still remain in the infantile stage of observation. I have read, in some work of literary criticism, that Dickens could walk up one side of a long, busy street and down the other, and then tell you in their order the names on all the shop-signs; the fact was alleged as an illustration of his great powers of observation. Dickens was a great observer, but he would assuredly have been a still greater observer had he been a little less preoccupied with trivial and uncoordinated details. Good observation consists not in multiplicity of detail, but in coordination of detail according to a true perspective of relative importance, so that a finally just general impression may be reached in the shortest possible time. The skilled observer is he who does not have to change his mind. One has only to compare one's present adjusted impression of an intimate friend with one's first impression of him to perceive the astounding inadequacy of one's powers of observation. The man as one has learnt to see him is simply not the same who walked into one's drawing-room on the day of introduction.

There are, by the way, three sorts of created beings who are sentimentally supposed to be able to judge individuals at the first glance: women, children, and dogs. By virtue of a mystic gift with which rumour credits them, they are never mistaken. It is merely not true. Women are constantly quite wrong in the estimates based on their "feminine instinct"; they sometimes even admit it; and the matrimonial courts prove it *passim*. Children are more often wrong than women. And as for dogs, it is notorious that they are forever being taken in by plausible scoundrels.

One of the most important gifts of many poets is that they see things sharply and describe them accurately, making simple things become vividly interesting and helping others to "see" things around them that have been there all the time but they have never noticed before. As examples, study the following five little poems by Tennyson, Emily Dickinson, Rupert Brooke, and Bernice Burton Holmes:

The Eagle[2]

Alfred Lord Tennyson

He clasps the crag with crooked hands;
Close to the sun in lonely lands,
Ringed with the azure world, he stands.

The wrinkled sea beneath him crawls;
He watches from his mountain walls,
And like a thunderbolt he falls.

------

[2]Observe with what crisp precision Tennyson (who doesn't write this vividly in all his poems) describes the eagle, the sea beneath, and the plunging of the one to meet the other.

I Like to See It Lap the Miles[3]

Emily Dickinson

I like to see it lap the miles,
And lick the valleys up,
And stop to feed itself at tanks;
And then, prodigious, step

Around a pile of mountains,
And, supercilious, peer
In shanties by the sides of roads;
And then a quarry pare

To fit its sides, and crawl between,
Complaining all the while
In horrid, hooting stanza;
Then chase itself down hill

And neigh like Boanerges;
Then, punctual as a star,
Stop—docile and omnipotent—
At its own stable door.

A Bird Came Down the Walk[4]

Emily Dickinson

A bird came down the walk:
He did not know I saw:
He bit an angle-worm in halves
And ate the fellow, raw.

And then he drank a dew
From a convenient grass,
And then hopped sidewise to the wall
To let a beetle pass.

---

[3]Emily Dickinson (1830-1886) is probably America's greatest poetess. (See p. 93 of Volume 1 of *Out of the Best Books*, pp. 111-112 of Volume 2, and pp. 9-10 of Volume 3.) Note in this poem how vividly she describes the run of an old-fashioned steam-engine railroad train. And note how much better the poem is because its description is imagistic rather than merely literal.

[4]How successful in this poem is Emily Dickinson in changing what would ordinarily be a commonplace or even ugly incident into a genuinely poetic experience?

He glanced with rapid eyes
That hurried all abroad,—
They looked like frightened beads, I thought
He stirred his velvet head

Like one in danger; cautious,
I offered him a crumb,
And he unrolled his feathers
And rowed him softer home

Than oars divide the ocean,
Too silver for a seam,
Or butterflies, off banks of noon,
Leap, splashless, as they swim.

From "The Great Lover"[5]

Rupert Brooke

These I have loved:
    White plates and cups, clean-gleaming,
Ringed with blue lines; and feathery, faery dust;
Wet roofs, beneath the lamp-light; the strong crust
Of friendly bread; and many-tasting food;
Rainbows; and the blue bitter smoke of wood;
And radiant raindrops couching in cool flowers;
And flowers themselves, that sway through sunny hours,
Dreaming of moths that drink them under the moon;
Then, the cool kindliness of sheets, that soon
Smooth away trouble; and the rough male kiss
Of blankets; grainy wood; live hair that is
Shining and free; blue-massing clouds; the keen
Unpassioned beauty of a great machine;
The benison of hot water; furs to touch;
The good smell of old clothes; and other such—
The comfortable smell of friendly fingers,
Hair's fragrance, and the musty reek that lingers
About dead leaves and last year's ferns. . . .

----

[5]Rupert Brooke (1887-1915) was a gifted young British soldier-poet who died of blood poisoning early in World War I. In the passage here quoted, how many of the five senses does he draw upon in reminiscently "describing" the things he loves? Point out specific examples of each.

Rain Song[6]

Bernice Burton Holmes

I shall miss the rain more than the snow.
I shall miss the rain most when I go.
The snow is feathery, deep, and white;
But the rain will talk to me all the night,
The rain will tell what I want to know.
I shall miss the rain most when I go.
Snow is voiceless and does not talk.
Rain will whisper; rain will walk
Upon the roof in dark of night;
Rain will silver the evening light.
I hear the silvery tongues of rain;
They talk to me through the windowpane.
Far off the thunder, dull, aloof;
But rain dances crystal feet on the roof.
I have missed the great white shawls of the snow;
But I shall miss the rain most when I go.

So enchanting is the world of nature made vivid for us by the poets that we are ready to say with A. E. Housman (1859-1936) in one of his little poems from *The Shropshire Lad* that life is too fleeting, even seventy years of it, to drink in all the beauties around us:

Loveliest of trees, the cherry now
Is hung with bloom along the bough,
And stands about the woodland ride
Wearing white for Eastertide.

Now, of my threescore years and ten,
Twenty will not come again,
And take from seventy springs a score,
It only leaves me fifty more.

And since to look at things in bloom
Fifty springs are little room,
About the woodlands I will go
To see the cherry hung with snow.

---

[6]This poem won second place out of 203 poems submitted in the 1961 Relief Society Poetry Contest, a contest conducted annually since 1924. A poem of genuine lyrical loveliness, it too is sharply and musically descriptive—a further example added to several already printed in these volumes of the work of some of our talented L.D.S. writers. The poem was published in the January 1962 issue of *The Relief Society Magazine*, along with a brief biographical sketch of Mrs. Holmes.

Up to this point we have been exploring the excitement of discovery with the eyes and the other physical senses. We all know, however, that there are even greater kinds of discovery. Seeing at its best is more than just seeing with the eyes, even as poetry at its best begins in experience but ends in thought. Or, as Robert Frost once said it better, "A poem begins in delight but ends in wisdom." The end of a poem (a good poem, that is) is therefore not so much an ending as a beginning—as illustrated by Walt Whitman's "When I Heard the Learn'd Astronomer":[7]

When I heard the learn'd astronomer,
When the proofs, the figures, were ranged in columns before me,
When I was shown the charts and diagrams, to add, divide, and measure them,
When I sitting heard the astronomer where he lectured with much applause in the lecture-room,
How soon unaccountable I became tired and sick
Till rising and gliding out I wander'd off by myself,
In the mystical moist night-air, and from time to time,
Look'd up in perfect silence at the stars.

The intent in quoting this poem by Whitman is not to belittle the study of astronomy, or any science. Scientific study is tremendously significant in our modern world. Beyond the factual details of science lie, however—as all first-quality scientists know—the great laws of the universe, and the highest study is contemplation of the eternal principles of the Great Astronomer. Apparently it was something like this that Carlyle had in mind when he said, "Thought without reverence is barren, perhaps poisonous."

If seeing at its best stimulates thinking, so discovery is more than just discovery of the physical world. And one of the richest sources of discovery, as we all know, is the world of books. For the poet's testament, again we turn to Emily Dickinson:

---

[7]For a discussion of Whitman's life and writings, see pp. 284-286 of Volume 2 and pp. 139-141 of Volume 3 of *Out of the Best Books.*

There is no frigate like a book
To take us lands away,
Nor any coursers like a page
Of prancing poetry.
This traverse may the poorest take
Without oppress of toll;
How frugal is the chariot
That bears a human soul!

More extensively Keats[8] also paid tribute to the exciting discoveries that may come through reading books:

On First Looking into Chapman's Homer

Much have I travelled in the realms of gold,
And many goodly states and kingdoms seen;
Round many western islands have I been
Which bards in fealty to Apollo hold.
Oft of one wide expanse had I been told
That deep-brow'd Homer ruled as his demesne
Yet did I never breathe its pure serene
Till I heard Chapman speak out loud and bold:
Then felt I like some watcher of the skies
When a new planet swims into his ken;
Or like stout Cortez when with eagle eyes
He star'd at the Pacific—and all his men
Look'd at each other with a wild surmise—
Silent, upon a peak in Darien.

When Keats wrote this poem he had never been outside England and had traveled very little within England. He had, however, traveled widely in the "realms of gold"—that is, of imagination quickened by reading. He knew the indebtedness poets felt for the great culture of ancient Greece. In particular, he had often been told that in epic poetry ("one wide expanse") Homer, author of *The Iliad* and *The Odyssey*, ruled as the supreme poet. Yet he never appreciated the greatness of Homer as an epic poet until he read an English translation by George Chapman, an Elizabethan poet and translator. Then he tingled with the excitement of a great new discovery, like an

---

[8]For discussions of John Keats (1795-1821) and his poetry, see pp. 22-24 of Volume 1 and pp. 74-76 of Volume 2.

astronomer who has discovered a new planet, or like Cortez[9] when he discovered the Pacific Ocean. Keats, who could not read Greek, spent all one night with a friend reading passages from the Chapman translation, and it opened for him a whole new world of great poetry. Books, great books, can do this, not only for Keats but for everyone —as millions of the world's readers can personally testify.

If we are to know the excitement of discovery throughout our lives and not just in childhood, we must keep an enquiring mind, for curiosity is the beginning of discovery. As the great Joseph Conrad dramatized in his short story "Youth," youth is an attitude of mind more than a scarcity of years. Some people are world-weary in their teens, and others are reaching out, stretching their minds for new ideas and experiences into their eighties and nineties. There is no age at which adventure must stop, as Tennyson suggests in "Ulysses," one of the best of his short dramatic poems:[10]

Ulysses

It little profits that an idle king,
By this still hearth, among these barren crags,
Matched with an aged wife, I mete and dole
Unequal laws unto a savage race,
That hoard, and sleep, and feed, and know not me.
I cannot rest from travel; I will drink
Life to the lees. All times I have enjoyed
Greatly, have suffered greatly, both with those
That loved me, and alone; on shore, and when
Through scudding drifts the rainy Hyades
Vexed the dim sea. I am become a name;
For always roaming with a hungry heart
Much have I seen and known—cities of men,
And manners, climates, councils, governments,
Myself not least, but honored of them all—

----

[9]As students of history will know, it was Balboa, not Cortez, who discovered the Pacific Ocean. Why then did Keats say Cortez? Because the name "Cortez" fit his poetic meter better than "Balboa"? I doubt this. Keats was too skilled a poet not to be able to use "Balboa" as easily as "Cortez." Besides, if anything, "Balboa" is more musical than "Cortez" as a word. I suspect the truth is that Keats was simply confused. He was a better poet than historian. Is the poem then ruined by this factual error? I hope your answer is, "Not very seriously." Unless you are a descendant of Balboa, that is.

[10]For discussions of Tennyson and his poetry, see pp. 476-477 of Volume 1 and pp. 165-166 of Volume 3.

And drunk delight of battle with my peers,
Far on the ringing plains of windy Troy.
I am a part of all that I have met;
Yet all experience is an arch wherethrough
Gleams that untraveled world whose margin fades
Forever and forever when I move.
How dull it is to pause, to make an end,
To rust unburnished, not to shine in use!
As though to breathe were life! Life piled on life
Were all too little, and of one to me
Little remains; but every hour is saved
From that eternal silence, something more,
A bringer of new things; and vile it were
For some three suns to store and hoard myself,
And this gray spirit yearning in desire
To follow knowledge like a sinking star,
Beyond the utmost bound of human thought.
    This is my son, mine own Telemachus,
To whom I leave the scepter and the isle—
Well-loved of me, discerning to fulfill
This labor, by slow prudence to make mild
A rugged people, and through soft degrees
Subdue them to the useful and the good.
Most blameless is he, centered in the sphere
Of common duties, decent not to fail
In offices of tenderness, and pay
Meet adoration to my household gods,
When I am gone. He works his work, I mine.
    There lies the port; the vessel puffs her sail;
There gloom the dark, broad seas. My mariners,
Souls that have toiled, and wrought, and thought with me—
That ever with a frolic welcome took
The thunder and the sunshine, and opposed
Free hearts, free foreheads—you and I are old;
Old age hath yet his honor and his toil;
Death closes all. But something ere the end,
Some work of noble note, may yet be done,
Not unbecoming men that strove with Gods.
The lights begin to twinkle from the rocks;
The long day wanes; the slow moon climbs; the deep
Moans round with many voices. Come, my friends.
'Tis not too late to seek a newer world.
Push off, and sitting well in order smite

The sounding furrows; for my purpose holds
To sail beyond the sunset, and the baths
Of all the western stars, until I die.
It may be that the gulfs will wash us down;
It may be we shall touch the Happy Isles,
And see the great Achilles, whom we knew.
Though much is taken, much abides; and though
We are not now that strength which in old days
Moved earth and heaven, that which we are, we are—
One equal temper of heroic hearts,
Made weak by time and fate, but strong in will
To strive, to seek, to find, and not to yield.

Ulysses, hero of *The Odyssey*, has returned home, an old man, to rule in Greece. But he hungers for new adventures, new experiences. Leaving his kingdom in the hands of his son, Telemachus, he sets sail for whatever unknown adventures may await him in the remaining years before he dies. He wants to die as he has always lived—on the frontier of new adventures. Not everyone can, or should, live as heroically as Ulysses, and certainly Christian readers will not share his pagan view of death. Even so, the robust, courageous, adventure-seeking attitude of Ulysses stands as a symbol of an attractively vigorous approach to life. Not many of us can be Ulysses, but a bit more of Ulysses in most of us would abundantly enrich middle age and old age.

The world around us, waiting to be explored, consists not only of places and books, but also of people, who are more interesting and more important than all other things. I think the most beautiful statement I have ever read concerning the world of people and human inter-relationships was written by the great John Donne (1572-1631)[11] as part of his Meditation 17:

All mankind is of one author, and is one volume; when one man dies, one chapter is not torn out of the book, but translated into a better language; and every chapter must be so translated. God employs several translators; some pieces are translated by age, some by sickness, some by war, some by justice; but God's hand is in every translation, and his hand shall bind up

---

[11] For a brief discussion of Donne and his works, see pp. 455-456 of Volume 1 of *Out of the Best Books.*

all our scattered leaves again for that library where every book shall lie open to one another. . . . No man is an island entire of itself; every man is a piece of the continent, a part of the main. If a clod be washed away by the sea, Europe is the less, as well as if a promontory were, as well as if a manor of thy friend's or of thine own were. Any man's death diminishes me, because I am involved in mankind, and therefore never send to know for whom the bell tolls; it tolls for thee. Neither can we call this a begging of misery, or a borrowing of misery, as though we were not miserable enough of ourselves but must fetch in more from the next house, in taking upon us the misery of our neighbors. Truly it were an excusable covetousness if we did, for affliction is a treasure, and scarce any man hath enough of it. No man hath affliction enough that is not matured and ripened by it and made fit for God by that affliction. . . . Tribulation is a treasure in the nature of it, but it is not current money in the use of it, except we get nearer and nearer our home, heaven, by it. Another man may be sick too, and sick to death, and this affliction may lie in his bowels as gold in a mine and be of no use to him; but this bell that tells me of his affliction digs out and applies that gold to me, if by this consideration of another's danger I take mine own into contemplation, and so secure myself by making my recourse to my God, who is our only security.

The thought that each person is a leaf from the book of mankind that will be bound into a single harmonious volume by the loving hand of God is developed in beautifully metaphorical language. And the "no man is an island" thought is developed with at least equal beauty. Finally, the thought that affliction and tribulation are treasures and we never have enough of them until we are "matured" and "ripened" and "made fit for God" is also both beautiful and profound.

Questions for discussion: (1) What responsibilities of compassion, understanding, and helpfulness are suggested by Donne's "no man is an island" statement? How does this harmonize with our responsibilities as members of the Church, both to other members and to those outside the Church? (2) How can we be "matured" and "ripened" and "made fit for God" by affliction and tribulation?

The preceding passage by John Donne not only points up the inter-linking of human lives but also illustrates another kind of discovery that we wish to emphasize in this section—the discovery of truth that literature can give. To be more accurate, the writer of literature doesn't really "discover" truth, for truth is eternal, and all of us are surrounded with it in experience and observation all our lives. The writer, however, especially the poet, puts these "truths" in remembrable phrases so that others can say, "How true! I wish I had said that." As Alexander Pope observed in "An Essay on Criticism":

> True wit is nature to advantage dressed,
> What oft was thought, but ne'er so well expressed;
> Something, whose truth convinced at sight we find,
> That gives us back the image of our mind.

Almost everything that we have included in these four volumes also illustrates how literature "discovers" and expresses truth, but as further examples here are three tiny poems:

From "Grace of the Way"

Francis Thompson[12]

> Now of that vision I, bereaven,
>   This knowledge keep, that may not dim:
> Short arm needs man to reach to Heaven,
>   So ready is Heaven to stoop to him.

Epitaph on an Ohio Tombstone

> Under this sod and beneath these trees
> Lies the body of Solomon Pease.
> He's not here, just his pod;
> He shelled out his soul and went up to God.[13]

---

[12]For a discussion of Thompson's life and poetry, see pp. 348-351 of Volume 1.

[13]Etheline Taylor of Lakeview, Utah, came across this charming epitaph when doing research in the Salt Lake Genealogical Library. Although metrically uneven in its fourth line, the quatrain nevertheless expresses in startlingly picturesque language a fundamental religious truth.

Prayer

Carol Lynn Pearson[14]

This radio set
Called prayer
Is designed
For remarkably
Simple repair.
When the lines fail,
There is no doubt
Which half
Of the set
Is out.

---

[14]Carol Lynn Pearson is a gifted young L.D.S. poet. For several further examples of her poetry and for some comments on her life and writing, see pp. 82-83 of this volume.

Introduction to "The Buried Life"

As one more example of man's search for discovery we turn to "The Buried Life" by Matthew Arnold.[15] In this beautifully melancholy poem we find Arnold groping for discovery in three directions:

First, a yearning for better communication, better understanding between people. Arnold realized that even people who are very close, even people who love each other, even husbands and wives, sometimes have difficulty communicating their inmost selves. "Alas! is even love too weak/To unlock the heart, and let it speak?" he asks. "Are even lovers powerless to reveal/To one another what indeed they feel?" He pleads for more understanding, more communication in complete harmony, confidence, and trust by those who love.

Second, Arnold yearns for a better understanding of self. Not only do we have trouble communicating with and understanding others, but also we have trouble understanding ourselves. Hidden deep within each of us are the complexities of personality and the mysteries of soul. Arnold feels keenly a need to surmount the essential loneliness of each person's isolated existence, and he realizes that the first step is to discover and know one's self. Even as it is almost impossible to know another person fully so it is almost impossible to know one's self fully—but we need to try.

Third, Arnold expresses a groping desire to look deep within to find the ultimate meaning and nature of life itself, the "buried stream" of humanity—"to know whence our lives come and where they go." Arnold felt an eternalness in the flow of human life from generation to generation and from civilization to civilization even though his faith was troubled by the philosophical problems of his day. And as he looked at the history of the world, he saw culture and religion working towards the same end—the perfection of man, as the following passage from his book *Culture and Anarchy* indicates:

Culture is then properly described . . . as having its origin in the love of perfection. . . . And religion, the greatest and most important of the efforts

---

15For a discussion of Matthew Arnold and his famous poem "Dover Beach," see pp. 246-247 of Volume 3. Arnold (1822-1888) was a great poet, essayist, humanist, and social-literary critic of Victorian England.

by which the human race has manifested its impulse to perfect itself—religion, that voice of the deepest human experience—does not only enjoin and sanction the aim which is the great aim of culture, the aim of setting ourselves to ascertain what perfection is and to make it prevail; but also, in determining generally in what human perfection consists, religion comes to a conclusion identical with that which culture . . . likewise reaches. Religion says: *The kingdom of God is within you;* and culture, in like manner, places human perfection in an *internal* condition. . . . Not a having and a resting, but a growing and a becoming, is the character of perfection as culture conceives it; and here, too, it coincides with religion. . . . The pursuit of perfection, then, is the pursuit of sweetness and light. He who works for sweetness and light, works to make reason and the will of God prevail. Culture . . . is not satisfied till we *all* come to a perfect man; it knows that the sweetness and light of the few must be imperfect until the raw and unkindled masses of humanity are touched with sweetness and light.

The Buried Life

Matthew Arnold

Light flows our war of mocking words, and yet,
Behold, with tears mine eyes are wet!
I feel a nameless sadness o'er me roll.
Yes, yes, we know that we can jest,
We know, we know that we can smile!
But there's a something in this breast,
To which thy light words bring no rest,
And thy gay smiles no anodyne.
Give me thy hand, and hush awhile,
And turn those limpid eyes on mine,
And let me read there, love! thy inmost soul.

Alas! is even love too weak
To unlock the heart, and let it speak?
Are even lovers powerless to reveal
To one another what indeed they feel?
I knew the mass of men concealed
Their thoughts, for fear that if revealed
They would by other men be met
With blank indifference, or with blame reproved;
I knew they lived and moved
Tricked in disguises, alien to the rest
Of men, and alien to themselves—and yet
The same heart beats in every human breast!

But we, my love!—doth a like spell benumb
Our hearts, our voices?—must we too be dumb?

Ah! well for us, if even we,
Even for a moment, can get free
Our heart, and have our lips unchained;
For that which seals them hath been deep-ordained!

Fate, which foresaw
How frivolous a baby man would be—
By what distractions he would be possessed,
How he would pour himself in every strife,
And well-nigh change his own identity—
That it might keep from his capricious play
His genuine self, and force him to obey
Even his own despite his being's law,
Bade through the deep recesses of our breast
The unregarded river of our life
Pursue with indiscernible flow its way;
And that we should not see
The buried stream, and seem to be
Eddying at large in blind uncertainty,
Though driving on with it eternally.

But often, in the world's most crowded streets,
But often, in the din of strife,
There rises an unspeakable desire
After the knowledge of our buried life;
A thirst to spend our fire and restless force
In tracking out our true, original course;
A longing to inquire
Into the mystery of this heart which beats
So wild, so deep in us—to know
Whence our lives come and where they go.
And many a man in his own breast then delves,
But deep enough, alas! none ever mines.
And we have been on many thousand lines,
And we have shown, on each, spirit and power;
But hardly have we, for one little hour,
Been on our own line, have we been ourselves—
Hardly had skill to utter one of all
The nameless feelings that course through our breast,
But they course on forever unexpressed.
And long we try in vain to speak and act

Our hidden self, and what we say and do
Is eloquent, is well—but 'tis not true!
And then we will no more be racked
With inward striving, and demand
Of all the thousand nothings of the hour
Their stupefying power;
Ah yes, and they benumb us at our call!
Yet still, from time to time, vague and forlorn,
From the soul's subterranean depth upborne
As from an infinitely distant land,
Come airs, and floating echoes, and convey
A melancholy into all our day.

Only—but this is rare—
When a beloved hand is laid in ours,
When, jaded with the rush and glare
Of the interminable hours,
Our eyes can in another's eyes read clear,
When our world-deafened ear
Is by the tones of a loved voice caressed—
A bolt is shot back somewhere in our breast,
And a lost pulse of feeling stirs again.
The eye sinks inward, and the heart lies plain,
And what we mean, we say, and what we would, we know.
A man becomes aware of his life's flow,
And hears its winding murmur; and he sees
The meadows where it glides, the sun, the breeze.

And there arrives a lull in the hot race
Wherein he doth forever chase
That flying and elusive shadow, rest.
An air of coolness plays upon his face,
And an unwonted calm pervades his breast.
And then he thinks he knows
The hills where his life rose,
And the sea where it goes.

People and Ants[16]

Peter Balgha

The hot air quivered and the paving-stones threw back waves of heat at passers-by. A man was kneeling in the shadow of the monument, his shoulders hunched as he stared fixedly at the ground. The children abandoned their wet sand castles and approached him, full of curiosity.

"Well, of all the disgusting things!" fumed one of the mothers. "Drunk in the middle of the day, in this heat." The red of her dress was loud in the sun.

"Oh, but perhaps he's ill," said another pityingly.

"He's tight, that's what he is." The ample bosom shook indignantly under the transparent red material. "Sozzled. I know the likes of him!"

The women's laughter quickly fizzled out in the torrid air. The bulky figure in the red frock turned towards an approaching police sergeant.

"I call this disgusting!" she cried. "Our children having to look at drunks making a spectacle of themselves!"

The sergeant got her message. He went up to the kneeling man and tapped him on the shoulder.

"Now then, get up! You ought to be ashamed of yourself! In broad daylight, too!"

The man looked up at him with astonished, sober eyes. Then he glanced down at the pavement again.

"Didn't you hear what I said? Get up!" The sergeant's voice grew stern. "What do you think you're doing?"

"There are ants here," said the man without moving.

Nonplussed, the sergeant looked down as well. A procession of minute black bodies was marching along there. An endless procession.

"Well, and what about them?"

"They're moving house," the man replied. "The whole tribe is moving. They must have met with some misfortune. See this multitude? It's an entire ant-hill."

"Well, and so what?" asked the sergeant without interest, treating the man to a look full of suspicion.

"Have you ever seen a whole ant-hill on the march?"

The sergeant said nothing.

"It's a very rare occurrence, you know. They're running away from some catastrophe, and on their way they've run slap into the city. Have you ever seen ants on the pavement? I haven't."

The sergeant waved his hand, but the man went on before he could say anything:

---

[16]Translated by George Theiner.

"I don't mean one or two, you see. Those you can always drop out of vegetables or a bunch of flowers. But a whole ant-hill on the march . . . I've certainly never seen *that* before."

Now the man and the sergeant were no longer alone. Curious people can always be found, even in seemingly deserted places. The children stopped fidgeting and looked on. The red frock flashed in the sun above the kneeling man.

"Have you ever tried to dig up an ant-hill? Right from the bottom, I mean? The ants will come swarming out, and in a couple of days they will have put it to rights again. These were probably taken by surprise by a fire or something. I once saw large forest ants on the move. An oil plant had been put up next to their ant-hill. I suppose they didn't like the smell of it. But for ants to march like this through a city. . . ."

Someone's leg drew near the swarm. A bureaucratic leg.

"Look out!" the man warned its owner. "You'll tread on them if you're not careful."

"Seeing pink elephants, eh?" exclaimed the bureaucrat, drawing back.

"Yes, yes, that's it—delirium tremens!" the woman in red concurred eagerly.

"Oh, shut up, will you!" said another voice. The man gave a smile in its direction. "This is very interesting. Go on, tell us more about them."

"What for?" grumbled the bureaucrat. "Listening to all this tripe about ants!"

"Well, nobody's keeping you, are they?" said the voice.

The bureaucrat stiffened.

"There's room enough in the street for us all, I should hope."

"The ant-hill is a maze of passageways," the kneeling man explained. "A huge underground city. All you can see above is the roof. The architecture is colossal. Something like the old Incas and Aztecs used to have on a much larger scale."

The bureaucrat's high-pitched laughter rose higher and higher.

"I once read a book about ants. *The Small Versus the Big* it was called, or something of that sort," confided another voice. It belonged to a tall fellow in a faded green shirt. "I thought it was just a lot of fairy-tales. It said something about a city, too. . . ."

The bureaucrat went on pretending laughter.

"Well, some of it may well be a fairy-tale," said the man on the ground. "But their ant-hills are all built in exactly the same way, everything is where it should be. It makes you think, doesn't it? Just insects, you might say, yet look what they're capable of."

"Oh, rot!" exclaimed the woman in red, taking her little boy by the hand. He held back. "It's a sin, that's what it is, messing about with a heap of earth like this." Her eyes met the level blue gaze of the kneeling man.

Her shiny double chin quivered. "I'm not blaming anyone, am I?" she added.
"Some people make a fuss about bees, others about ants. What do I care—
but at least bees give honey." She felt that people were looking at her; there
was silence. "Still, I suppose it's better than collecting stamps," she conceded.
"That's what my brother-in-law does. I ask you, collecting stamps. . . ."

"Amazing," exclaimed the man in the faded green shirt. "It's incredible,
isn't it. Almost as if these creatures could think."

The bureaucrat turned to the woman in red.

"I wonder what he'll say to that."

"Well, not quite perhaps," said the man on the ground, smiling. "But
they're perfect of their kind, and we're frequently baffled by them."

Five people now knelt on the hot paving-stones. The woman in red
took up a squatting position next to them and, breathing hard, followed the
strange procession with her eyes.

"These are the nurses," said the man. "They look after the new generation."

"Sort of a kindergarten, eh?" trilled the bureaucratic falsetto.

"Yes, if you like. A sort of kindergarten."

The ants were dragging along white eggs so large that they could hardly be
seen under them. Small-bodied ants with huge heads scurried forward by the
side of the caravan.

"And what are these?" asked the man in the faded green shirt.

"Well, you might call them the ant police. They're responsible for the
safety of the tribe. The differentiation begins in the egg. Every group has
its exact tasks to perform. And their bodies are shaped accordingly."

The young man might have been about twenty-two, and he wore a crew
cut. The girl had a beehive hair-do. They were embracing, but nobody took
any notice, so intent were they all on the ants.

"You know him?" the girl asked.

"He's a local character," replied the young man. "A writer. Writes
about animals—weasels, does, hamsters. . . ."

"Oh, a colleague of ours, then," said the girl, and laughed.

"A writer?" drawled the bureaucrat, suddenly wiping the sneer off his
face. "Now I understand. You're a writer too, I take it?"

"Well, that depends. Not been published yet, you know. Only in
magazines. . . ."

But the bureaucrat was not listening any more, whispering instead to
the woman in red:

"He's a writer." And he bent down to look at the ants.

"A monarchy with a rigid disciplinary code," the man was saying.

The bureaucratic voice squealed with enthusiasm: "Would you believe it!"

"He once took me to look at an ant-hill. There were two ants wandering
about there, and he said they were drunken pensioners," the young man told

his girl. "He said they intoxicated themselves on the fermented secretion of green-flies."

"And were they really drunk?"

The young man tapped his forehead significantly.

"Don't be silly! Trying to make out that ants behave like people. He's nuts about them. I bet he doesn't even hear what I'm saying."

"To think that there still are people like him," said the girl. "Why haven't you ever mentioned him?"

"Whatever for? Writing about animals in the space age! Probably he's about to launch a novel on ant psychology."

"Yes, you've guessed it," said the man. "Or perhaps not really guessed, because I believe I told you as much myself."

"You did?" wondered the young man, trying to look nonchalant.

"Yes, that's right. Vercors wrote about beavers—you read that and didn't think it absurd. You even found it enlightening. But, of course, I know—that's Vercors. . . . He's a writer after your own heart. . . ."

Bringing up the rear of the endless procession was a troop of ants without any burdens.

"Are they police, too?"

"Just a second," said the man, turning again to the young fellow. "While we're on the subject of space flights. . . . To be able to conquer space we must have knowledge. And ants are a part of that knowledge; they, too, belong to our world. People like Bradbury know that very well, so does Lem. You haven't grasped it yet. . . . Perhaps you'll write something about astronauts, but you'll be writing as a beginner." He turned back to the man in the faded green shirt. "What was it you were asking?"

"If these were also policemen."

"Demagogy, that's what it is," muttered the young man.

"They're warriors," explained the man. "Notice their large mandibles."

"What do ants need an army for?" enquired the bureaucratic falsetto. "Surely they don't wage wars?"

"When two tribes come up against one another, hundreds of thousands of ants get killed," said the man.

The young man was quick to ridicule him:

"Then they say wars are not inevitable!"

The man's face was tranquil. Slowly he got to his feet and carefully brushed his knees.

"Ants are perfect insects," he said, "but we are human beings."

The last black specks vanished from sight at the end of the shadow thrown by the monument.

Discussion of "People and Ants"

"People and Ants" is the first story by a Czechoslovakian author
to be included in the *Out of the Best Books* series. The author, Peter
Balgha, was born in 1935 in Dolny Kubin, a town in Slovakia, the
eastern province of Czechoslovakia. Early in World War II his father
was executed as a political prisoner by the Nazis, and Peter, then
a little boy, was imprisoned with his mother in the Nazi concentra-
tion camp at Terezin. However, he survived this ordeal and, after
the war, became a professional drama student and writer, producing
television dramas and short stories. Although only 33 years old, he
has already published two volumes of short stories: *House for the
Living* in 1962 and *The Quiet You Left Behind You* in 1964. As
Ervin Hrych, one of the leading Czechoslovakian literary critics, has
said, Balgha's stories "explore the thoughts and emotions of contemporary people with a sensitive understanding of wider psychological and social problems."

On the surface "People and Ants" is a relatively simple story
about the world of ants, but it also has deeper implications. In fact,
it is not really so much about ants as about people. Observe, for
one thing, the different reactions of the various people when they
see the strange man on his knees: (1) the children, who are immediately curious and interested; (2) the large woman in the red dress,
who at first loudly accuses the man of drunkenness but gradually
grows interested in spite of herself; (3) the gruff police sergeant,
dutifully official and indifferent; (4) the pompous bureaucrat, who
abruptly changes his attitude as soon as he learns that the kneeling
man is "a *writer*"; (5) the tall man in a faded green shirt, filled
with awed interest from the beginning; (6) the young girl and her
smart-alecky boy-friend, who thinks of himself as also a writer.

Beyond just letting us observe these different reactions, the
story likewise plunges us into thought from time to time as in our
minds we compare the warring ants and their "civilization" with
the warring human nations and our "civilization." What, for example, are the implications of the following comment at the end of
the story? "Ants are perfect insects, but we are human beings." Have

people with their "higher intelligence" solved their international problems better than the ants?

Our reason for including "People and Ants" in this section on "The Excitement of Discovery" is that the story illustrates the wonder of the world around us once we start to look at things—really look, that is. Ants on a city street! What could be interesting about them? But as the story unfolds they become very interesting indeed, not only for some of the people in the story but also, and especially, for us as readers. This is a simple story, but it moves with delight and leaves us thinking. It also does what Arnold Bennett advised early in this section: it turns miscellaneous details into correlated meaning.

SECTION TWO

The Power of Discipline

by Robert K. Thomas

"Chestnut Trees"
by Paul Cezanne (1839-1906), French (Minneapolis Institute of Arts)

Commentary by
Floyd E. Breinholt, Associate Professor of Art, Brigham Young University

Each style of art had its inventor. Each artist believed implicitly in the importance of the truth for which he was searching. Each tenaciously clung to his concept—sometimes at great personal expense in other areas of his life. It has been said that great revolutionary leaders are men with a single and simple idea, and it is the very persistency and discipline with which they pursue this idea that endows it with power. Paul Cezanne was one of these.

In spite of his great desire to have his work accepted by the officials of the art world, and the public who rejected and often ridiculed it, he gave up trying to be accepted and pursued his single idea the rest of his life in semi-seclusion. Herbert Read, well known art critic, described this single idea as follows:

> There is no doubt that what we call the modern movement in art begins with the single-minded determination of a French painter to see the world objectively. There need be no mystery about this world: what Cezanne wished to see was the world, or that part of it he was contemplating, as an object, without any intervention either of the tidy mind or the untidy emotions. His immediate predecessors, the Impressionists, had seen the world subjectively—that is to say, as it presented itself to their senses in various lights, or from various points of view. Each occasion made a different and distinct impression on their senses, and for each occasion there must necessarily be a separate work of art. But Cezanne wished to exclude this shimmering and ambiguous surface of things and penetrate to the reality that did not change, that was present beneath the bright but deceptive picture presented by the kaleidoscope of the senses.

Cezanne believed that even though each brick and timber in a piece of architecture is important in its construction it is the building as a whole we see. Likewise, in a painting each part must contribute to the whole. He thought that in all nature—the landscape, the still life, and the human figure, there is reality which exists in substance and is more than surface. He tried to get away from the decorative element and present what was real. His struggle to do this was often very frustrating and he destroyed many of his paintings to try again and again.

In the painting "Chestnut Trees at Jas de Bouffan" you sense that the artist was struggling with technical difficulties—that it was not easy. You notice how he broke up the surface into separate independent colors. These in turn serve to build an architectural structure which gives the appearance of solidity—of existing in space —of being real, a generalization about nature rather than a literal reproduction of nature.

THE POWER OF DISCIPLINE

*"A stern discipline pervades all nature, which is a little cruel that it may
be very kind."*
                                                              —Edmund Spenser

It is probably revealing—if not comforting—to admit that
discipline awakens memories of correction or even punishment in
many minds. The teacher who is a "good disciplinarian" maintains
tight control of his class, and "military discipline" too often suggests
order that is enforced by rigid regulation. To be undisciplined is to
throw off all external restraint. Yet external restraints are rarely dis-
carded if internal guides remain strong and meaningful.

As any successful teacher can testify, rigidly enforced order in
the classroom may teach a child to hate school more effectively than
it teaches him arithmetic. And any soldier who has felt the *esprit de
corps* that men united in a cause can generate knows that he can
willingly subject himself to the most rigorous control.

That which gives discipline significance is commitment, and
commitment is always internal. As the quotation which precedes this
section suggests, all nature conspires to help us discipline ourselves.
But discipline must carry more than a negative connotation, a suggestion of external restraint, if it is to be a truly developing attribute.
Until we can control our thoughts and actions because of a basic
moral imperative, a deeply felt conviction that some values are far
more important than others, we will never experience the positive
meaning of discipline.

In the selections which make up this section, there are manifestations of control which are both external and internal, but emphasis is
given to discipline which is the result of moral choice. In Yeats'
"The Balloon of the Mind" we see a man subjecting himself to
intellectual discipline. In the paragraphs from *Nature* we experience
with Emerson the developing awareness of how much our total
environment provides direction if we are sensitive to its promptings.
Whittier's "Abraham Davenport" gives an impressive picture of a

man who achieves that participation in yet triumph over his surroundings which Emerson has just described.

"The Character of a Happy Life" celebrates the well being which self-control alone can promise, and "The Death of Socrates" provides a classic example of that promise fulfilled. The final two selections, "Command" by Wetjen and "Ordeal by Handcart" by Stegner give extended treatment to discipline which is based on secular and sacred ideals.

As we read the above selections it will be evident that discipline easily shades into courage, responsibility, devotion, faith, steadfastness and serenity. Perhaps its distinctive contribution is an emphasis upon conscious choice. The disciplined man or woman has not simply become involved in a situation needing courage and then groped within himself until he found that courage. There should be no note of desperation in discipline. His basic, deliberate choices have prepared the disciplined person for whatever happens to him.

The Balloon of the Mind

William Butler Yeats

Hands, do what you're bid:
Bring the balloon of the mind
That bellies and drags in the wind
Into its narrow shed.

Discussion of "The Balloon of the Mind"

For a brief biography of William Butler Yeats (1865-1939) see volume two of *Out of the Best Books*, where his celebrated "A Prayer for My Daughter" was discussed. "The Balloon of the Mind" is not one of Yeats' better known poems. Perhaps its very size makes it easy to overlook. Yet by the time this poem was written there was beginning to be an unmistakable change in Yeats' poetry. The romantic aura that had surrounded much of his early work was being dispelled by a passionate involvement in politics. Apparently he was beginning to feel that a practical concern for Irish liberty took precedence over a dreamy interest in Irish folklore. But disciplining a mind that had been at home in the fairyland of Irish myth to operate skillfully in the real world of political tactics proved to be unusually difficult. The cryptic injunction of this little poem suggests how taxing it was to keep his mind focused on immediate problems.

We needn't share Yeats' personal dilemma to share his problem. Many of us, for instance, did not forego a childish attention span when we became adults. If you have difficulty in giving a speaker an attentive hearing, if you find your mind wandering when you are trying to study or if you find yourself restless at a concert, at least one of your problems is mental discipline. The physical image that Yeats uses—the "hands" that must reel in the balloon—is aptly descriptive of the physical effort that is necessary to keep your mind focused on the matters that should be holding your attention.

Finally, of course, the problem is one of will. We often speak of those whose skill or personality keep us watching or listening to them raptly. The real test, however, is not whether someone or something can gain and keep our attention but whether we can *give* attention to that which deserves it.

"Discipline" from Nature

Ralph Waldo Emerson

In view of the significance of nature, we arrive at once at a new fact, that nature is a discipline. This use of the world includes the preceding uses, as parts of itself.

Space, time, society, labor, climate, food, locomotion, the animals, the mechanical forces, give us sincerest lessons, day by day, whose meaning is unlimited. They educate both the Understanding and the Reason. Every property of matter is a school for the understanding,—its solidity or resistance, its inertia, its extension, its figure, its divisibility. The understanding adds, divides, combines, measures, and finds nutriment and room for its activity in this worthy scene. Meantime Reason transfers all these lessons into its own world of thought, by perceiving the analogy that marries Matter and Mind.

1. Nature is a discipline of the understanding in intellectual truths. Our dealing with sensible objects is a constant exercise in the necessary lessons of difference, of likeness, of order, of being and seeming, of progressive arrangement; of ascent from particular to general; of combination to one end of manifold forces. Proportioned to the importance of the organ to be formed, is the extreme care with which its tuition is provided,—a care pretermitted in no single case. What tedious training, day after day, year after year, never ending, to form the common sense; what continual reproduction of annoyances, inconveniences, dilemmas; what rejoicing over us of little men; what disputing of prices, what reckonings of interest,—and all to form the Hand of the mind;—to instruct us that "good thoughts are no better than good dreams, unless they be executed!"

The same good office is performed by Property and its filial systems of debt and credit. Debt, grinding debt, whose iron face the widow, the orphan, the sons of genius fear and hate;—debt which consumes so much time, which so cripples and disheartens a great spirit with cares that seem so base, is a preceptor whose lessons cannot be foregone, and is needed most by those who suffer from it most. Moreover, property, which has been well compared to snow,—"if it fall level to-day, it will be blown into drifts tomorrow,"—is the surface action of internal machinery, like the index on the face of a clock. Whilst now it is the gymnastics of the understanding, it is hiving in the foresight of the spirit, experience in profounder laws.

The whole character and fortune of the individual are affected by the least inequalities in the culture of the understanding; for example, in the perception of differences. Therefore is Space, and therefore Time, that man may know that things are not huddled and lumped, but sundered and individual. A bell and a plough have each their use, and neither can do the office of the other. Water is good to drink, coal to burn, wool to wear; but wool cannot be drunk, nor water spun, nor coal eaten. The wise man shows his wisdom in separation, in gradation, and his scale of creatures and of merits is as wide as nature. The foolish have no range in their scale, but suppose every man is as every other man. What is not good they call the worst, and what is not hateful, they call the best.

In like manner, what good heed Nature forms in us! She pardons no mistakes. Her yea is yea, and her nay, nay.

The first steps in Agriculture, Astronomy, Zoology (those first steps which the farmer, the hunter, and the sailor take), teach that Nature's dice are always loaded; that in her heaps and rubbish are concealed sure and useful results.

How calmly and genially the mind apprehends one after another the laws of physics! What noble emotions dilate the mortal as he enters into the councils of the creation, and feels by knowledge the privilege to Be! His insight refines him. The beauty of nature shines in his own breast. Man is greater that he can see this, and the universe less, because Time and Space relations vanish as laws are known.

Here again we are impressed and even daunted by the immense Universe to be explored. "What we know is a point to what we do not know." Open any recent journal of science, and weigh the problems suggested concerning Light, Heat, Electricity, Magnetism, Physiology, Geology, and judge whether the interest of natural science is likely to be soon exhausted.

Passing by many particulars of the discipline of nature, we must not omit to specify two.

The exercise of the Will, or the lesson of power, is taught in every event. From the child's successive possession of his several senses up to the hour when he saith, "Thy will be done!" he is learning the secret that he can reduce under his will not only particular events but great classes; nay, the whole series of events, and so conform all facts to his character. Nature is thoroughly mediate. It is made to serve. It receives the dominion of man as meekly as the ass on which the Saviour rode. It offers all its kingdoms to man as the raw material which he may mould into what is useful. Man is never weary of working it up. He forges the subtle and delicate air into wise and melodious words, and gives them wing as angels of persuasion and command. One after another his victorious thought comes up with and reduces all things, until the world becomes at last only a realized will,—the double of the man.

2. Sensible objects conform to the premonitions of Reason and reflect the conscience. All things are moral; and in their boundless changes have an unceasing reference to spiritual nature. Therefore is nature glorious with form, color, and motion; that every globe in the remotest heaven, every chemical change from the rudest crystal up to the laws of life, every change of vegetation from the first principle of growth in the eye of a leaf, to the tropical forest and antediluvian coal-mine, every animal function from the sponge up to Hercules, shall hint or thunder to man the laws of right and wrong, and echo

the Ten Commandments. Therefore is Nature ever the ally of Religion: lends all her pomp and riches to the religious sentiment. Prophet and priest, David, Jesus, Isaiah, have drawn deeply from this source. This ethical character so penetrates the bone and marrow of nature, as to seem the end for which it was made. Whatever private purpose is answered by any member or part, this is its public and universal function, and is never omitted. Nothing in nature is exhausted in its first use. When a thing has served an end to the uttermost, it is wholly new for an ulterior service. In God, every end is converted into a new means. Thus the use of commodity, regarded by itself, is mean and squalid. But it is to the mind an education in the doctrine of Use, namely, that a thing is good only so far as it serves; that a conspiring of parts and efforts to the production of an end is essential to any being. The first and gross manifestation of this truth is our inevitable and hated training in values and wants, in corn and meat . . .

Discussion of "Discipline"

As he returned home from England in 1833 Ralph Waldo Emerson (1803-1882) entered in his diary, "I like my book about Nature." When it was finally published in 1836 the reasons for this fondness are not difficult to see. Although less than 100 pages in length, it summarizes Emerson's early thought memorably while foreshadowing most of his later work.

Divided into an introduction and eight sections, it apparently sets out to present an idealistic philosophy of life which will show the unity of man and Nature (Emerson often capitalizes it.) The style of this brief treatise is one that Emerson was to make famous as both writer and lecturer: Epigrammatic sentences sparkle in almost every paragraph, but they often stand alone; and the reader must leap from one idea to another without the transition he expects. Fortunately, Emerson's work is most rewarding when we let ourselves be stimulated by individual ideas rather than trying to connect each insight with those that precede and follow it.

Despite some confusing terminology (when Emerson writes Reason he means something we might call intuition, and when he talks of Understanding we might say practical life), the paragraphs in which he discusses Nature as a discipline are among Emerson's most perceptive. Note, for instance, his memorable phrasing of

Nature's consistency: "She pardons no mistakes. Her yea is yea and her nay, nay." We smile ruefully with him in the next paragraph when he suggests that "Nature's dice are always loaded." We may rail at circumstance which displeases us or lament at situations we can't control; but, says Emerson, neither our tears nor our despair will alter the facts; we must discipline ourselves to acceptance.

Yet such acceptance need not justify passivity. Emerson is equally quick to point out that "Nature is thoroughly mediate. It is made to serve." We needn't change facts to use them. To the really imaginative man or woman a fact is more challenge than limitation.

In his final paragraph, Emerson presents one of his most interesting ideas. He insists that "All things are moral." All choices, finally, are either right or wrong. We can't escape responsibility for our acts by insisting certain things don't really matter. The moral consequences of some choices may be hard to see, but no choice can be neutral. If we are sensitive to our surroundings, says Emerson, we can see moral distinctions everywhere, and in recognizing such distinctions we are helped in bringing our own ethical life under control.

Abraham Davenport

John Greenleaf Whittier

In the old days (a custom laid aside
With breeches and cocked hats) the people sent
Their wisest men to make the public laws.
And so, from a brown homestead, where the Sound
Drinks the small tribute of the Mianas,
Waved over by the woods of Rippowams,
And hallowed by pure lives and tranquil deaths,
Stamford sent up to the councils of the State
Wisdom and grace in Abraham Davenport.

'Twas on a May-day of the far old year
Seventeen hundred eighty, that there fell
Over the bloom and sweet life of the Spring,
Over the fresh earth and the heaven of noon,
A horror of great darkness, like the night
In day of which the Norland sagas tell,—
The Twilight of the Gods. The low-hung sky
Was black with ominous clouds, save where its rim
Was fringed with a dull glow, like that which climbs
The crater's sides from the red hell below.
Birds ceased to sing, and all the barn-yard fowls
Roosted; the cattle at the pasture bars
Lowered, and looked homeward; bats on leathern wings
Flitted abroad; the sounds of labor died;
Men prayed, and women wept; all ears grew sharp
To hear the doom-blast of the trumpet shatter
The black sky, that the dreadful face of Christ
Might look from the rent clouds, not as he looked
A loving guest at Bethany, but stern
As Justice and inexorable Law.

Meanwhile in the old State House, dim as ghosts
Sat the lawgivers of Connecticut,
Trembling beneath their legislative robes.
"It is the Lord's Great Day! Let us adjourn,"
Some said; and then, as if with one accord,
All eyes were turned to Abraham Davenport.
He rose, slow cleaving with his steady voice
The intolerable hush. "This well may be
The Day of Judgment which the world awaits;

But be it so or not, I only know
My present duty, and my Lord's command
To occupy till He come. So at the post
Where He hath set me in his providence,
I choose, for one, to meet Him face to face, —
No faithless servant frightened from my task,
But ready when the Lord of the harvest calls;
And therefore, with all reverence, I would say.
Let God do his work, we will see to ours.
Bring in the candles." And they brought them in.

Then by the flaring lights the Speaker read,
Albeit with husky voice and shaking hands,
An act to amend an act to regulate
The shad and alewives fisheries. Whereupon
Wisely and well spake Abraham Davenport,
Straight to the questions, with no figures of speech
Save the ten Arab signs, yet not without
The shrewd dry humor natural to the man:
His awe-struck colleagues listening all the while,
Between the pauses of his argument,
To hear the thunder of the wrath of God
Break from the hollow trumpet of the cloud.

And there he stands in memory to this day,
Erect, self-poised, a rugged face, half seen
Against the background of unnatural dark,
A witness to the ages as they pass,
That simple duty hath no place for fear.

Discussion of "Abraham Davenport"

In the second volume of *Out of the Best Books* "First-Day Thoughts" introduced us to the poetry of John Greenleaf Whittier (1807-1892). "Abraham Davenport" is a slightly different kind of poem, but it is no less typical of Whittier in its terse understatement.

The entire poem simply introduces the last line: "That simple duty hath no place for fear." It is the setting, however, which gives this statement its force. Whittier's prose description of the circumstance to which he gives poetic extension in "Abraham Davenport" is worth recounting:

The famous Dark Day of New England, May 19, 1780, was a physical puzzle for many years to our ancestors but its occurrence brought something more than philosophical speculation into the minds of those who passed through it. The incident of Colonel Abraham Davenport's sturdy protest is a matter of history.

Whittier's imaginative re-creation of this situation presents the reaction of the general public in revealing contrast to that of the doughty old Colonel. Note that his stand is not taken because he doesn't believe this could be the Day of Judgment. Abraham Davenport's serenity stems from daily preparation, constant discipline. He can still smile and he is not put off from doing what his position calls him to do.

If, in our striving for exaltation, we think of duty as a rather telestial attribute, this poem helps us see its basic importance. It is not easy to be consistently dutiful. The discipline that is involved in grasping and holding the iron rod cannot be discounted. If the Lord would not have us commanded in all things, he surely must command us in many. The extent to which we can see and do what is expected of us is the extent to which we are ready for greater opportunities.

The Character of a Happy Life

Sir Henry Wotton

How happy is he born or taught
  That serveth not another's will,
Whose armor is his honest thought,
  And simple truth his highest skill;

Whose passions not his masters are;
  Whose soul is still prepared for death,
United unto the world with care
  Of princes' grace or vulgar breath;

Who envies none whom chance doth raise,
  Or vice; who never understood
The deepest wounds are given by praise,
  By rule of state but not of good;

Who hath his life from rumors freed,
  Whose conscience is his strong retreat,
Whose state can neither flatterers feed
  Nor ruins make accusers great;

Who God doth late and early pray
  More of his grace than goods to send,
And entertains the harmless day
  With a well-chosen book or friend.

This man is free from servile bands
  Of hope to rise or fear to fall,
Lord of himself, though not of lands,
  And having nothing, yet hath all.

Discussion of "The Character of a Happy Life"

Sir Henry Wotton (1568-1639) from college days was a friend of the celebrated English poet, John Donne, but he did not begin writing poetry himself until the 1590's. Much of his life was spent abroad in private travel or diplomatic service. Only in 1624 did Wotton settle down as provost of Eton. During the latter part of his life he began a biography of Donne which he did not live to complete.

Wotton's verse is characterized by the graceful paradoxes that flowed easily from the pens of cavalier poets. The final lines to "The Character of a Happy Life" are just what we might expect. Yet this poem has survived the obscurity in which most of Wotton's work now lies by an occasional insight that exhibits the thoughtful discipline the poem celebrates.

In the midst of the rather pedestrian comparisons in the opening stanza, for instance, we come upon the fresh idea that "simple truth" may demand our "highest skill." How neatly this pricks the comfortable illusion that simplicity, at least, is ours without effort. When we think about this, we recognize that seeing through fashionable complexity to simple truth *does* require all the skill we can summon.

Similarly, consider the point of stanza four. It is a well-worn idea that the person who is in control of his life is not easily tempted by flattery, but the concluding point of this verse is arrestingly different. Part of the responsibility of disciplined, proper living is to deprive those who champion the wrong from citing our fall in support of their position.

It is worth noting that the emphasis of the entire poem is less on self-knowledge than on self-control. In our introspective day there is such a stress on self-understanding that many dubious actions seem justified if they can be explained. Wotton's "simple truth" is that control of self rather than knowledge of self provides true mastery.

"The Death of Socrates" from Phaedo

Plato

A man of sense ought not to say, nor will I be very confident, that the description which I have given of the soul and her mansions is exactly true. But I do say that inasmuch as the soul is shown to be immortal, he may venture to think, not improperly or unworthily, that something of the kind is true. The venture is a glorious one, and he ought to comfort himself with words like these, which is the reason why I lengthen out the tale. Wherefore, I say, let a man be of good cheer about his soul, who having cast away the pleasures and ornaments of the body as alien to him and working harm rather than good, has sought after the pleasures of knowledge, and has arrayed the soul, not in some foreign attire, but in her own proper jewels, temperance, and justice, and courage, and nobility, and truth—in these adorned she is ready to go on her journey to the world below, when her hour comes. You, Simmias and Cebes, and all other men, will depart at some time or other. Me already, as a tragic poet would say, the voice of fate calls. Soon I must drink the poison; and I think that I had better repair to the bath first, in order that the women may not have the trouble of washing my body after I am dead.

When he had done speaking, Crito said: And have you any commands for us, Socrates—anything to say about your children, or any other matter in which we can serve you?

Nothing particular, Crito; he replied; only, as I have always told you, take care of yourselves; that is a service which you may be ever rendering to me and mine and to all of us, whether you promise to do so or not. But if you have no thought for yourselves, and care not to walk according to the rule which I have prescribed for you, not now for the first time, however much you may profess or promise at the moment, it will be of no avail.

We will do our best, said Crito; And in what way shall we bury you?

In any way that you like; but you must get hold of me, and take care that I do not run away from you. Then he turned to us, and added with a smile: —I cannot make Crito believe that I am the same Socrates who has been talking and conducting the argument; he fancies that I am the other Socrates whom he will soon see a dead body—and he asks, How shall he bury me? And though I have spoken many words in the endeavour to show that when I have drunk the poison I shall leave you and go to the joys of the blessed,— these words of mine, with which I was comforting you and myself, have had, as I perceive, no effect upon Crito. And therefore I want you to be surety for me to him now, as at the trial he was surety to the judges for me: but let the promise be of another sort; for he was surety for me to the judges that I would remain, and you must be my surety to him that I shall not remain, but go away and depart; and then he will suffer less at my death, and not be grieved when he sees my body being burned or buried. I would not have him sorrow at my hard lot, or say at the burial, Thus we lay out Socrates, or, Thus we follow him to the grave to bury him; for false words are not only evil in themselves, but they inflict the soul with evil. Be of good cheer then, my dear Crito, and say that you are burying my body only, and do with that whatever is usual, and what you think best.

When he had spoken these words, he arose and went into a chamber to bathe; Crito followed him and told us to wait. So we remained behind, talking and thinking of the subject of discourse, and also of the greatness of our sorrow; he was like a father of whom we were being bereaved, and we were about to pass the rest of our lives as orphans. When he had taken the bath his children were brought to him (he had two young sons and an elder one); and the women of his family also came, and he talked to them and gave them a few directions in the presence of Crito; then he dismissed them and returned to us.

Now the hour of sunset was near, for a good deal of time had passed while he was within. When he came out, he sat down with us again after his bath, but not much was said. Soon the jailer, who was the servant of the Eleven, entered and stood by him, saying:—To you, Socrates, whom I know to be the noblest and gentlest and best of all who ever came to this place, I will not impute the angry feeling of other men, who rage and swear at me, when, in obedience to the authorities, I bid them drink the poison—indeed, I am sure that you will not be angry with me; for others, as you are aware, and not I, are to blame. And so fare you well, and try to bear lightly what must needs be—you know my errand. Then bursting into tears he turned away and went out.

Socrates looked at him and said: I return your good wishes, and will do as you bid. Then turning to us, he said, How charming the man is: since I have been in prison he has always been coming to see me, and at times he would talk to me, and was as good to me as could be, and now see how generously he sorrows on my account. We must do as he says, Crito; and therefore let the cup be brought, if the poison is prepared: if not, let the attendant prepare some.

Yes, said Crito, the sun is still upon the hill-tops, and I know that many a one has taken the draught late, and after the announcement has been made to him, he has eaten and drunk, and enjoyed the society of his beloved: do not hurry—there is time enough.

Socrates said: Yes, Crito, and they of whom you speak are right in so acting, for they think that they will be gainers by the delay; but I am right in not following their example, for I do not think that I should gain anything by drinking the poison a little later; I should only be ridiculous in my own eyes for sparing and saving a life which is already forfeit. Please then to do as I say, and not to refuse me.

Crito made a sign to the servant, who was standing by; and he went out, and having been absent for some time, returned with the jailer carrying the cup of poison. Socrates said: You, my good friend, who are experienced in these matters, shall give me directions how I am to proceed. The man answered: You have only to walk about until your legs are heavy, and then to lie down, and the poison will act. At the same time he handed the cup to Socrates, who in the easiest and gentlest manner, without the least fear or change of colour or feature, looking at the man with all his eyes, Echecrates, as his manner was, took the cup and said: What do you say about making a libation out of this cup to any god? May I, or not? The man answered: We only prepare, Socrates, just so much as we deem enough. I understand, he said: but I may and must ask the gods to prosper my journey from this to the other world—even so— and so be it according to my prayer. Then raising the cup to his lips, quite readily and cheerfully he drank off the poison. And hitherto most of us had been able to control our sorrow; but now when we saw him drinking, and saw too that he had finished the draught, we could no longer forbear, and in spite of myself my own tears were flowing fast; so that I covered my face and wept, not for him, but at the thought of my own calamity in having to part from such a friend. Nor was I the first; for Crito, when he found himself unable to restrain his tears, had got up, and I followed; and at that moment, Apollo- dorus, who had been weeping all the time, broke out in a loud and passionate cry which made cowards of us all. Socrates alone retained his calmness: What is this strange outcry? he said. I sent away the women mainly in order that they might not misbehave in this way, for I have been told that a man should die in peace. Be quiet then, and have patience. When we heard his words we were ashamed, and refrained our tears; and he walked about until, as he said, his legs began to fail, and then he lay on his back, according to directions, and the man who gave him the poison now and then looked at his feet and legs; and after a while he pressed his foot hard, and asked him if he could feel; and he said, No; and then his leg, and so upwards and upwards, and showed us that he was cold and stiff. And he felt them himself, and said: When the poison reaches the heart, that will be the end. He was beginning to grow cold about the groin, when he uncovered his face, for he had covered himself up, and said—they were his last words—he said: Crito, I owe a cock to Asclepius; will you remember to pay the debt? The debt shall be paid, said Crito; is there anything else? There was no answer to this question; but in a minute or two a movement was heard, and the attendants uncovered him; his eyes were set, and Crito closed his eyes and mouth.

Such was the end, Echecrates, of our friend; concerning whom I may truly say, that of all men of his time whom I have known, he was the wisest and justest and best.

Discussion of "The Death of Socrates"

So far as scholars have been able to discover, Socrates was a citizen of ancient Athens who made it his business to discuss the great issues of the day with his fellow Athenians. By vocation a stonemason, Socrates himself wrote nothing. What we know about him comes mainly from the writings of his pupil Plato (429?-347 B.C.) who was a philosophical writer of the first rank. It is difficult, if not impossible, to distinguish between what Socrates actually said and what Plato puts in his mouth. If this is historically important, it makes little difference to us today. The dialogues are as fresh and provocative now as they have ever been, and they still speak clearly to man's basic problems.

Apparently Plato was present at the trial of Socrates in 399 B.C. and heard his teacher condemned to death by poisoning for corrupting the youth of Athens. In the account of Socrates' last hours which is included in this section, Phaedo, who was present at the execution, gives his friend Echecrates a description of the final scene. Many of his friends were with Socrates on this day, including Crito, Simmias and Cebes. These last two had been arguing with Socrates about the immortality of the soul. As we pick up the narrative, Socrates is concluding his argument in support of a meaningful after life.

Few accounts in all literature present more graphically the results of a life spent in obedience to principle. It is particularly noteworthy that most of his friends are able to remain in control of themselves before the actual drinking of the poison. But when they see that Socrates has emptied the entire cup of hemlock, they all break down. One particularly loud and passionate cry from Apollodorus, recounts Phaedo, "made cowards of us all."

The distinction between control which is merely temporary inhibition and control which stems from disciplined commitment could not have been made more effectively. To those who must still argue about immortality control never goes beyond the stiff-upper-lip level. Only Socrates has so committed his life to what he calls its "own proper jewels—temperance, and justice, and courage, and nobility, and truth," that he is prepared for any eventuality. External restraints are subject to external pressures, but internal discipline is not at the mercy of the world.

Command

Albert Wetjen

He had been trained in such a school that the normal state of his features was one of impassiveness. His jaw was granite, not prominent but terribly firm. It had had to cope with a good deal in its time. The eyes were steady and very clear in the tan of the lined face.

At the temples the brown hair was a little white, though he had not yet reached his forty-fifth birthday. He walked with a firm, confident tread. He was aloof, remote, and tranquil. No one, save, perhaps, another master, knew what years and immense happenings, fears, and hopes had gone into making him like he was.

His name was Arthur Stewart Taplow, and he commanded the three-funnelled liner Santhia. She was a mighty craft, thirty thousand tons. She flew the flag of a great line. She ran to a clocklike schedule. She was the finest sort of thing that man had built for navigating the great waters.

Below her decks the engines spun ceaselessly. They did not stamp and reel and grunt after the manner of old. They were the latest turbines, as quiet, almost as electric motors. The men tending them were alert and neat, not the tired, grimy men the sea was used to. In her stokehold there was no rattle and clang of shovels in coal or the jarring clamour of the ash hoist to torture the air. The Santhia burned oil. She was modern in every detail. Her chart room bristled with scientific devices. Wireless stations ashore kept in touch and gave her her position in case she was not sure of it. A whisper of trouble on her sea journeys, and nations sprang to her assistance.

Going down the river with the Santhia were two other craft. One was a coast barge, laden with cement. Her sails were dun-coloured, and her hull was daubed with tar. The other vessel was a rusty, red-sided tramp, laden with coal for Mexico. On her bridge walked her captain, a fat man with a walrus moustache and dressed in greasy serges.

On the poop of the sailing barge, steering, was a man almost as fat and attired in blue dungaree pants and a flannel shirt with the sleeves rolled up. He wore a dirty peaked cap and smoked a clay pipe. The peculiar part of it all was that each man bore the same ageless, impassive look that graced the face of Captain Taplow on the Santhia.

For you must understand that the mark of the sea is imprinted on all alike, and it does not matter, really, when the test comes, whether you command a smack out of Lowestoft or a white-walled liner flying the flag of a great line. And scientific devices are not of much use when the rack rips across the sky and the white-capped combers are roaring in from the horizon.

Which was why Captain Taplow, for all he walked a broad bridge and was surrounded by calm and efficient men, was just a little nervous under his outward tranquilness. He was so keyed up, so fully a creature of ships and the sea, that his ears absorbed every sound and his eyes missed nothing.

He might be saying to the pilot, "Yes, old Hamlin's a good man. Best president the line ever had." But he was thinking, "The red-and-white buoy over by Scrop's Landing is not in place. Oh, yes, it was reported removed for repairs. There's the substitute."

And even as he listened to the pilot's reply about Hamlin, he heard the hoarse shouting of a man on the fore deck of the collier, and he noticed the captain of the sailing barge spin his wheel sharply as his great mainsail commenced to shiver. Not only did he hear and note these small matters. He was hearing and noting every other such matter that impinged upon his senses — the swirl of black water over a mud bank, the bow wave lifted by a racing launch that gave a good idea of the speed, the man standing by the collier's windlass, which indicated she was very likely going to anchor; the various screechings and hootings of sirens up and down the mighty river. That was his business. Command—

Later, he sat at his table in the brilliantly lighted saloon and smiled gravely as he listened to a New York banker dilate on the war debts. Over by the great curving main stairway a gray-haired passenger was in hot argument with the chief steward. There had been some mistake about seating him. He desired to be at the captain's table. He was a pompous and wealthy man with a vast opinion of himself, but he was also a shareholder in the company. He had brought a letter from old Hamlin, the president.

The chief steward glanced across, over the heads of the diners, and caught the captain's eye. The captain nodded imperceptibly, and the steward grew all at once urbane and smiling. He deftly whisked an astonished young lady from her chair near the captain and flourished a shareholder into it. But by that time the captain was murmuring a very discreet joke to the stern-looking woman seated on his left.

He had barely finished and was reaching for his soup spoon when a quartermaster came down the stairway and tapped the chief steward on the shoulder. The chief crossed the saloon with a slip of paper and the captain read from between the cover of his palms: "Ice reported latitude 47° 12', longitude 47° 06'. Large berg drifting S.S.E."

He nodded to the chief, who shook his head at the waiting quartermaster. The stern-faced lady was saying, "Do you know Captain, I feel so very nervous crossing the ocean. I suffer from the heart—leaking valve—you know."

The captain inclined his head, smiling, tranquil, courteous. He had heard it too many times before. A few minutes later he was deep in a calm argument about the merits and demerits of spiritualism. And no one knew that he was thinking all the time about that ice floating in latitude 47° 12' and longitude 47° 06'.

The dining saloon emptied slowly. The orchestra put its instruments away while it fed. Later it would appear on the promenade deck. The captain went to his bridge, his face impassive, his hands in his side pockets. He looked at the compass, at the sky, at the windward horizon, at the bridge log. He stared then straight ahead into the gathering dusk for over a quarter of an hour.

A few sharp words to the mates on watch, and he went slowly down the companion to the boat deck and his cabin. He sat there for a while, signing some papers, looking over reports. The surgeon came in, prim, white-bearded, professional looking even in his evening dress. He tapped on his thumb nail with his pince-nez glasses and waited until the captain was ready.

"Well?"

"Just a seaman, sir. Came on board intoxicated. Rather old. I'm afraid we'll lose him."

The captain frowned. He disliked deaths at sea. It was bad on a passenger ship. Women grew nervous. Superstition, of course. But it had spoiled many people's voyages before.

"His name?"

"Just Smith, sir. William Smith. He's a bos'n's mate, I believe."

The captain nodded. "Ah! Smith. An old shipmate, so to speak. He was with me first on the Brixton City. Good man. Keep me informed."

"Very well, sir." The surgeon commenced to withdraw. The captain gestured and stopped him.

"Not a word if he—er—dies. No alarm."

"I understand, sir." The surgeon was rather stiff. As if he didn't know that. He closed the cabin door quietly behind him. The captain stared at the papers on his desk. William Smith. Plain Bill Smith, bos'n mate. He remembered the man. He had been an able seaman on the Brixton City when he, Taplow, was an apprentice. How time flew! And Smith had sailed on his ships pretty nearly ever since. Sort of understanding between them. Never had time to talk together, of course. Master and man. Bad for discipline. Why didn't the fo'c's'le hands leave liquor alone?

He rose with a sigh, put his papers away. He adjusted his uniform cap and his black wing tie. The miniature medals tinkled on his left lapel. He caught sight of himself in a glass and stopped to grin a trifle. The impassiveness wiped away.

He was a bit different from the sweating kid who'd furled royals on many an icy night and tarred down the backstays in the tropics. A bit different from the scared youngster on his first responsible watch with his certificate brand new in his sea chest. He was a captain now. But thirty-odd years had gone into putting him behind a starched shirt front and into a dinner jacket with miniature medals in a row. They thought it was easy, the youngsters.

He appeared below and moved through the lounge with unhurried strides, smiling, dropping courteous words here and there. The orchestra was playing softly behind some palms. Women were chatting in groups, a few men attending. The captain stopped by each group, listened, told a delicate set joke, rendered, perhaps, a little information, and passed on. An hour later, he reached the smoking room.

The purser and assistant surgeon were seated at a table playing bridge. They greeted him with a jovial "Have a hand, sir?" that contained just the correct amount of respect. They each offered to rise and deliver their hands, but he waved them to be seated. The chief steward and the chief engineer were smoking cigars and drinking Scotch with a group of American salesmen.

The captain made for a table in the corner where he noticed the gray-headed man who was a shareholder in the line. "Treat him kindly," Hamlin had written in his grim way. It was hard, sometimes, but it had to be done. The home office couldn't be bothered with petty grievances.

The shareholder called loudly for the best cigars the smoke room possessed. The captain accepted one from the box and lighted it with care. He declined whisky and called for ginger ale. The shareholder settled himself and began to talk.

He was a good talker, a loud talker. He knew everything, and constantly asserted he was a self-made man. He'd always worked and always would work. Some men had easy jobs—he glared at the captain—but not he. No, he toiled ten hours a day, sometimes twelve, when in his office. Nothing like it. A man's business would go to bits if he wasn't paying attention.

The captain smiled and agreed. He always agreed, with everyone. It was part of his job, as it was his job to listen to small men and women trying to impress on him what a great figure they cut ashore. He had gained the art of listening to a fine degree. He could answer logically almost any question that cropped up, look interested and smile when required, while all the time his mind could be miles away.

The smoke-room crowd thinned out. Some men went to turn in. Some joined the women. More cards were produced and bridge tables occupied. The captain played with the shareholder, the purser, and a sandy-haired man from Chili. The second game of the rubber was halfway through when the captain paused in the act of playing a card and listened. The three other men looked at him, wondering, and waited. Then the purser relaxed. He had caught the sound. The other two men, land-trained, heard nothing.

It was a little thing, scarcely sounding above the noise of the smoke room. It was merely a change in the perpetual note of the wind singing by the open portholes. But it was enough to check Captain Taplow in his game, make him murmur an apology, lay down his cards and walk to the door. He was only gone a minute, just stepped on the deck and looking over the darkling sea, but the shareholder fumed and grumbled.

"Fine way t'go off and leave everything. How the devil. . . ."

"He'll be right back," murmured the purser soothingly, and added, "Here he is," as the captain returned. The game was finished. The rubber was won and lost. And no one in the smoke room, save the ship's officers who happened to be present, knew that the captain had gone to look over the sea because of the faintest of faint changes in the noise of the wind.

He had just finished dressing when the surgeon entered his room next morning. The white-bearded man stood on the mat inside the door and tapped his thumb nail with his glasses.

"He's dead," he said shortly.

"Smith?"

The surgeon nodded. "Overstrained heart and arteries almost hard. Too much drink."

"No one knows?"

"Only my hospital attendants, sir."

"We'll bury him at ten o'clock."

"Very well, sir."

The captain stood shaking his head when the surgeon had gone. Just like Bill Smith. Couldn't leave liquor alone. He pressed a bell and a quartermaster knocked at the door.

"Send the mate here."

The mate came, a white-headed, reliable old man, stopped only from high command because of a moroseness that made him a bad man to mix with passengers.

"Have the sailmaker sew up Smith. He's in the after hospital, Mr. Hopkins."

"Aye, aye, sir. Shall I inform the chaplain what time the burial?"

"I'll conduct service myself. He was an old shipmate — a very old shipmate—when I was 'prenticed." The mate nodded, understanding. The captain paused a moment and went on: "Have four A.B.'s aft at ten—sailing-ship men, if you can find them. Clear the third-class promenade. An ensign over the canvas. That'll be all."

"Very good, sir." The mate withdrew, nodding. The captain reached for his uniform cap and went on the bridge. An hour later he strolled aft along the first-class promenade, chatting with passengers, inquiring of ladies if they found everything all right. He straightened out two or three small matters, heard two complaints, found a child's lost ball wedged in the scupper port, and reprimanded the salon deckman for carelessly splicing grommets. Then, almost unnoticed, he dropped down the companion to the third-class deck and went right aft to where the screws shook and vibrated underfoot.

A long canvas bundle with the red ensign over it rested on a grating, balanced on the bulwarks. Four bareheaded A.B.'s held it level. The mate stood by. The surgeon stood by. The palefaced ship's chaplain was in his robes and holding a prayer book.

He said, in a thin voice, as the captain approached. "You know, sir, I consider it is my duty. . ."

The captain smiled and pulled a little black-leather book from his own pocket. He answered, gently, "He wasn't much of a Christian, Mr. Winch. I don't think he'd properly appreciate it. And we were old shipmates. He's been with me a long time, since we were in wind-jammers."

"But—" protested the chaplain, quivering. He was really distressed that a soul should go out on the water without a proper sending. But then he wasn't a sailor.

The captain was still smiling. "He saved my life one night — at least, I think so. It was icy on the yard and I slipped from the footrope. I'm sure you won't mind."

The chaplain opened his mouth, but shut it again, for, looking at the captain, he felt his will battered down to a little whimpering thing. The face he gazed at was so ageless, tranquil, confident. The face of the sea itself. He gestured wearily and stepped back.

The captain cleared his throat. He looked for a gentle moment at the ensign covering the canvas, and then at Mother Carey's chickens skimming the bubbling wake. A good drop for a sailor, the sea birds and the sun. He started to read the service in a subdued voice, but he was thinking of that night on the icy yard long ago.

The grating tilted. There was a splash, lost in the roar of the wake. So a sailor sent a sailor to Fiddler's Green.

Three days out something happened. Many of the passengers would have talked about it for the rest of their lives had they known. But ugly things are always hidden from people who pay for cabins. The Santhia caught fire somewhere just forward of her midship fuel tank. The smoke was cleverly stifled. Men went down in the thick of it with grotesque masks over their heads. The fuel tank was pumped out, but the danger did not decrease because there was enough oil gas left inside to rupture things severely if a spark chanced to catch.

The turbines whirled without end. The Santhia made her steady twenty-one knots. The band still played at meal times and in the evening. The day the fire was discovered there was a dance on the promenade.

The captain followed his daily programme as nearly as he was able. He ate in the saloon, listened to passengers, helped entertain them. He smiled always, was always unruffled and calm. And not one of the two thousand souls he was paid to deliver safely knew he was a man exhausted with worry, or that overhead the wireless was crashing out half-hourly reports to four ships almost as big as the Santhia herself.

It was a grim, anxious time. The captain played bridge nightly in the smoking room. He laughed heartily at the shareholder's jokes despite the fact he had heard them all before. And when the shareholder had gone comfortably to bed, the captain repaired to his cabin, pulled dun-coloured overalls over his evening suit, and went diving down into the bowels of his ship, where men searched and fought at his order.

They were twelve hours finding the seat of the fire and just fifteen minutes extinguishing the whole thing! Had they been a little later the empty fuel tank would have blown up. As it was, matters were smoothed and there was no trouble. Nothing was changed save that a few more lines were etched in Captain Taplow's face.

When it was all over he went to try and get some sleep, but his foot was only over his cabin storm step when a wireless message was handed to him. The ice was lower. Latitude 43°12'. Longitude 48°20'. A berg, six hundred feet long and two hundred feet high, had been sighted across the main sailing route. The captain closed his cabin door, went up on the navigation bridge, called for a cup of strong, black coffee, and settled himself to watch and pilot his course with care.

That night he sent his regrets to the shareholder. He was unable to play bridge with him. He was going to be busy. And the shareholder, who had no understanding, only grumbled: "What for? Pretty easy he's got it. Enough officers to run a dozen ships."

It was true. There were enough officers to cover with their sharp eyes every point of the compass. Right at that moment, while Captain Taplow was on the bridge, there were two mates with him. From each bridge wing watched an apprentice. Two quartermasters eyed the sea from where they stood near the chart house. There was even a man on the fo'c's'le head.

Yet Captain Taplow, who needed sleep, must walk his bridge, as nervous as the newest master out of London. And this because it was no light thing to hold in trust thirty thousand tons and two thousand souls. Whatever might befall, the responsibility was his. The officers might be efficient. They were.

But if they made a mistake it was the captain who was broken. He was responsible. Officers were given him for him to command and order, not to take responsibility from him. And officers had been known to make mistakes before. So how could a master mariner sleep when there was ice abroad and to a certainty fogs as well? That was what it meant—command.

The shareholder who grumbled so much, who considered that Captain Taplow might have come down to have his game of bridge, never knew that at one o'clock that morning the Santhia shot suddenly into a night mist and was slowed to half speed. Nor did he know that half an hour later she barely skimmed a berg as large as a mountain, so that the hair of every watcher stood on end and the heart of at least one man contracted until it pained in his breast.

The dawn broke gray and chilly, strangely chilly after the summer weather that had gone. The ice blink was on the northern horizon, but straight ahead the sea appeared clear. It was a gray sea, a steely sort of swelling with little jumbles of white foam capping it. The sky was blue between patches of gray cloud. The horizon was a little dim.

As the light strengthened and day settled into being, a haggard, unshaven Captain Taplow took a good look around and sighed with relief that he had come safely through the night. There was danger still, great danger ahead. But it could be seen approaching, and even a new officer could steer a ship out of the way.

"I'm going below, Mr. Stevens. Got to get some sleep. We dock to-morrow, and it'll be hard work going up to the harbour. Give me a call if it gets thick."

"Aye, aye, sir. Call you if it thickens."

"Don't forget! We don't want another Titanic!" He frowned irritably as he turned away. There was no need for him to use such a tone of voice to a junior. Of course, he was tired—that accounted for it. He went down the companion to his room and sank to a chair.

He rang and a steward brought him some coffee and an omelette. He managed to consume that and then pulled off the high rubber sea boots he had been wearing. When he had them off he padded across the room in his socks to look at the barometer and frowned worriedly.

Two decks below, the shareholder was turning over under the warm sheets and gazing up at the deck head. He was very comfortable and rested. He smiled, thinking of the breakfast he was going to eat. He was disturbed when he caught the faint sound of the third mate's voice shouting to a quartermaster. He didn't know what it was and he didn't care, but he wished whoever it was would be quieter.

As a matter of fact, the third mate was anxious, which was why his voice was raised. As a consequence, a somewhat surly quartermaster tapped at the door of the captain's cabin and poked his head inside. The captain was just peeling off his jacket.

He looked up and said, "Well?"

The quartermaster blinked. "Third mate says it's getting thick, sir."

The captain sighed. He slipped on his jacket and reached for his sea boots. "I'll be right up," he said. He sighed again as he stamped out on to the boat deck and started for the navigation bridge, the first thin wisps of the fog wrapping about him.

The third mate peered at him as he came up the companion and started, "Sorry, sir. Didn't like to disturb you."

"That's all right," murmured the captain wearily. "Half speed. Siren, there!" And so he took over again to bring his thirty thousand tons and his two thousand souls to safety.

That was what it meant. Command.

Discussion of "Command"

Albert Richard Wetjen (1900-1948) was born in England but ran away to sea at the age of fourteen. By the time he was sixteen he had been in two shipwrecks. At eighteen he began writing. Most of his best work was produced during the 1920's when he moved to America and devoted himself to short stories about the sea.

Although "Command" is often reprinted in anthologies which are expected to appeal to men, the impact of this story is almost unlimited. Anyone who has had to take charge, from simple presiding in meetings to directing a large work force, knows the almost unbearable weight which such responsibility can entail.

It is interesting to note that, although the word command suggests the giving of orders, most of the details of this story show Captain Taplow obeying. He is sensitive to the authority of the circumstances in which he is involved. He needs to placate the testy old man who is a shareholder in the company which owns the Santhia. He must soothe the nervous lady with the bad heart. His meals and sleep are interrupted, but no delegation of responsibility really shifts the burden of making the ultimate decisions. Before we have read much of this story it dawns on us that Captain Taplow is first of all in command of himself. He can control others and bring order out of complex difficulties because his own life is a harmonious whole.

Unlike Bill Smith, the sailor who was an able-bodied seaman when the captain was only an apprentice, Captain Taplow had not succumbed to the sailor's curse of heavy drinking. When a hidden fire or an unknown iceberg threatens the safety of all aboard the ship, the Captain not only works alongside his crew, he keeps his passengers relaxed and entertained.

If such calmness under pressure seems almost inhuman, a comparable achievement can be documented in thousands of homes in which mothers assume their "command." As with the Captain of our story, most good mothers spend more time answering demands than they do in giving orders. The apparent chaos of school mornings, the constant care which a half-sick child expects, the affectionate sympathy a tired husband looks forward to, the deadening routine of household tasks—such varied demands can only be met successfully by a woman whose personal discipline is so complete it hardly shows. Perhaps only another mother can know the cost of such discipline—and only another mother can appreciate the rewards of such effort.

Ordeal by Handcart

by

Wallace Stegner

(The first part of this article details the preparation of the handcart companies which came across the plains during 1856. The story of the Martin and Willie companies which follows is the climax to Mr. Stegner's account.)

Two weeks after the first 500 left Iowa City, a group composed mainly of Welshmen took out after them. This third party had such phenomenally lucky passage, discounting the usual discomforts of the trail, and the occasional and expected deaths, that they seemed to demonstrate beyond all doubt the excellence of Brigham Young's handcart plan. In spite of the presence of many old people—one woman of seventy-three walked every step of the way— this company averaged 20 miles a day, as against the ordinary ox-train average of little better than 10. They came into Salt Lake Valley with loud hosannas only a week behind the first parties.

But later that summer two more companies would try it, and theirs was a different story.

Some of them didn't sail from Liverpool until the end of May. It was July before they assembled in Iowa City, where they found no handcarts prepared and no seasoned lumber to build them from. More than 1,000 strong, they waited a long, worrisome time until 260 carts could be made from green wood. On July 15, 500 of them finally got away. The other 576 did not get on the road until July 26th.

As far as the Missouri they fared well. The first party, under Captain Willie, arrived on August 11th, the second under Captain Martin on the 22d, while the Willie company was still resting in Florence and mending its carts.

Reunited in a great mass meeting, the two companies debated whether or not to take the chance of starting across so late in the season. They made the mistake that many a party of Western travelers more seasoned than they had made: they gambled on weather. Eager to reach Zion, they persuaded themselves that the Lord would temper the wind to His lambs, and hold back the winter.

On each cart, as insurance, they laid an extra hundred pounds of flour, and the human draft animals pulled this overload bravely enough, and the carts bore it, until they crossed that invisible line that divides the humid Midwest from the arid West. Then their green carts began to warp and dis- integrate and collapse; their shrieking wooden axles wore down under the grinding of the sand. Patching every night, greasing the axles with soap or bacon rind or whatever would slip, they hurried on, the two companies about a week apart. Behind both came two Mormon parties traveling by ox-drawn wagon and hurrying even more belatedly to beat the onset of winter.

Knowing they were dangerously late, the pilgrims on foot hated the delays of their collapsing carts. And then came something more serious: one night a stampeding herd of buffalo came right through their camp, and when they crawled out from under the carts and rounded up all the cattle they could find, they were 30 head short. Those had had been not only draft animals for their commissary wagons but beef insurance, and the flour they had to unload from the wagons and pull on the handcarts strained their crazy carts as much as their endurance.

Fort Laramie saw the Willie company on September 1st. Ahead lay 500 more miles, the hardest 500, mountainous all the way, and at high altitudes where the cold came early. They had had their deaths, but they were still in fair condition. Counting heads and estimating daily marches, Willie cut their flour allowance from a pound a day per head to three quarters of a pound. The harder the road and the longer the marches, the smaller their rations and the frailer their strength. Some of them threw away belongings, lightening the carts for the last lap. They could not hope to reach Salt Lake Valley on the food they had, but they hoped for supplies at South Pass or Fort Bridger, and they sent word on ahead by some fast-traveling returning missionaries.

Nights were cold and got colder as they labored up the Sweetwater and climbed the long hard grade toward the Continental Divide. There were more deaths. The older and weaker members drooped and failed under the grind, stumbled into camp with faces drawn and set with exhaustion, and sometimes they lay down for a moment's rest and died without ever knowing how completely worn out they were. "Life went out," a survivor wrote afterward, "as smoothly as a lamp ceases to burn when the oil is gone. At first the deaths occurred slowly and irregularly, but in a few days at more frequent intervals, until we soon thought it unusual to leave a campground without burying one or more persons. . . . Many a father pulled his cart with his little children on it, until the day preceding his death."

There was a gray day in October when the people plodding along in a long ragged column felt something brush their faces, and looked up. Snow. They did not stop their patient dull plodding. Even when two mounted strangers who said they were messengers from a relief party en route from Salt Lake appeared out of the snow-filled afternoon, the pilgrims had little left to rally with. Foot after tired foot, they forced themselves on a few more miles and camped in some willows. When they awoke, the snow was a foot deep, their few starving draft animals were scattered in the storm, and there were five new corpses to be buried.

Without strength to hunt their stock or walk farther, they stalled there in the snow, and because the ground was hard-frozen and their strength was gone, they could not now even dig graves for their dead, but simply buried them together in a snowdrift.

Several days' travel behind them, the Martin party had reached Red Buttes and the last crossing of the Platte. They had not lost as many oxen as the Willie party, and had thus fared a little better, but their situation was even more desperate because they had farther to go. The hundred buffalo robes they had bought in Fort Laramie were a mixed blessing: a family might keep warmer because of them, but die of hauling the extra weight. Some families had already thrown theirs away. Before them the Platte ran slush ice, and there was no ferry.

Grimly fathers picked up their children and waded out into the river; women hiked their skirts and waded after them. Blue, shivering, starving, they huddled into camp on the other side, and that was where the first snow caught them.

For three days they sat there; they could do nothing else. Deaths got so frequent they had to appoint a burial squad of the strongest men. Margaret Dalglish, a stout Scotch girl worn down to skin and bones, but still keeping up, looked across at another young girl by the fire one evening and saw her die in the act of raising a cracker to her mouth. A day or two later she watched as 18 of their company were buried in one snow grave.

When the storm blew out, they wallowed on a few miles toward the Sweetwater, but before they reached it another three-day storm halted them.

A woman named Elizabeth Kingsford, alarmed when her husband was not even able to swallow his morsel of supper, wrapped him in their blankets and lay down beside him with all her clothes on.

About midnight, terribly cold, she rolled closer and put her hand on him and knew that he was dead. She cried out, but her cries brought no one. The rest of the nights she lay grim and dry-eyed beside her husband's corpse, and when the camp could move again, she struggled on with her three children.

A night or two later they were so worn out that nobody in the group had strength to pitch their tent. The mother sat down on a rock with one child in her lap and one huddled against each side, and so sat out the night—without hope, almost without thought, without anything left except the indomitable spark that would not quite flicker out.

In Salt Lake City the missionaries bearing news of the Willie and Martin companies arrived during the October Conference of the Church, when all the settlers from all the settlements in Zion were gathered for exhortation and renewal. Brigham Young promptly adjourned the conference and called for wagons, supplies and volunteers. This was the sort of operation at which the Mormon people had always been as good as anyone in the world. They had met enough crises together to know how, and they were bound by a sense of brotherhood to the converts struggling toward them across the mountains. Twenty-seven young men took off with wagonloads of food, warm clothing and bedding.

The rescuers themselves had nothing easy to look forward to—a forced drive across three or four hundred miles of wintry mountains. They crowded their teams recklessly day after day, looking ahead for the vanguard of the walkers. But the mountain valleys reached on snowy and empty, the ramparts of Echo Canyon bounced back the thud and rattle of their broad tires, they rose out of the canyon and saw the shining Uintas to the southward and the great high Wyoming plain ahead, and still no one appeared.

By Fort Bridger they were seriously alarmed, and would have pushed on even faster, but a new storm came blindingly out of the north and stopped them. That was the night of October 20th. That same night Captain Willie and one companion, frostbitten and exhausted and riding two worn-out animals, appeared out of the blizzard to tell them that if they didn't come at once there was no use to come at all.

They broke camp at once and started again. Even these, trailwise and hardy and young and well fed, had all they could do, but they did not stop again until they reached the camp where the Willie company lay. The night before rescue reached them nine more had died. The rest had not eaten for 48 hours.

The rescuers built up great fires, distributed clothes and bedding, handed out food. But even though the company had lost a sixth of its original number, there were still more than 400 people, far more than the rescue party could feed or clothe. And beyond them lay the Martin company, as bad off or worse. The rescuers divided, one-half staying to help the Willie company on toward Fort Bridger, the others pushing on to find the Martin party. They found it camped and waiting for the end between Red Buttes and the Sweetwater. In their hurry and weakness many had thrown away too much. Some of them now were without bedding, and some of the children were barefoot in the snow. They had no food except a little stringy beef from draft animals that had worn themselves out in the harness, and even that food had given them dysentery. Since the party crossed the Platte nine days before, 56 had died. Even then, with both handcart companies located, and the stalled wagon trains still farther back reached with supplies and encouragement, rescue was far from sure. Exhaustion and death were not rendered impossible because a few men had arrived with a few pounds of food and a great load of hope. The deaths went on, and it took days of toil and agony to work the stricken camps along the road to the Green River, where they met more supply wagons rushed through by Brigham Young, and where there were shelter and firewood. As quickly as they could, the rescue wagons loaded up the weakest and started them for Salt Lake City. The stronger ones came along under their own power, but with a broad, broken trail to follow and constant help when they needed it. Much of the Martin company's gear was left with that of the two wagon trains at Devil's Gate, with a wintering party to look after it. The wagon trains never did reach Salt Lake that season, but wintered at Fort Bridger.

It is hard to imagine the emotions of rescue, the dazed joy of being snatched from the very toppling brink, and hard to feel how hope that had been crushed little by little, day by day, until it is apparently dead, can come back with a rush like life itself returning. It is quite as hard to visualize the hardship that even rescue entailed—that jolting, racking, freezing, grief-numbed, drained and exhausted 300 miles on through the winter mountains to sanctuary. In Echo Canyon, between the battlements of red sandrock, a child was born in one of the wagons. How his mother survived long enough to bring him to life will never be fully understood by anyone who read his story. Against all probability, both he and his mother lived.

The first of the rescued reached Salt Lake on November 9th, a day of tears and thanksgiving. For many days afterward the others were straggling in, some riding the wagons, some still grimly hauling their battered carts, still defiantly on their own legs. Margaret Dalglish, that gaunt image of Scotch fortitude, dragged her pitiful handful of possessions to the very rim of the valley, but when she looked down and saw the end of it, safety, the City of the Saints, she did something extraordinary. She tugged the cart to the edge of the road and gave it a push and watched it roll and crash and tumble and burst apart, scattering down the ravine the last things she owned on earth. Then she went on into Salt Lake to start a new life with nothing but her gaunt bones, her empty hands, her stout heart.

These stories tell of one of the worst disasters in all the history of Western settlement. Other tragedies have taken the imaginations of historians more, for some reason, perhaps because the Mormons have been considered a "peculiar" people and the civilization they established in the valleys of the mountains an eccentric one. The three successful handcart caravans and the two tragic ones are an overlooked episode in our histories of the West. The grisly story of the Donner party in the Sierra Nevada in 1846, and the almost-as-grisly experience of John Charles Fremont's party in the San Juan Mountains of Colorado two years later are known to hundreds where the story of the handcart companies is known to one. But Fremont lost 11 men, the Donner party about 40. The Willie and Martin handcart companies, never able to count their casualties with accuracy, lost well over 200 people. If the nerve and endurance and faith necessary to break the Western wilderness had a single climactic illustration, it was here.

Perhaps their suffering seems less dramatic because the handcart pioneers bore it meekly, praising God, instead of fighting for life with the ferocity of animals and eating their dead to keep their own life beating, as both the

Fremont and Donner parties did. And assuredly the handcart pilgrims were less hardy, less skilled, less well equipped to be pioneers. But if courage and endurance make a story, if human kindness and helpfulness and brotherly love in the midst of raw horror are worth recording, this half-forgotten episode of the Mormon migration is one of the great tales of the West and of America.

Discussion of "Ordeal by Handcart"

Wallace Stegner (1909-   ) spent his youth and undergraduate days in Salt Lake City. Although not a member of the Church, he has developed a deep affection for Utah and the pioneer settlers who claimed the Salt Lake Valley as their new home. Since 1945, Stegner has been professor of English at Stanford University where he directs the program in creative writing.

"Ordeal by Handcart" is Stegner's touching tribute to the handcart pioneers. If their story has often been told in the Church, Stegner is correct in saying that this account is almost unknown to the world. We offer it here as the most powerful narrative of human discipline we know. For all the courage, fortitude, and faith of those who pushed and pulled their meager possessions and boundless hopes across the plains would lack their ultimate significance if they did not stem from a commitment that was more important than life itself. Their discipline exhibited none of that desire to spurn the flesh which has occurred from time to time in the name of religion. To them discipline was never an end—only a means. The flesh was not to be debased in order that the spirit might be exalted, but the flesh and spirit together were to be subjected to the will of God. For each person who died en route or who lived to dwell in Zion knew that only in that Will is there present peace and eternal happiness.

SECTION THREE

The Comfort of Faith

by Bruce B. Clark

THE COMFORT OF FAITH

By Bruce B. Clark

The saddest thing that can befall a soul is to lose faith in God and woman.
—Alexander Smith

Introductory Comments

Already, in the preceding three volumes in this series, we have extensively sampled the literature of faith.[1] Already, too, all of us through reading, thought, experience, and observation know that faith as a principle is very broad. It includes not only faith in God and His eternal plans but also faith in humanity, faith in husbands, wives, and children, faith in friends, faith in ourselves and our abilities, faith in the future, faith that right will ultimately triumph over wrong, etc. Not merely hundreds but actually tens of thousands of poems, songs, stories, novels, dramas, essays, and sermons have been published exploring faith and its lack; and great men of all kinds have commented upon one or another aspect of faith. For example, William Faulkner in his Nobel Prize Acceptance Speech of 1950 expressed his faith in man and the future:

> I decline to accept the end of man. It is easy enough to say that man is immortal simply because he will endure. . . . I believe that man will not merely

---

[1] In Volume 1 see especially Section 2, entitled "Faith in God and Man" (pp. 47-107), which includes "Ode: Intimations of Immortality," "Character of the Happy Warrior," and excerpts from *The Prelude* by William Wordsworth, "A Grammarian's Funeral" and "An Epistle of Karshish" by Robert Browning, "The Lamb" by William Blake, "I Never Saw a Moor" by Emily Dickinson, "Little Jesus" by Francis Thompson, "The Windhover" and "God's Grandeur" by Gerard Manley Hopkins, and "Still Falls the Rain" by Edith Sitwell. Other selections in Volume 1 especially illustrating faith are "The Hound of Heaven" by Francis Thompson (pp. 343-351), "Michael" by Wordsworth (pp. 405-419), Sonnet 146 by Shakespeare (pp. 453-454), "Death Be Not Proud" by John Donne (pp. 455-456), "And Death Shall Have No Dominion" by Dylan Thomas (pp. 457-458), "Prospice" and "Rabbi Ben Ezra" by Browning (pp. 459-468), and "We Are Seven" by Wordsworth (pp. 469-472). In Volume 2 see especially "Where Love Is, There God Is Also" by Leo Tolstoy (pp. 270-282), and "The Leaden Echo and The Golden Echo" by Gerard Manley Hopkins (pp. 347-350). And in Volume 3 see especially "Lead, Kindly Light" by John Henry Newman (pp. 149-150), "To Utah" by Edward Hart (pp. 151-155), "The Mantle of the Prophet" by Clinton Larson (pp. 156-160), "The Cotter's Saturday Night" by Robert Burns (pp. 189-199), and all of Section 6 entitled "The Substance of Faith" (pp. 239-282).

endure: he will prevail. He is immortal, not because he alone among creatures has an inexhaustible voice, but because he has a soul, a spirit capable of compassion and sacrifice and endurance.

A few years later President John F. Kennedy in a speech at Amherst College affirmed his faith in poetry and art:

When power leads man towards arrogance, poetry reminds him of his limitations. When power narrows the area of man's concern, poetry cleanses. For art establishes the basic human truths which must serve as the touchstones of our judgment. . . . I see little of more importance to the future of our country and our civilization than full recognition of the place of the artist. If art is to nourish the roots of our culture, society must set the artist free to follow his vision wherever it takes him.

And many years earlier Thomas Carlyle in *Sartor Resartus*, with his typically vivid language, described the power of faith to endure:

For man's well-being, faith is properly the one thing needful; how, with it, martyrs, otherwise weak, can cheerfully endure the shame and the cross; and without it, worldlings puke-up their sick existence, by suicide, in the midst of luxury.

Obviously from among the world's tens of thousands of writings on faith we can print only the merest fraction of samplings, and perhaps the best place to begin is with a few short affirmative poems, from which we will turn to other works exploring facets and problems of faith. Taken all together these selections are intended to suggest that men of literature join with men of religion in concluding that faith is the foundation for happy living.

Psalm 8

O Lord our Lord, how excellent is thy name in all the earth! who hast set thy glory above the heavens.

Out of the mouth of babes and sucklings hast thou ordained strength because of thine enemies, that thou mightest still the enemy and the avenger.

When I consider thy heavens, the work of thy fingers, the moon and the stars, which thou hast ordained;

What is man, that thou art mindful of him? and the son of man, that thou visitest him?

For thou hast made him a little lower than the angels, and hast crowned him with glory and honour.

Thou madest him to have dominion over the works of thy hands; thou hast put all things under his feet:

All sheep and oxen, yea, and the beasts of the field;

The fowl of the air, and the fish of the sea, and whatsoever passeth through the paths of the seas.

O Lord, our Lord, how excellent is thy name in all the earth!

Psalm 23

The Lord is my shepherd; I shall not want.

He maketh me to lie down in green pastures: he leadeth me beside the still waters.

He restoreth my soul: he leadeth me in the paths of righteousness for his name's sake.

Yea, though I walk through the valley of the shadow of death, I will fear no evil: for thou art with me; thy rod and thy staff they comfort me.

Thou preparest a table before me in the presence of mine enemies: thou anointest my head with oil; my cup runneth over.

Surely goodness and mercy shall follow me all the days of my life: and I will dwell in the house of the Lord forever.

Discussion of Psalm 8 and Psalm 23

These are two of the loveliest of the Psalms (song-poems) of David in the Old Testament. Both are filled with faith and religious adoration, acknowledging the power and the love of God. No analysis or commentary seems needful; they speak beautifully to all levels of readers.

Song from "Pippa Passes"

Robert Browning

The year's at the spring
And day's at the morn;
Morning's at seven;
The hillside's dew-pearled;
The lark's on the wing;
The snail's on the thorn.
God's in his heaven—
All's right with the world!

Discussion of "Song from Pippa Passes"

Without question this *is* affirmative. The trouble is, it is *too* affirmative—as Browning well knew. He puts the song in the mouth of a little girl who dances gaily over the hillsides singing pretty songs about a world she doesn't understand, except from the naive point of view of a child. God *is* in heaven, and nature *is* beautiful, as the first seven lines say. But the last line goes too far. All is *not* right with the world—as God knows, as all mature people know, and as Browning fully knew. (See his many poems describing wrongs in the world.) Sometimes this poem has been pointed to as typical of Browning's philosophy and of romanticism. It is typical of neither, for both Browning and the romantic movement in literature were rooted in a profound understanding of man and his complex problems. If God is to work through men in solving the many problems of the world as we strive towards the ultimate goals of the human race, then as thinking adults we must recognize that much is wrong with the world, and it is our responsibility to help correct these wrongs. I believe it was Voltaire who once said, "The price of intelligence is unhappiness"—meaning that intelligence brings with it an increased awareness of complex problems in the world, and hence a sobering concern. If our lives are guided by high personal integrity, if we are at peace with our own conscience, we can find personal happiness; but even here we are probably fooling ourselves if we think that we are perfect, needing no improvement. And as soon as we start to examine the world around us, we must either close our eyes and pretend not to see, or share with God a deep concern over all the wrongs that need correcting. There is danger in being too pessimistic: there is also danger—and unrealism—in being too optimistic.[2]

————————

[2] As humorously suggested by the following poem, entitled "Optimist"

> An optimist fell ten stories.
> At each window bar
> He shouted to his friends.
> "All right so far."

Easter Wings

George Herbert

Lord, who createdst man in wealth and store,
Though foolishly he lost the same,
Decaying more and more
Till he became
Most poor:

✝

With thee
O let me rise
As larks, harmoniously,
And sing this day thy victories:
Then shall the fall further the flight in me.

My tender age in sorrow did begin:
And still with sicknesses and shame
Thou didst so punish sin
That I became
Most thin.

✝

With thee
Let me combine,
And feel this day thy victory;
For, if I imp my wing on thine,
Affliction shall advance the flight in me.

Discussion of "Easter Wings"

George Herbert (1593-1633) was a late English Renaissance religious poet. He not only helped develop and fashion the devotional lyric into a popular literary type, but he delighted in delicate visual experiments in poetry. For example, he wrote one poem called "The Altar" whose lines were printed in the shape of an altar, and "Easter Wings" is printed in the shape of two sets of larks' wings.

In substance "Easter Wings" is a lovely poem of conventional religious faith, telling in the first stanza how man cut himself off from God through the "fall" and thus became spiritually poor, but how he aspires through the fall to rise in flight to God. In the second stanza Herbert first refers to his life of sorrow and sickness (he suffered a great deal of sickness before he died at 40), then expresses his faith that, harmonizing his life with God, he will fly to eternal victory. The whole poem develops on an elaborate "wing" metaphor and is also delicately constructed so that the first half of each stanza is a lament whereas the second half of each is an expression of the triumph of faith. The word "imp" in the next-to-last line is a term from falconry; to mend the damaged wing of a hawk by grafting to it feathers from another bird. When we know this, note how the comment "if I imp my wing on thine" takes on richer meaning.

A Psalm of Life

Henry Wadsworth Longfellow

Tell me not, in mournful numbers,
    Life is but an empty dream!—
For the soul is dead that slumbers,
    And things are not what they seem.

Life is real! Life is earnest!
    And the grave is not its goal;
Dust thou art, to dust returnest,
    Was not spoken of the soul.

Not enjoyment, and not sorrow,
    Is our destined end or way;
But to act, that each tomorrow
    Find us farther than today.

Art is long, and Time is fleeting,
    And our hearts, though stout and brave,
Still, like muffled drums, are beating
    Funeral marches to the grave.

In the world's broad field of battle,
    In the bivouac of Life,
Be not like dumb, driven cattle!
    Be a hero in the strife!

Trust no Future, howe'er pleasant!
    Let the dead Past bury its dead!
Act,—act in the living Present!
    Heart within, and God o'erhead!

Lives of great men all remind us
    We can make our lives sublime,
And, departing, leave behind us
    Footprints in the sands of time;

Footprints, that perhaps another,
    Sailing o'er life's solemn main,
A forlorn and shipwrecked brother,
    Seeing, shall take heart again.

Let us, then, be up and doing,
With a heart for any fate;
Still achieving, still pursuing,
Learn to labor and to wait.

Discussion of "A Psalm of Life"

For over a century one of the most popular poems of faith has been "A Psalm of Life" by the American poet Henry Wadsworth Longfellow (1807-1882). The openly didactic tone of Longfellow's early poems such as this, although rather out of fashion today, won masses of new readers for poetry in generations past, and continues to find a responsive appeal in the hearts of many people. Emphasis in the poem, written when Longfellow was only 31, is upon the importance of robust living, with high goals and high energy to achieve them—that is, upon faith in man and his ability to accomplish. Underlying this emphasis, however, is a strong faith in God and a God-controlled universe.

Questions for discussion: What elements in this poem would tend to make it more popular among readers in years past than it may be today? Is the poem too obvious and too general? What enduring truths, nevertheless, does it encompass?

Crossing the Bar[3]

Alfred Lord Tennyson

Sunset and evening star,
   And one clear call for me!
And may there be no moaning of the bar,
   When I put out to sea,

But such a tide as moving seems asleep,
   Too full for sound and foam,
When that which drew from out the boundless deep
   Turns again home.

Twilight and evening bell,
   And after that the dark!
And may there be no sadness of farewell,
   When I embark;

For though from out our bourne of Time and Place
   The flood may bear me far,
I hope to see my Pilot face to face
   When I have crossed the bar.

Discussion of "Crossing the Bar"

In 1833 when Tennyson was only 24 years old his close friend Arthur Henry Hallam died and Tennyson was plunged into a grief which dominated his life for many years thereafter. For seventeen years he worked on a long poem, *In Memoriam*, in which he exposes his grief to the world and tries to reconcile the death of a gifted young man with the will of God. At one place or another in the poem he explores not only most of the facets of grief but also most of the facets of faith and its absence. Throughout much of the poem the grief dominates, but gradually the "lame hands of faith" grow stronger as the poem ends with a repeated assertion that "all is well" if we will trust in God and His plan for mankind. Although Tennyson's faith lacks the robust vigor and unwavering confidence of his great

---

[3]The "bar" here referred to is an underwater sand uprising at the mouth of a harbor or river. There is an old folk superstition that the tide moans in grief as it passes over a sandbar when someone has died or is about to die.

contemporary Robert Browning, nevertheless Tennyson too is a poet of religious faith.

Best known of Tennyson's short poems is "Crossing the Bar," written in 1889 when he was 81 years old. Partly the poem lives by its lyrical loveliness, and partly by the quality of its faith— not a sure knowledge, such as a few people have, but a firm hope, which many people share. A few days before Tennyson died in 1892 he instructed that this poem should end all editions of his poetry— a request that has seldom been violated.

Question for discussion: Why does Tennyson want no "moaning of the bar" when he "puts out to sea"?

Uphill

Christina Rossetti[4]

Does the road wind uphill all the way?
    Yes, to the very end.
Will the day's journey take the whole long day?
    From morn to night, my friend.

But is there for the night a resting-place?
    A roof for when the slow dark hours begin.
May not the darkness hide it from my face?
    You cannot miss that inn.

Shall I meet other wayfarers at night?
    Those who have gone before.
Then must I knock, or call when just in sight?
    They will not keep you standing at that door.

Shall I find comfort, travel-sore and weak?
    Of labor you shall find the sum.
Will there be beds for me and all who seek?
    Yea, beds for all who come.

Discussion of "Uphill"

Another poem of conventional religious faith by a famous author is Christina Rossetti's "Uphill." Although written allegorically, its meaning will be clear to all readers. The only problem in reading will be to note that it is a conversation poem, with the questions in the first and third lines of each stanza asked by one person and the answers in the second and fourth lines given by another, wiser person —as if the Saviour Himself were giving reassurance.

Question for discussion: What is the full meaning of the line "Of labor you shall find the sum" in the last stanza? What is the "sum"?

[4]For a discussion of Christina Rossetti (1830-1894) and her writings, see pp. 291-294 of Volume 2.

Ah, Sun-flower

William Blake[5]

Ah, Sun-flower! weary of time,
Who countest the steps of the Sun,
Seeking after that sweet golden clime
Where the traveller's journey is done:

Where the Youth pined away with desire,
And the pale Virgin shrouded in snow
Arise from their graves, and aspire
Where my Sun-flower wishes to go.

Discussion of "Ah, Sun-flower"

The great romantic mystic William Blake (1757-1827) centered his poetry in symbols. Here the sunflower, rooted in the earth but reaching skyward, symbolizes man bound by the flesh and the mortal world yet ever aspiring towards heaven and spiritual freedom. This, too, represents man's faith that he can transcend his present limitations to climb towards life with God. The poetry is metaphoric and symbolic rather than explicit and didactic, but the central idea is not far afield from the more direct poems by Longfellow, Tennyson, and Christina Rossetti which we have just examined.

---

[5]For a discussion of Blake and his works, see pp. 91-92 of Volume 1. For other works by Blake, see also pp. 285-286 of Volume 1 and pp. 295-296 of Volume 2.

Five Poems by Carol Lynn Pearson

Of the Mysteries

I know only as much of God and the world
As a creature with two eyes must;
But what I do understand I love,
And what I don't understand, I trust.

The Lord Speaks to a
Literary Debauché
Newly Arrived in Heaven

Impressive indeed, this shelf of books
On which all the earth-critics dote.
But oh, my son, how I wish that you
Had read the book I wrote.

To a Beloved Skeptic

I cannot talk with you of God
Since sober wise you grew;
So my one recourse in charity
Is to talk with God of you.

Guilt

I have no vulture sins, God,
That overhang my sky,
To climb, grey-feathering the air
And swoop carnivorously.

It's just the tiny sins, God,
That from memory appear
Like tedious, buzzing flies to dart
Like static through my prayer.

Day-Old Child

My day-old child lay in my arms.
With my lips against his ear
I whispered strongly, "How I wish—
I wish that you could hear;

"I've a hundred wonderful things to say
(A tiny cough and a nod),
Hurry, hurry, hurry and grow
So I can tell you about God."

My day-old baby's mouth was still
And my words only tickled his ear.
But a kind of a light passed through his eyes,
And I saw this thought appear:

"How I wish I had a voice and words;
I've a hundred things to say.
Before I forget I'd tell you of God—
I left Him yesterday."

Discussion of Five Poems by Carol Lynn Pearson

Earlier in this volume we printed a little poem by Carol Lynn Pearson called "Prayer." Now it is our pleasure—and we mean pleasure—to include five more little poems by this gifted young L.D.S. writer, taken from her first small book of poems, called *Beginnings.* Mrs. Pearson is a native Utahn, born in Salt Lake City. She is now living in Provo with her husband Gerald, where she is employed as a scriptwriter for the B.Y.U. Motion Picture Department. Although still a young woman, already she has published both poetry and essays in quite a few places, and two of her plays—*Pegora the Witch* and *Think Your Way to a Million*—have won first-place awards in statewide playwriting contests. Another play, *Martyr-in-Waiting,* is being published by the Mutual Improvement Association of the L.D.S. Church.

As these five tiny poems delightfully illustrate, Mrs. Pearson has a combination of delicate word-usage with stimulating word-meanings that are both thought-provoking and charmingly simple. Nothing further need be said of them. The little poems speak clearly for themselves.

Sonnet 29

William Shakespeare

When in disgrace with fortune and men's eyes
I all alone beweep my outcast state,
And trouble deaf heaven with my bootless cries,
And look upon myself, and curse my fate,
Wishing me like to one more rich in hope,
Featured like him, like him with friends possessed,
Desiring this man's art, and that man's scope,
With what I most enjoy contented least;
Yet in these thoughts myself almost despising,
Haply I think on thee,—and then my state,
Like to the lark at break of day arising
From sullen earth, sings hymns at heaven's gate;
  For thy sweet love remembered such wealth brings
  That then I scorn to change my state with kings.

Discussion of Shakespeare's "Sonnet 29"

This sonnet, part of the total of 154 sonnets written by Shakespeare, is included here to emphasize that one kind of faith is faith in other people. Just thinking of a beloved person, says Shakespeare, can lift one out of a mood of despondency. Some readers may feel that Shakespeare exaggerates the power of love and friendship (in Shakespeare's case the person referred to in the sonnet was a cherished friend); other readers, having known the healing power of love and friendship, will see more meaning in Shakespeare's words.

Ode to the West Wind

Percy Bysshe Shelley

I

O, Wild West Wind, thou breath of Autumn's being,
Thou, from whose unseen presence the leaves dead
Are driven, like ghosts from an enchanter fleeing,

Yellow, and black, and pale, and hectic red,
Pestilence-stricken multitudes: O, thou,
Who chariotest to their dark wintry bed

The wingèd seeds, where they lie cold and low,
Each like a corpse within its grave, until
Thine azure sister of the spring shall blow

Her clarion o'er the dreaming earth, and fill
(Driving sweet buds like flocks to feed in air)
With living hues and odours plain and hill:

Wild Spirit, which art moving everywhere;
Destroyer and preserver: hear, oh, hear!

II

Thou on whose stream, 'mid the steep sky's commotion,
Loose clouds like earth's decaying leaves are shed,
Shook from the tangled boughs of Heaven and Ocean,

Angels of rain and lightning: there are spread
On the blue surface of thine aery surge,
Like the bright hair uplifted from the head

Of some fierce Maenad,[6] even from the dim verge
Of the horizon to the zenith's height
The locks of the approaching storm. Thou dirge

Of the dying year, to which this closing night
Will be the dome of a vast sepulchre,
Vaulted with all thy congregated might

Of vapors, from whose solid atmosphere
Black rain, and fire, and hail will burst: oh, hear!

[6]A frenzied female worshiper of Bacchus.

III

Thou who didst waken from his summer dreams
The blue Mediterranean, where he lay,
Lulled by the coil of his crystalline streams,

Beside a pumice[7] isle in Baiae's bay,[8]
And saw in sleep old palaces and towers
Quivering within the wave's intenser day,

All overgrown with azure moss and flowers
So sweet, the sense faints picturing them! Thou
For whose path the Atlantic's level powers

Cleave themselves into chasms, while far below
The sea-blooms and the oozy woods which wear
The sapless foliage of the ocean, know

Thy voice, and suddenly grow grey with fear,
And tremble and despoil themselves: oh, hear!

IV

If I were a dead leaf thou mightest bear;
If I were a swift cloud to fly with thee;
A wave to pant beneath thy power, and share

The impulse of thy strength, only less free
Than thou, O, uncontrollable! If even
I were as in my boyhood, and could be

The comrade of thy wanderings over heaven,
As then, when to outstrip thy skiey speed
Scarce seemed a vision; I would ne'er have striven

As thus with thee in prayer in my sore need.
Oh! lift me as a wave, a leaf, a cloud!
I fall upon the thorns of life! I bleed!

A heavy weight of hours has chained and bowed
One too like thee: tameless, and swift, and proud.

V

Make me thy lyre, even as the forest is:
What if my leaves are falling like its own!
The tumult of thy mighty harmonies

—————
[7]Of light, porous volcanic lava.
[8]An ancient Roman summer resort near Naples.

Will take from both a deep, autumnal tone,
Sweet though in sadness. Be thou, Spirit fierce,
My spirit! Be thou me, impetuous one!

Drive my dead thoughts over the universe
Like withered leaves to quicken a new birth!
And, by the incantation of this verse,

Scatter, as from an unextinguished hearth
Ashes and sparks, my words among mankind!
Be through my lips to unawakened earth

The trumpet of a prophecy! O, wind,
If Winter comes, can Spring be far behind?

Discussion of "Ode to the West Wind"

Shelley (1792-1822) was the next to youngest of the six lyric geniuses (Blake, Wordsworth, Coleridge, Byron, Shelley, and Keats) who crowned the movement of English romanticism in the early nineteenth century. Independent, fiery, and idealistic, Shelley saw poetry as the hope of the world that would ultimately lift mankind to universal freedom through universal love. His masterpiece is *Prometheus Unbound*, for which he wrote a preface acknowledging that he had "a passion for reforming the world" through poetry. Later in his famous essay "A Defence of Poetry" he argued that "poetry is the record of the best and happiest moments of the happiest and best minds" and that "poets are the unacknowledged legislators of the world," meaning that they are the spokesmen for humanity as well as the shapers of human destiny.

With this information as background we are now ready to examine "Ode to the West Wind," one of the most carefully constructed of Shelley's poems.[9] The first 14-line section describes the power of the wind to scatter the leaves and seeds hither and yon until they settle like corpses in their graves awaiting the coming of spring. This first section is also a plea that the wind will listen to the voice of the poet. The second 14-line section is much the same—

---

[9]Note that each 14-line section is carefully built of iambic pentameter lines rhyming aba bcb cdc ded ee, a variation of the famous terza rima stanza developed by Dante for *The Divine Comedy*.

again an appeal for the wind to hear the poet's voice, and a description
of the powers of the wind over the clouds. The third section once
more parallels the structure of the first two—the power of the wind
over the sea-currents, the ocean-tides, the waves, and a third plea
that the wind will listen to the imploring voice of the poet. The
fourth section then summarizes, referring in its first three lines to
the power of the wind over the "dead leaf" (first section), "swift
cloud" (second section), and "wave" (third section). The fourth
section also contrasts, a little self-pityingly, the soaring freedom of
the wind with the present ineffectualness of the poet. Finally the
fourth section actually turns to prayer, as the poet prays to the wind.
Obviously no poet would pray to a mere wind unless the wind
symbolized something greater than itself. Here the wind is a symbol
of regenerative power that brings a re-birth of life each year. As
trees and flowers die in autumn, the wind scatters their leaves and
seeds where they lie on the ground until the spring winds bring
life-giving rains and the earth bursts forth in a re-awakening of life.
All of this is made clear in the fifth and closing section, where the
central point of the poem is also identified as the poet prays that,
like the life-giving wind, his thoughts may be driven over the universe
among mankind to "quicken a new birth." And the closing line is
one of optimistic faith for the future of the earth and mankind as
Shelley asks, "If Winter comes, can Spring be far behind?"

The enduring appeal of the poem, one of Shelley's finest, results
probably more from its soaring, image-filled, music-rich lyricism, its
vivid descriptive phrases, and its carefully executed form than from
its ideas. The strength of the ideas, nevertheless, is also considerable,
as he expresses his faith in the redemptive power of poetry and also
in the future, both for the earth and for man.

Thoughts for discussion: (1) Point out the qualities of the
wind that make it a good symbol of regenerative power. (2) How
can poetry help to cleanse and regenerate the world?

The Darkling Thrush

Thomas Hardy

I leaned upon a coppice gate
  When Frost was specter-gray,
And Winter's dregs made desolate
  The weakening eye of day.
The tangled bine-stems scored the sky
  Like strings from broken lyres,
And all mankind that haunted nigh
  Had sought their household fires.

The land's sharp features seemed to be
  The Century's corpse outleant.
His crypt the cloudy canopy,
  The wind his death-lament.
The ancient pulse of germ and birth
  Was shrunken hard and dry,
And every spirit upon earth
  Seemed fervorless as I.

At once a voice burst forth among
  The bleak twigs overhead
In a full-hearted evensong
  Of joy illimited;
An aged thrush, frail, gaunt, and small,
  In blast-beruffled plume,
Had chosen thus to fling his soul
  Upon the growing gloom.

So little cause for carolings
  Of such ecstatic sound
Was written on terrestrial things
  Afar or nigh around,
That I could think there trembled through
  His happy good-night air
Some blessed Hope, whereof he knew
  And I was unaware.

Discussion of "The Darkling Thrush"

Thomas Hardy (1840-1928), great English novelist, short-story writer, and poet, was often gloomy and harshly pessimistic in his writings. Like many people of the modern world, he looked around and saw so much misery, cruelty, and injustice that he had difficulty believing the world is under God's control. Nevertheless, underlying the general pessimism of his philosophy is a hungering desire to believe, as expressed in this famous little poem. Perhaps it is not a grossly untrue generalization to say that the world is divided into two types of people—those who have faith, and those who wish they could.

Introduction to "Invictus" and "Work Without Hope"

Up to this point in this section we have been exploring various kinds and degrees of faith. Not all literature, of course, expresses faith. Hardy's poem, just examined, has only a glimmering, and some works have even less. In fact, much of the literature of the twentieth century, powerful and artistically vivid though it may be, tends to challenge rather than affirm traditional religious beliefs. In Volume 1 (pp. 448-451) we printed several poems by James Thomson, A. C. Swinburne, and Robinson Jeffers portraying life as a misery to endure and death as an oblivion of nothingness to anticipate. Here we have space to print just two little poems illustrating problems resulting from a lack of faith.

The first is "Work Without Hope" by Samuel Taylor Coleridge (1772-1834).[10] Coleridge's problem was not that he did not believe in God, for he was a devout Christian, nor that he did not believe in life after death, for he did, but that he did not believe in himself. "The fearful unbelief is unbelief in yourself," said Carlyle. Coleridge was a brilliant and gifted man, in many ways the most brilliant and gifted writer of the English romantic movement. But he was also beset with terrible personal insecurity, unhappiness, and lack of self-discipline which resulted in agonizing drug addiction, insomnia, and wrecking of health, both physical and mental. In a moment of despair a few years before his death he wrote "Work Without Hope," one of the most beautiful yet dejected little poems ever written. Here we feel the suffering anguish of a man who has lost faith in himself.

Work Without Hope

Samuel Taylor Coleridge

All Nature seems at work. Slugs leave their lair—
The bees are stirring—birds are on the wing—
And Winter slumbering in the open air,
Wears on his smiling face a dream of Spring!
And I the while, the sole unbusy thing,
Nor honey make, nor pair, nor build, nor sing.

---

[10]For a discussion of Coleridge and his masterpiece, "The Rime of the Ancient Mariner," see Volume 1, pp. 321-328.

Yet well I ken the banks where amaranths blow,
Have traced the fount whence streams of nectar flow.
Bloom, O ye amaranths! bloom for whom ye may,
For me ye bloom not! Glide, rich streams, away!
With lips unbrightened, wreathless brow, I stroll:
And would you learn the spells that drowse my soul?
Work without Hope draws nectar in a sieve,
And Hope without an object cannot live.

The problem of William Ernest Henley (1849-1903) is different. If anything, he has too much confidence in himself—and too little in God. In fact, he doesn't really believe in God, nor in a Christian life after death. "Invictus" has sometimes been recited by people in Church as an example of a devoutly religious Christian with an admirable faith. I shudder every time I hear the famous little poem referred to in this manner. It is a powerful poem, but it is hardly Christian. The phrase "whatever gods may be" seems more pagan than Christian, "the fell clutch of circumstance" is the deadly grip of fate, and the "horror of the shade" which "looms" after death is about as un-Christian a view of eternal life as could be. The poem is printed here partly to show the importance of not mis-interpreting literature (a reading of Henley's other poems will confirm that the interpretation given here is correct), and partly to illustrate an arrogantly un-Christian attitude towards life. The speaker in the poem may exhibit a courageous capacity to endure whatever difficulties mortal life has in store for him, but he hardly exhibits personal humility or faith in a benevolent God.

Invictus[11]

William Ernest Henley

Out of the night that covers me,
    Black as the Pit from pole to pole,
I thank whatever gods may be
    For my unconquerable soul.

In the fell clutch of circumstance
    I have not winced nor cried aloud.

─ ─ ─ ─ ─ ─
[11]The title means "unconquered."

Under the bludgeonings of chance
   My head is bloody, but unbowed.

Beyond this place of wrath and tears
   Looms but the Horror of the shade.
And yet the menace of the years
   Finds, and shall find, me unafraid.

It matters not how strait the gate,
   How charged with punishments the scroll,
I am the master of my fate.
   I am the captain of my soul.

Christ in Flanders

Honoré de Balzac

At a time somewhat indeterminate in Brabantine history, connection between the island of Cadzant and the coast of Flanders was kept up by a boat used for passengers to and fro. The capital of the island, Middleburg, afterward so celebrated in the annals of Protestantism, counted then hardly two or three hundred hearths. Rich Ostend was then an unknown harbor, flanked by a village thinly peopled by a few fisherfolk, and poor dealers, and pirates who plied their trade with impunity. Nevertheless, the borough of Ostend, composed of about twenty houses and three hundred cottages, cabins, and hovels—made with the remains of wrecked ships—rejoiced in a governor, a militia, a gallows, a convent, and a burgomaster, in fact, all the institutions of advanced civilization. Who was reigning at that time in Brabant, Belgium, and Flanders? On this point tradition is mute.

Let us admit that this story is strangely imbued with that vagueness, indefiniteness, and love of the marvelous which the favorite orators of Flemish vigils love to intermingle in their legends, as varied in poetry as they are contradictory in detail. Told from age to age, repeated from hearth to hearth, by grandmothers and by storytellers night and day, this chronicle has received each century a different coloring. Like those buildings planned according to the architectural caprice of each epoch, whose dark, crumbling masses are a pleasure to poets alone, this legend would drive commentators, and wranglers over facts, words, and dates, to desperation. The narrator believes in it, as all superstitious souls in Flanders have believed in it, without being for that reason either more learned or more weak-minded. Admitting the impossibility of harmonizing all the different versions, here is the story, stripped perhaps of its romantic naiveté—for this it is impossible to reproduce—but still with its daring statements disproved by history, and its morality approved by religion; its fantastic flowers of imagination, and hidden sense which the wise can interpret each to his own liking. Let each one seek his pasture herein and take the trouble to separate the good grain from the tares.

The boat which served to carry over the passengers from the island of Cadzant to Ostend was just about to leave the village. Before undoing the iron chain which held his boat to a stone on the little jetty where people embarked, the skipper blew his horn several times to call the loiterers, for this journey was his last. Night was coming on, the last fires of the setting sun scarcely gave enough light to distinguish the coast of Flanders or the tardy passengers on the island wandering along the earthen walls which surrounded the fields or among the tall reeds of the marshes. The boat was full. "What are you waiting for? Let us be off!" they cried. Just then a man appeared a few steps from the jetty. The pilot, who had neither heard nor seen him approaching, was somewhat surprised. The passenger seemed to have risen from the earth on a sudden. He might have been a peasant sleeping in a field, waiting for the hour for starting, whom the horn had wakened up. Was it a thief, or was it someone from the Customs House or police? When he arrived on the jetty to which the boat was moored, seven persons who were standing in the stern hastened to sit down on the benches, in order to have them to themselves and prevent the stranger from seating himself among them. It was a sudden instinctive feeling, one of those aristocratic instincts which suggest themselves to rich people. Four of these personages belonged to the highest nobility of Flanders.

First of all, there was a young cavalier, with two beautiful grey-hounds, wearing over his long hair a cap decked with jewels. He clinked his gilded spurs, and now and again curled his mustache, as he cast disdainful looks at the rest of the freight.

Then there was a proud damosel, who carried a falcon on her wrist and spoke only to her mother or to an ecclesiastic of high rank, a relative, no doubt. These persons made as much noise talking together as if they were the only people on the boat. All the same, next to them sat a man of great importance in the country, a fat merchant from Bruges, enveloped in a large mantle. His servant, armed to the teeth, kept by his side two bags full of money. Beside them was a man of science, a doctor of the University of Louvain, with his clerk. These people, who all despised one another, were separated from the bows by the rower's bench.

When the late passenger put his foot into the boat he gave a swift look at the stern, but when he saw no room there he went to seek a place among the people in the bows. It was the poor who sat there. At the sight of a man bare-headed, whose brown cloth coat and fine linen shirt had no ornament, who held in his hand neither hat nor cap, with neither purse nor rapier at his girdle, all took him for a burgomaster—a good and gentle man, like one of those old Flemings whose nature and simple character have been so well rendered by the painters of their country. The poor passengers welcomed the stranger with a respectful demeanor, which excited mocking whispers among the people in the stern. An old soldier, a man of toil and trouble, gave him his place on the bench, and sat himself at the end of the boat, keeping himself steady by putting his feet against one of the transverse beams which knit the planks together like the backbone of a fish.

A young woman, a mother with her little child, who seemed to belong to the working class of Ostend, moved back to make room for the newcomer. In this movement there was no trace either of servility or disdain. It was merely a mark of that kindliness by which the poor, who know so well how to appreciate a service, show their frank and natural disposition—so simple and obvious in the expression of all their qualities, good or bad.

The stranger thanked them with a gesture full of nobility, and sat down between the young mother and the old soldier. Behind him was a peasant with his son, ten years old. A poor old woman, with a wallet almost empty, old and wrinkled, and in rags—a type of misery and neglect—lay in the prow, crouched upon a coil of ropes. One of the rowers, an old sailor, who had known her when she was rich and beautiful, had let her get in for what the people so beautifully call "the love of God." "Thank you kindly, Thomas," the old woman had said; "I will speak special prayers for you in my prayers this evening."

The skipper blew his horn once more, looked at the silent country, cast the chain into his boat, ran along the side to the helm, took the tiller, and stood erect; then, having looked at the sky, called out in a loud voice to the rowers, when they were well in the open sea, "Row hard, make haste; the sea smiles evilly—the witch! I feel the swell at the helm and the storm at my wound." These words, spoken in the language of the sea—a tongue only understood by those accustomed to the sound of the waves—gave to the oars a hastened but ever-cadenced movement, as different from the former manner of rowing as the gallop of a horse from its trot. The fine people sitting at the stern took pleasure in seeing the sinuous arms, the bronzed faces with eyes of fire, the distended muscles, and the different human forms working in unison, just to get *them* the quicker over this narrow strait. So far from being sorry for their labor, they pointed out the rowers to each other, and laughed at the grotesque expressions which their exertion printed on their anxious faces. In the prow the soldier, the peasant, and the old woman regarded the mariners with that kind of compassion natural to people who, living by toil, know its hard anguish and feverish fatigue. Besides, being accustomed to life in the open air, they all divined by the look of the sky the danger which threatened them; so *they* were serious. The young mother was rocking her child to sleep, singing to it some old hymn of the church.

"If we *do* get over," said the old soldier to the peasant, "God will have taken a deal of trouble to keep us alive."

"Ah! He is master," said the old woman; "but I think it is His good pleasure to call us to Himself. Do you see that light, there?" and by a gesture of the head she pointed out the setting sun. Bands of fire streaked vividly the brown-red tinted clouds, which seemed just about to unchain a furious wind. The sea gave forth a suppressed murmur, a sort of internal groan, something like the growling of a dog whose anger will not be appeased.

After all Ostend was not far off. Just now the sky and the sea showed one of those sights to which it is impossible for words or painting to give longer duration than they have in reality. Human creations like powerful contrasts, so artists generally demand from nature its most brilliant aspects, despairing per-haps to be able to render the great and beautiful poetry of her ordinary appearance, although the human soul is often as profoundly moved by calm as by motion, by the silence as much as by the storm.

There was one moment when everyone on the boat was silent and gazed on the sea and sky, whether from presentiment or in obedience to that religious melancholy which comes over nearly all of us at the hour of prayer, at the fall of day, at the moment when nature is silent and the bells speak. The sea cast up a faint, white glimmer, but changing like the color of steel; the sky was mostly gray; in the west, long, narrow spaces looked like waves of blood, whereas in the east, glittering lines, marked as by a fine pencil, were separated from one another by clouds, folded like the wrinkles on an old man's forehead. Thus the sea and the sky formed a neutral background, everything in half tints, which made the fires of the setting sun glare ominously. The face of nature inspired a feeling of terror. If it is allowable to interweave the daring hyperboles of the people into the written language, one might repeat what the soldier said, "Time is rolling away," or what the peasant answered, that the sky had the look of a hangman. All of a sudden the wind rose in the west, and the skipper, who never ceased to watch the sea, seeing it swell toward the horizon, cried, "Ho, ho!" At this cry the sailors stopped immediately, and let their oars float.

"The skipper is right," said Thomas. The boat, borne on the top of a huge wave, seemed to be descending to the bottom of the gaping sea. At this extraordinary movement and this sudden rage of the ocean the people in the stern turned pale, and gave a terrible cry, "We perish!"

"Not yet," answered the skipper quietly. At this moment the clouds were rent in twain by the force of the wind exactly above the boat. The gray masses spread out with ominous quickness from east to west, and the twilight, falling straight down through a rent made by the storm wind, rendered visible every face. The passengers, the rich and the noble, the sailors and the poor, all stopped one moment in astonishment at the aspect of the last comer. His golden hair. parted in the middle on his tranquil, serene forehead, fell in many curls on his shoulders, and outlined against the gray sky a face sublime in its gentleness, radiant with divine love. He did not despise death; he was certain not to perish. But if at first the people at the stern had forgotten for an instant the tempest whose implacable fury menaced them, they soon returned to their selfish sentiments and life-long habits.

"It's lucky for him, that dolt of a burgomaster, that he does not know the danger we are all in. There he stands like a dog, and doesn't seem to mind dying," said the doctor.

Hardly had he completed this judicious remark when the tempest unchained its legions; wind blew from every side, the boat spun round like a top, and the sea swamped it.

"Oh, my poor child! my child! who will save my child?" cried the mother, in a heartrending voice.

"You yourself," replied the stranger. The sound of this voice penetrated the heart of the young woman and put hope therein. She heard this sweet word, in spite of the raging of the storm, in spite of the shrieks of the passengers.

"Holy Virgin of Perpetual Succor, who are at Antwerp, I promise you twenty pounds of wax and a statue if you will only get me out of this," cried the the merchant, falling on his knees upon his bags of gold.

"The Virgin is no more at Antwerp than she is here," replied the doctor.

"She is in heaven," said a voice, which seemed to come forth from the sea.

"Who spoke?"

"The devil," said the servant; "he's mocking the Virgin of Antwerp."

"Shut up with your blessed Virgin," said the skipper to the passengers; "take hold of the bowls and help me get the water out of the boat. As to you," he continued, addressing the sailors, "row hard, we have a moment's grace, and in the devil's name, who has left you in this world until now, let us be our own Providence. This little strip of water is horribly dangerous, I know from thirty years' experience. Is this evening the first time I have had a storm to deal with?" Then standing at the helm, the skipper continued to look alternately at the boat, the sea, and the sky.

"The skipper mocks at everything," said Thomas in a low voice.

"Will God let *us* die with these wretched people?" asked the proud damosel of the handsome cavalier.

"No! no! Noble damsel, listen to me." He put his arm round her waist, and spoke in her ear. "I can swim—don't say anything about it; I will take you by your beautiful hair and bring you safely to the shore; but I can save you only."

The damosel looked at her old mother; the dame was on her knees asking absolution from the bishop, who was not listening to her. The cavalier read in the eyes of his beautiful mistress some faint sentiment of filial piety, so he said to her in a low voice, "Submit yourself to the will of God; if He wishes to call your mother to Himself, it will doubtless be for her happiness—in the other world," he added, in a voice still lower, "and for ours in this."

The dame Rupelmonde possessed seven fiefs, besides the barony of Gavres. The damosel listened to the voice of life, to the interests of love, speaking through the mouth of the handsome adventurer, a young miscreant, who haunted churches, seeking for prey—either a girl to marry or else good ready money.

The bishop blessed the waves and ordered them to be calm, not knowing exactly what to do; he was thinking of his concubine awaiting him with a delicate feast, perhaps at this moment in her bath perfuming herself, or arraying herself in velvet, and fastening on her necklaces and jewels. So far from thinking of the powers of the Church, and consoling these Christians, and exhorting them to trust in God, the perverse bishop mingled worldly regrets and words of lust with the sacred words of the Breviary.

The light, which lit up the pale faces, showed all their varying expressions, when the boat was borne up into the air by a wave, or cast down to the bottom of the abyss; then, shaken like a frail leaf, a plaything of the autumn wind, it cracked its shell, and seemed nigh to break altogether. Then there were horrible cries alternating with awful silence.

The demeanor of the people seated in the prow of the boat contrasted singularly with that of the rich and powerful in the stern. The young mother strained her child to her bosom every time that the waves threatened to engulf the frail bark; but she held to the hope with which the words of the stranger had filled her heart: each time she turned her eyes toward this man she drank in from his face a new faith, the strong faith of a weak woman, the faith of a mother. Living by the divine word, the word of love, which had gone forth from this man, the simple creature awaited trustfully the fulfillment of the sort of promise he had given her, and scarcely feared the tempest any more. Sticking to the side of the boat, the soldier ceased not to contemplate this singular being, on whose impassibility he sought to model his own rough, tanned face, bringing into play all his intelligence and strength of will, whose powerful springs had not been vitiated in the course of a passive mechanical life. He was emulous to show himself tranquil and calm, after the manner of this superior courage; he ended by identifying himself in some measure with the secret principle of its interior power. Then his imagination became an instinctive fanaticism, a love without limit, a faith in this man, like that enthusiasm which solders have for their commander when he is a man of power, surrounded with the glory of victories, marching in the midst of the splendid prestige of genius. The poor old woman said in a low voice, "Ah! what a miserable sinner I am! Have I not suffered enough to expiate the pleasures of my youth? Miserable one, why hast thou led the gay life of a Frenchwoman? Why hast thou consumed the goods of God with the people of the Church, the goods of the poor 'twixt the drink shop and the pawn shop? Ah! how wicked I was! Oh! my God! my God! let me finish my hell in this world of misery. Holy Virgin, Mother of God, take pity on me."

"Console yourself, mother, God is not a Lombard; although I have killed here and there good people and wicked, I do not fear for the resurrection."

"Ah! Sir, how happy they are, those beautiful ladies who are near the bishop, holy man!" the old woman went on; "they will have absolution from their sins. Oh! if I could only hear the voice of a priest saying to me, 'Your sins are forgiven you,' I could believe him."

The stranger turned toward her, and his look, full of charity, made her tremble. "Have faith," he said, "and you will be saved."

"May God reward you, good sir," she answered. "If you speak truly, I will go for you and for me on a pilgrimage to Our Lady of Loretto, barefooted."

The two peasants, father and son, remained silent, resigned, and submitting to the will of God, as people accustomed to follow instinctively, like animals, the convulsions of nature.

So on one side there were riches, pride, knowledge, debauchery, crime, all human society such as it is made by arts, thought, and education, the world and its laws; but also on this side, only shrieks, terror, the struggles of a thousand conflicting feelings, with horrible doubt—naught but the anguish of fear. And, towering above these, one powerful man, the skipper of the boat, doubting nothing, the chief, the fatalist king, making his own Providence, crying out for bailing bowls and not on the Virgin to save him, defying the storm, and wrestling with the sea, body to body.

At the other end of the boat, the weak: The mother, holding to her bosom a little child, who smiled at the storm. A wanton once gay, now given over to horrible remorse. A soldier, scarred with wounds, without other reward than his mutilated life, as a price for indefatigable devotion—he had hardly a morsel of bread, steeped in tears; all the same, he laughed at everything, and marched on without care, happy when he could drown his glory at the bottom of a pot of beer, or was telling stories thereof to wondering children; he commended gaily to God the care of his future. Lastly, two peasants, people of toil and weariness, labor incarnate, the work on which the world lives; these simple creatures were guileless of thought and its treasures, but ready to lose themselves utterly in a belief; having a more robust faith, in that they had never discussed or analyzed it; virgin natures, in whom conscience had remained pure and feeling strong. Contrition, misery, love, work had exercised, purified, concentrated, disculpated their will, the only thing which in man resembles that which sages call the soul.

When the boat, piloted by the marvelous dexterity of the skipper, came almost in view of Ostend, fifty paces from the shore, it was driven back by the convulsion of the storm, and suddenly began to sink. The stranger with the light upon his face then said to this little world of sorrow, "Those who have faith shall be saved; let them follow me." This man stood up and walked with a firm step on the waves. At once the young mother took her child in her arms and walked with him on the sea. The soldier suddenly stood at attention, saying in his rough language, "By my pipe! I follow you to the devil." Then, without seeming astonished, he marched on the sea.

The old streetwoman, believing in the omnipotence of God, followed the man, and walked on the sea. The two peasants said, "As they are walking on the sea, why should not *we?*" So they got up and hastened after the others, walking on the sea.

Thomas wished to do likewise; but his faith wavered, and he fell several times into the sea, but got out again; and after three failures he too walked upon the sea.

The daring pilot stuck like a leech to the bottom of his boat. The merchant had faith, and had risen, but he wanted to take his gold with him, and his gold took him to the bottom of the sea. Mocking at the charlatan and the imbeciles who listened to him, at the moment when he saw the stranger proposing to the passengers to walk on the sea, the man of science began to laugh, and was swallowed up in the ocean. The damosel was drawn down into the abyss by her lover. The bishop and the old lady went to the bottom, heavy with sin, perhaps, heavier still with unbelief and confidence in false images; heavy with devotional practices, light of alms and true religion.

The faithful troop, who trod with firm, dry feet on the plain of the raging waters, heard around them the horrible howling of the storm; great sheets of water broke in their path; irresistible force rent the ocean in twain. Through the mist these faithful ones perceived on the shore a little feeble light, which flickered in the window of a fisherman's cabin. Each one as he marched bravely toward this light seemed to hear his neighbor crying through the roaring sea, "Courage!" Nevertheless, absorbed each in his own danger, no one said a single word. And so they reached the shore. When they were all seated at the hearth of the fisherman, they sought in vain the guide who had a light upon his face. From his seat upon the summit of a rock, at the base of which the hurricane had cast the pilot clinging to his plank with all the strength of a sailor in the throes of death, the MAN descended, picked up the shipwrecked man almost dashed to pieces; then he said, as he held out a helping hand over his head, "It is well this once, but do as thou *hast* done no more; the example would be too bad." He took the mariner on his shoulders, and carried him to the fisherman's cottage. He knocked for the unfortunate man, so that someone would open the door of this humble refuge to him; then the Savior disappeared.

In this place the sailors built the Convent of Mercy, where were long to be seen the prints that the feet of JESUS CHRIST had, it was said, left on the sand.

Afterward, when the French entered Belgium, some monks took away with them this precious relic, the testimony of the last visit JESUS ever paid to the earth.

Discussion of "Christ in Flanders"

Honoré de Balzac (1799-1850) is one of the giants of French literature and one of the great novelists of the world. Especially important in the development of the massive school of realism that has dominated western-world literature for the past hundred years, Balzac devoted twenty years to writing his huge several-volumed masterpiece, *Comédie Humaine* (The Human Comedy).

"Christ in Flanders," an internationally famous story, is written in the form of an old folk tale. The first two paragraphs, and the last two, are intended to give it an authentic yet timeless setting. Balzac realizes that the old story may not be true—may just be a folk myth—but realizes also that whether the events are factual or not, the message that the story delivers is both true and universal. For L.D.S. readers there is a slightly special problem in that occasional phrases reflect a Catholic origin and setting for the story, but these in no way lessen the central truth of the story—and so we print it here.

The incident of Christ walking on the storm-tossed waters followed by some of the boat-passengers is intended to symbolize faith. Those who have sufficient faith walk with Christ on the water, and those without sufficient faith sink to the bottom. The whole story is written in the simple method of a parable. Each character is developed only to the extent needed to show his faith or lack of faith. That is, they are caricatures rather than rounded characters. The merchant is fat and money-loving. The scientist is learned but skeptical, priding himself in his intellect and scorning all things spiritual. The pretty damosel and the dashing cavalier are fleshly pleasure-lovers. And so forth.

Thoughts and questions for discussion: (1) Examine each character and point out what qualities in each result in his being saved or not being saved. (2) To what extent does Christ save each person and to what extent does each one save himself—or otherwise? (3) Is Balzac in the story too severe on the people of wealth and nobility? Is it their wealth and nobility that destroy them or their qualities of character? (4) Why does Christ save the pilot, who did not obey His command?

SECTION FOUR

The Satisfaction of Growth

by Robert K. Thomas

"Lady Jean"

by George Bellows (1882-1925) American (Yale University Art Gallery)
Bequest of Stephen Carlton Clark, B.A., 1903

Commentary by
Floyd E. Brienholt, Associate Professor of Art, Brigham Young University

We can be sure of one thing. That is change. Nothing remains static. Whether change means growth is a matter of question. Growth implies a movement toward a better or more ideal state or situation. History is a record of this change and art history reflects this change in some tangible form. The paintings of George Bellows reflect changes in a growing America. It is for you to decide whether or not this change is growth.

During the late 19th and early 20th centuries a group of artists who called themselves "The Eight" wished to get away from the repetitious and sentimental in landscape and figure painting. They painted uninhibited scenes of life in the streets or crowded tenements of the big city, claiming that this was real life. They were self-termed American realists.

Although George Bellows was not one of "The Eight," he admired them and was a friend of most of them. He chose similar subject matter and worked in the same manner—rebelling against the academic and trite. His subjects covered many facets of the changing American life—city streets, sports, romantic landscapes, and, in his later mature life, character portraits. He never went to Europe to study, as was common practice among artists at that time, but treated his subject matter in an expressive technique with bold draftsmanship, slashing strokes, and heavy paint. His remarkable visual memory made it possible for him to work rapidly to give a strong impression of actuality.

In the painting "Lady Jean," we see the artist's younger daughter dressed in her mother's "grown-up" clothes. It has a nostalgic quality for most of us because we remember our own experiences at that age or because we see our own children dressing up and imitating adults. Although much less dramatic and active than his paintings of prize fights and the rugged reality of his time, it is appealing in its youthful beauty—one of the best loved paintings in American art history.

The great artist (Bellows in this example) finds beauty and truth in the commonplace and paints it so that we almost feel as if it is our own discovery. As one writer so aptly put it, most discoveries are "suddenly seen things that were always there."

THE SATISFACTION OF GROWTH

"We are born to grow and can only develop by keeping ourselves in vital communication with the world without and within us." —J. S. Spalding

The Greek philosopher Pythagoras divided human life into four equal parts: between one and twenty, one is a child; between twenty and forty, one is a youth; between forty and sixty, one is a human being; and between sixty and eighty, a human being who is beginning to lose some of his powers. For those who live beyond eighty Pythagoras had no description—and he prudently died at seventy-five. One suspects that, had he lived to ninety-five, he might have revised his views.

If there is some neatness in establishing categories by which to describe human life, the arbitrary nature of Pythagoras' division is exposed by reflecting on our own experience. We have all known those who retained the spontaneity and vitality of youth beyond forty or, sad to say, those who were childish at fifty. Genuine maturity, however, has some relationship to chronology. No matter how sensitive a young woman is to her environment, the time it takes to develop judgment cannot be shortened easily. We are proverbially told that experience is the best teacher; we need to realize that it is often a deliberate one as well. We may learn to avoid a hot stove very quickly, but the cultivation of taste is a slow process, and the attainment of wisdom may be a life-long one.

It is popular in our day to talk knowingly about the "mature mind" or the "mature personality." Usually, such discourses probe modern techniques for curing mental illness or achieving personal and social serenity. A possible danger here is that we allow those who do not share our beliefs to set our standards. An equal danger is posed if no standards are recognized. The gospel, however, provides the direction that is needed in establishing guide lines while encouraging the widest possible range of personal growth. Eternal, individual progression is the most exciting concept of human potential yet envisioned for man.

The first selection in this section, "Silence" by Marianne Moore, skillfully brings together several characteristics of maturity on which there would probably be general agreement. What are here called "superior" people have developed sensitivity to the feelings of others; they are not prone to indulge themselves; they take little pleasure in doing the usual, expected things, and they recognize the limits under which they function. What makes this poem effective is the way in which these ideas are presented. To begin with, the indirection of Miss Moore's lines forces us to think about what she is saying while the specific details she uses help us to participate in the situations she describes. The result is that we come away from a poem *about* growth having *experienced* growth.

The second selection—an excerpt from a larger work—is almost clinical in its forthright analysis, yet it exhibits a warmth and understanding that allows us to see our possible faults without destroying our ability to change. This article is particularly interesting in its implied insistence that our own growth should match the development of those who are dearest to us.

Ezra Pound's rather free translation of an ancient Chinese poem helps us to see how old, yet how fresh, are the stages in developing love. Anyone who is happily married can testify that falling in love is exciting, but growing in love is more deeply satisfying.

In John Donne's "Sonnet 7" we may recognize part of our own religious growth. As children our imaginations are primarily visual. We may have difficulty in comprehending some religious concepts, but we easily imagine what a day of Judgment might look like. As we grow older, we shift our emphasis from picturing such an occasion to preparing for it. We begin to appreciate Amos' blunt warning that "the day of the Lord is darkness and not light" to those who are still unrepentant when He comes to judge the world.

Our first short story in this section, "Early Marriage" by Conrad Richter, has a pioneer setting that focuses on the Southwest. While many of the problems faced by those who colonized this region were shared by the pioneers who came to the Rocky Mountains, the ever-present terror of Indian attack was not as great a problem in Utah as it was farther south. Yet this is no story of courage under actual fire. The young boy and girl who must make several days journey through hostile country are not called upon to fight Indians, but they must fight their own fears, develop enough self-control to strengthen each other, and grow up to the point that they can face whatever the next day brings.

"My Kinsman, Major Molineaux" is one of Nathaniel Hawthorne's earliest attempts at short story writing. Although it has often been neglected by critics, it is now being recognized as one of the few truly great stories which Hawthorne wrote. For it manages to touch such universal chords that this young man's initiation into adult life rings true for most readers.

Growing up is often painful because it involves changes we are not prepared to make. As we follow Robin in his search for the relative who is to make his fortune, we may remember our own uncertain encounters with forces which helped shape our lives when our young hearts were still disorderly with hope and expectation. As the final lines of this unusual story suggest, a certain amount of disillusionment is fairly certain as we "put off childish things," but this is fair payment for maturity. The Robin we leave is not the carefree, thoughtless youth we met in the beginning. But, as his understanding friend suggests, he is now prepared to make realistic decisions which do not depend upon indulgence by others. Whatever he now chooses to do, he decides as a responsible adult.

Silence

Marianne Moore

My father used to say,
'Superior people never make long visits,
have to be shown Longfellow's grave
or the glass flowers at Harvard.
Self-reliant like the cat—
that takes its prey to privacy,
the mouse's limp tail hanging like a
    shoelace from its mouth—
they sometimes enjoy solitude,
and can be robbed of speech
by speech which has delighted them.
The deepest feeling always shows it-
    self in silence;
not in silence, but restraint.'
Nor was he insincere in saying, 'Make
    my house your inn.'
Inns are not residences.

Discussion of "Silence"

Marianne Moore (1887-   ) recently celebrated her eightieth birthday, still vigorously writing poetry and maintaining interests which range from baseball to meticulous scholarship. She was educated at Bryn Mawr and the Metzger Institute in Pennsylvania. This joining of a liberal arts education with specific business training (her year at the Institute emphasized business administration) is typical of Miss Moore's insistence that the subject matter of poetry is only limited by the poet's sensitivity.

"Silence" is an excellent example of the effective use of sentence and phrase to point up or even over-emphasize a simple statement. Note that this poem is not so much about silence as it is an attempt to plumb desirable qualities which silence may be masking. The opening statement that "superior people never make long visits" would seem to be echoed by the closing line: "Inns are not residences." In between, however, we have grown in our appreciation

of the reasons why this is so. The silence which comes from restraint
is a developed silence which implies unusual awareness. The silence
which is the result of profound feeling suggests the respect we have
for that which has moved us. No casual applause or exclamation
is appropriate, and we do not need to call attention to our approval.
These are mature attitudes, and it is to these that Miss Moore would
call our attention.

There is one image in this poem that is so graphic that it is
unforgettable. Who will ever be able to erase from his memory the
picture of the cat who has just caught a mouse. It is probably meant
to jar a little, since we have just been lulled by brief descriptions
of standard, unthinking behavior. The contrast between generalized
sightseeing tour activity and that shockingly specific mouse tail
illustrates how different the worlds of sensitive and insensitive people
are.

The final lines are partially quoted from Edmund Burke, an
English statesman of the 18th century. They suggest the necessity
for constant improvement. If we are content to take up residence
when we should be moving on, we have substituted indulgence for
growth.

"The Mother's Dilemma" from Their
Mothers' Sons

Edward Strecker

Maturity is not an inborn trait; it is not hereditary. It is the result of early background, environment, training, and unselfish parental love.

Conversely, immaturity is caused by the lack of a good intelligent foundation in this business of living. It is not difficult to find basic reasons for immaturity. Often it is merely necessary to retrace the life of an immature person. Given the opportunity of having known, when he was eight to twelve years old, any one of the men who failed in his opportunity to serve in the armed forces because of neuro-psychiatric tendencies, and, particularly, of having known his mother, a competent psychiatrist could have forecast with reasonable accuracy the boy's future immaturity. In the vast majority of case histories, a "mom" is at fault.

Every woman who bears children is confronted by a dilemma from which there is no escape. The dilemma is as old as the human race, yet its implications and its dangers are peculiarly a part of our closely knit modern civilization and its intricate social cultures. Upon the successful solution of the dilemma depends not only the welfare of a mother's children but, in a large part, the basic survival of the nation of which her children are to be the future citizens and statesmen. The solution is not easy and the stakes are high. No nation is in greater danger of failing to solve the mother–child dilemma than our own nation. No nation would have to pay as great a penalty as the United States for not solving it.

The future social behavior of a child has its beginning and is patterned in the conflicting sensations and emotions that arise from the early relationship between the mother and child. For the child the mother is not only the great Dispenser of pleasure and love and the great Protectress, but also the source of pain, the ruthless Thwarter and Frustrator. So the dilemma of the mother is likewise the dilemma of the child. It is a delicately balanced conflict of clinging and rejecting and, depending on which way the balance is tipped, the child either learns to meet successfully the larger give-and-take aspects of mature living or he doesn't. If the give-and-take capacity is not developed, the child will fail to adjust himself to his own life and to society. As a result, the child never grows up. He remains emotionally immature.

Weaning is as much a part of motherhood as is nursing. Taking away from a child is as important as giving to it. Rejecting and emancipating a child are as significant as clinging to it. Furthermore, these seemingly contradictory phases of motherhood belong to each other both in nature and in sequence.

A play would be incomplete and meaningless if it stopped at the end of the first act, or if the last act were given without the first. Likewise with the mother-child relationship. The phase of taking away from or the rejection of the child by the mother would not only be ineffective but also senseless cruelty unless it had been preceded by the clinging and protective phase. On the other hand, the child who has known nothing but protection and has only learned to take and not to give has been sadly defrauded by his mother—so badly cheated that it would have been better if he had never been born.

Within the limits of the sensory, emotional, and social motherhood-relationship, there is in miniature each child's future. The world we live in drives a hard bargain in the business of giving and taking. It never gives of the largeness of its satisfactions, unless it receives an equally valuable deposit in the general social account. The adult who as a child was never taught to share and give and concede or to think and act independently can almost never learn to do so later in life. There is a tragic finality about childhood. Unfortunately, the vast majority of men and women are made or broken before the first ten years of their lives have been completed.

What happens to the child whose mother not only has failed to sever the emotional apron strings but often has not even loosened them? His natural gregarious instincts lead him to seek social relations with his fellow man. But, because he has only learned to take, he sooner or later is rebuffed. He becomes a bystander in the game of life—a sad, disillusioned and envious spectator. He cannot be a lone wolf, living apart from his fellow man. Few men succeed in doing that and he least of all. Psychologically, it would mean his eventual emotional annihilation. . . .

What constitutes a mom? How does she differ from a mother? Fundamentally, a mom is not a mother. Mom is a maternal parent who fails to prepare her offspring emotionally for living a productive adult life on an adult social plane. A mom does not untie the emotional apron string—the Silver Cord—which binds her children to her.

Moms are just about as old as parenthood. For years in my practice I have seen moms and the sad result of moms. My work in the Army and Navy, because it gave me the chance to study over a short period thousands of psycho-neurotics, served to add to my case histories of moms.

I look at mom without rancor or resentment and not without understanding. Mom is not of her own making. Various forces work together to produce her kind. The basic mosaic of her behavior in most cases was put together in her own childhood without her knowledge and without her consent. Furthermore, momism is the product of a social system veering toward a matriarchy in which each individual mom plays only a small part.

Outwardly, a mom is not distinctively marked. She may be fat or thin; tall or small; blond, brunette, or a redhead, or she may wear a halo of motherly silvered hair. She may be beautiful or uncomely, dress dashingly or dowdily. She may be a college graduate or she may not. She may be quite ignorant of Emily Post's dicta, or she may be gracious and charming.

However, she does have one thing in common—the emotional satisfaction, almost repletion, she derives from keeping her children paddling about in a kind of psychological amniotic fluid rather than letting them swim away with the bold and decisive strokes of maturity from the emotional maternal womb.

There is nothing stronger in this world than the child-mother cohesion. A mother song in a bar or from the stage of the cheapest burlesque will bring lumps in the throats and tears to the eyes of the roughest and toughest men. For all of us there is a natural pull back to mother. . . .

Discussion of "The Mothers' Dilemma"

Edward A. Strecker (1896-   ) has been a professor at the University of Pennsylvania since 1931. As the excerpt we have included suggests, Dr. Strecker has served as a consultant to both the Army and Navy and has done extensive research on behavior disorders. Unlike those who have popularized the distinction between "moms" and mothers through extravagant charges and emotional rhetoric, Dr. Strecker is almost clinically detached.

Yet the warmth of his writing keeps us aware that he realizes he is dealing with an intensely human problem which is not going to be resolved by reason alone.

This selection might well serve as a model of exposition. The key idea is stated at the very beginning, and supporting detail follows in persuasive, logical order. The scope of the problem is outlined broadly in paragraph three, and its source is given careful examination in the paragraphs that follow.

It is easy to point out that Dr. Strecker lacks some insights which the Gospel provides in establishing parent-child relationships, and his suggestion that the "social system" in which a woman lives is the primary force in producing momism might well be debated. Yet we should not discount part of the truth because the whole is not evident, and Dr. Strecker surely speaks significantly when he stresses the necessity for mothers to help their children grow into independence. The insistence of this article or the impact of early background ("the vast majority of men and women are made or broken before the first ten years of their lives") may be a bit shocking, yet child psychologists and other students of children's development are more and more in agreement that patterns established and reinforced in early childhood are particularly difficult to break later.

It is worth noting at this point that maturity is usually the result of repentance. We grow emotionally as we recognize our weaknesses and attempt to change. When we are not allowed to face our inadequacies, we are not prepared to repent. If, out of a mistaken and misdirected love, a mother clings to her children when they should be establishing emotional and spiritual resources of their own, she not only refuses to let them develop, but she denies her own needed growth.

The River Merchant's Wife

A Letter

by Ezra Pound

While my hair was still cut straight across my forehead
I played about the front gate, pulling flowers.
You came by on bamboo stilts, playing horse,
You walked about my seat, playing with blue plums.
And we went on living in the village of Chokan:
Two small people, without dislike or suspicion.

At fourteen I married My Lord you.
I never laughed, being bashful.
Lowering my head, I looked at the wall.
Called to, a thousand times, I never looked back.

At fifteen I stopped scowling,
I desired my dust to be mingled with yours
For ever and for ever and for ever.
Why should I climb the look out?

At sixteen you departed,
You went into far Ku-to-yen, by the river of swirling eddies,
And you have been gone five months.
The monkeys make sorrowful noise overhead.
You dragged your feet when you went out.
By the gate now, the moss is grown, the different mosses,
Too deep to clear them away!

The leaves fall early this autumn, in wind.
The paired butterflies are already yellow with August
Over the grass in the West garden;
They hurt me. I grow older.
If you are coming down through the narrows of the river Kiang,
Please let me know beforehand,
And I will come out to meet you
        As far as Cho-fu-sa.

Discussion of "The River Merchant's Wife"

Ezra Pound (1885-   ) was born in Hailey, Idaho, but he spent his formative years in the East. After teaching Romance languages at the University of Pennsylvania for two years, he went to Europe to do literary research. He settled more or less permanently in England in 1908 and became a major influence upon a number of writers who were rebelling against the rhetorical excesses of romantic poetry.

If Pound has often been the center of controversy, he is important in literary history as the person who introduced many readers to Japanese, Chinese, Italian, Latin and French poetry through his own skillful translations and as the champion of many important writers who have acknowledged his influence.

"The River Merchant's Wife" is a translation from Li Po (701-762) a great Chinese poet who has probably not been rendered into English as deftly by anyone else. The charm of this poem is so obvious that one is tempted not to analyze it at all lest the result be mere dissection. Yet awareness of the skill with which it is presented should only enhance our pleasure in this exquisite account of developing love.

Note how effectively the childhood stage is set by such details as having the young girl "pulling" flowers instead of picking them. Perhaps only those who have had the help of a pre-schooler in a flower garden can appreciate how perfectly this detail reinforces the scene that is being established. The second stanza documents the youthful, arranged marriage and shifts the scene gracefully with new details. For instance, the girl-bride is not completely cowed; she gazes at the wall and not the floor. The last line of this section probably suggests that she is determined to grow into a wife in spite of the pull of childhood memories. If this interpretation is correct, it provides transition to the next stanza in which she is freely and wholly in love.

A year later the husband must leave on an extended journey. In her loneliness and yearning the wife finds her entire environment affected. The sounds the monkeys make and the growing moss by the gate through which her husband left are almost more than she can bear. Yet this touching letter ends on a practical note that shows the resilience of youth.

In this foreshortened account of developing love we see the indifference of mere acquaintance, the uncertainty of beginning affection, the wonder of growing love and the security and identity of married devotion. Perhaps it should be mentioned that these stages are not automatic—or inevitable. The final lines of stanzas two and three help us see how anxious the girl is to become a woman her husband can love. That she is successful is testified to in the line which describes how his feet drag when he must leave her.

Sonnet 7 from Holy Sonnets

by John Donne

At the round earth's imagined corners, blow
Your trumpets, angels, and arise, arise
From death, you numberless infinities
Of souls, and to your scattered bodies go;
All whom the flood did, and fire shall o'erthrow;
All whom war, dearth, age, agues, tyrannies,
Despair, law, chance, hath slain, and you whose eyes
Shall behold God, and never taste death's woe.
But let them sleep, Lord, and me mourn a space,
For, if above all these, my sins abound,
'Tis late to ask abundance of Thy grace,
When we are there; here on this lowly ground,
Teach me how to repent; for that's as good
As if Thou hadst sealed my pardon, with Thy blood.

Discussion of "Sonnet 7"

Biographical details concerning John Donne (1571-1631) were given in volume one of *Out of the Best Books* and can easily be found in any major anthology of English literature. An examination of Donne's later life, however, does not yield much to account for the tone of anguish that characterizes the *Holy Sonnets*. There is a sense of personal unworthiness in these poems which verges on despair. Perhaps no other series of poems in English makes us feel so acutely the predicament of the natural man trying to be spiritual.

While there is identification with others in the poem, it is essentially a highly personal plea for time to repent, to prepare himself for judgment. The opening line obviously refers to Revelation 7:1: "And after these things, I saw four angels standing on the four corners of the earth, holding the four winds of the earth." Then in imaginative concourse those who are coming to judgment assemble. Once more we hear a Biblical echo in the phrase "never taste death's woe." Donne's source for this is Luke 9:27: "I tell you of a truth, there be some standing here which shall not taste of death 'till they see the kingdom of God."

In typical sonnet fashion, the problem has been presented in the first eight lines. Donne's answer, however, is a bit unexpected. He doesn't plead for mercy in the final sestet; he pleads for time—and help. There is implicit echo of the parable of the talents in the concluding lines. Donne wants to come to judgment worthily. The Savior's death might well have pardoned sinners as well as redeemed them. But it is the sinner's repentance that gives redemption its significance, and Donne asks for time to grow into the kind of person whose life does not mock the Savior's sacrifice.

All the *Holy Sonnets* emphasize personal pronouns. The request of this poem suggests a colloquy between servant and master in which there is no attempt at fanciful language or clever paradox. This is a straightforward plea for help in changing before it is too late, and Donne obviously thinks that there is something blameworthy in counting on future mercy rather than present repentance.

If, as it was suggested earlier in this section, all maturity is the result of repentance, spiritual maturity becomes synonymous with worthiness. Spiritual growth would describe that process by which we perfect ourselves. Yet spiritual development is not simply a matter of overcoming weaknesses. Whenever we replace indulgence with control, we become receptive to additional insights. The author of the 23rd psalm notes how quickly his "cup runneth over" when he contemplates the blessings available from the Lord. It is tragic to think that we may be limiting the Lord's blessings to us by our unwillingness to grow into persons capable of containing His bounty.

Early Marriage

by Conrad Richter

For two days the leathery face of Asa Putman had been a document in cipher to anyone who could read the code. Since Saturday but one traveler had passed his solitary post, a speck of adobe and picket corrals lost on the vast, sandy stretch of the Santa Ana plain. Far as the eye could see from his doorway, the rutted El Paso trail, unfenced, gutterless, innocent of grading, gravel, culverts or telephone poles, imprinted only by iron tires, the hoofs of horses, sheep and cattle, and the paw of the loping lobo wolf, lay with dust unraised.

Ordinarily, there were freighters with cracking whips and trailers rumbling on behind. Army trains to and from the forts set up their tents for the night beyond the springs. The private coaches of Santa Fe and Colorado merchants, of cattle kings and Government officials, stopped long enough for the Putman children to admire the ladies, the magnificent woodwork and the luxurious cushions inside. Trail herds of gaunt red steers bawled for the water in the earthen tank, and pairs and companies of horsemen rode up and down.

But since Saturday not even a solitary buckboard from the far settlements in the Cedar country had called for supplies or letters. Only a girl from the Blue Mesa had ridden in for her and her neighbors' mail. She had eaten dinner with the Putmans, refused to stay overnight and started her long ride home.

A stranger from the East would have spoken about the stillness, the deadly waiting, and asked uneasily why Uncle Gideon hadn't come as promised. But in the Putman household it was not mentioned.

Asa deliberately busied himself about the post, filling the bin beneath the counter with navy beans and green coffee, leafing through the packet of letters in the drawer and making a long rite out of feeding the occupants of the picket corrals—four horses of which two were fresh for the next stage.

Rife, just turned fifteen, carried water and gathered cow chips in an old hide dragged by a rope to his saddle horn. Ignacita, the Mexican housekeeper, spat sharply on her heavy irons in the torrid kitchen and kept glancing over her shoulder and out of the open door and windows.

And Nancy Belle, going on seventeen, packed and repacked the high, ironbound trunk that her father had brought for her at Santa Fe and sang softly to herself in the way that women sang fifty and sixty years ago.

Saturday she was being married at Gunstock, two hundred miles away— five days' journey in a wagon, four in a saddle or buckboard.

For six months she had thought of little else. The almanac fell apart at June as naturally as her mother's Bible did at the Twenty-third Psalm. So often had she run her finger down the page that anyone might tell from the worn line of type the very day she and Stephen Dewee would be man and wife. The Dewees lived four hundred miles west across the territory in the Beaverhead country. She and Stephen were taking a mountain ranch near his people, and the wedding had been compromised at Gunstock, nearly equidistant to both families and convenient to friends scattered up and down the Rio Grande.

She had lighted a candle in the dusk, when a figure appeared reluctantly in her doorway. Asa Putman had never been at ease in his daughter's bedroom. A tall, rawhide man in an unbuttoned, sagging vest, any furnishings that suggested refinement visibly embarrassed him. Invariably he kept his hat on in the house. He had it on now, a flat top and a flat brim, not so much like the Western hats you see now. Nancy Belle knew that her mother's people had never forgiven him for bringing his young wife and their two small children to this lonely post, at the mercy of outlaws and the worse Apaches.

Tonight she could see that something bothered him. He gave her a side-wise glance, so sharp and characteristic.

"I don't expect, Nancy Belle, you could put off your weddin'?"

The girl stood quietly gazing at him with a face like the tintype of her mother. But under her sedate gray dress, with tight waist and full skirts to the instep, she had frozen. She looked much older than her years. Her air of gentlefolk and her wide-apart gray eyes came from her mother. But the chin, tipped up with resolute fearlessness, was her father's.

"No, pappa!" Her two clear words held all the steady insistence of the desert.

"I figured how you'd feel," he nodded, avoiding her eyes. "I'd just wanted to put it up to you. I'd 'a' covered the *jornada* on foot to be on time at my own weddin', but I didn't have to count on Gideon to hold me up."

"Are you telling me, papa, that you can't go to Gunstock tomorrow?" Her voice remained quiet, but a coldness had seized her. Of all the people she had visualized at her wedding, the one next to Stephen she could least spare was the tall, grave figure of her father.

"I reckon I kind of can't, Nancy Belle," he said soberly. "Rife could tend to the stage all right and do the feedin'. But they's men come to this post no boy can handle." He shifted his position. "I figured once on closin' up the post till I got back. But the stage is comin' and the mail. And the freighters count on me for feed and grub. Then I got to protect my own property and the mail and freight for the Cedar Country that's in the storage room."

"I know," Nancy Belle said steadily. "I can get to Gunstock all right."

Far back in her father's assaying eyes, she fancied she saw a glint of pride.

"You're pretty nigh a woman now, Nancy Belle. And Rife's a good slice of a man. It's a straight trail to the Rio Grande, once you turn at the old post. Both you and Rife's been over it before. Of course, I'd like to be at the weddin', but the boy can can tell me about it." He went to the window. "Rife!" he called.

Nancy Belle's brother came in presently. A slight boy, with his father's blue eyes, he seldom made a fuss over anything, even when he shot a stray duck on the tank or when they braked down the last cedar hill into Santa Fe with all the open doors of the plaza shops in sight. And when his father told him now, he showed neither enthusiasm nor regret—merely straightened.

"Sure. I can take you, Nancy Belle," he said.

Something pulled under his sister's tight basque. She remembered the long miles they would have in the wagon, the camps at the lonely places, the ugly shadow ever hovering over the outposts of this frontier country and the blight that, since Saturday, seemed to have fallen on the trail. Her eyes swam. Now, at the last minute, she yielded.

"If you'll let me ride, papa, I'll wait another day for Uncle Gideon," she promised.

Her father's eyes moved to the ruffled red calico curtains at the shadeless windows.

"I don't hardly count on Gideon comin' any more, Nancy Belle. Besides, it's too long in the saddle to Gunstock—especially for a girl to get married. You'd be plumb wore out, and you wouldn't have your trunk. You couldn't get dressed for your weddin'."

He turned thoughtfully and went out, Rife close behind. Nancy Belle could hear her father's tones, slow and grave, coming from near one of the picket corrals.

It was too far to catch the words; but when they came in, she saw that her brother's features looked a little pale under the tan.

"You better get some sleep, Nancy Belle," her father said. "You and Rife are startin' before daylight. If Gideon comes, I'll ride after."

They had scarcely gone from the room when Ignacita came in from the kitchen, her black eyes glittering over a pile of freshly starched white in her arms.

"Nancy Belle, *chinita!*" she whispered, plucking at the girl's sleeve. "You don't say to your *papacito* I talk to you! I have wildness alone, *pobrecita!* Sometimes people go safe from one place to the other, oh, *si!* But sometimes, *chinita*, they don't come back! You have not the oldness like Ignacita. Ay, I tell you these old eyes have seen men and women quartered from a tree like sheep or maybe tied over a stove like I don't have the words to say to you."

Nancy Belle did not answer except to lay, one by one, the ironed pieces in her trunk—a bride's muslin underwear trimmed with red-and-blue feather stitching; long petticoats stiffly flounced with ruffles, and nightgowns long in the sleeve and high in the neck, with ruffles at wrist and throat. The Mexican woman went on hoarsely. The girl folded away her winter's cashmere dress, buttoned up the front and with a white fichu. She unwrapped and wrapped again in crumpled white tissue the red slippers the old gentleman on the stage had sent her as a wedding present from Philadelphia.

When Ignacita had left, she opened her keepsake box covered with colored shells. The mirror on the inside lid turned back a face as calm as the little golden clouds that hung of an evening over the east to catch the desert sunset. But after she had undressed and put on her nightdress, for a long time she was aware of the soft pound of her heart faintly swaying the bed on its rawhide springs.

At the first sound of Ignacita's hand on the kitchen stove, Nancy Belle sprang out of bed. She dressed on the brown pool of burro skin, the only carpet on her adobe floor. Through the west window she could see the morning star burning like a brilliant candle. It hung, she told herself, over Gunstock and the Beaverhead, where Stephen, at this moment, in their new log ranch house, lay thinking about her.

They ate in the kichen by lamplight. She had never been so conscious of every detail—the great white cups and saucers, the familiar steel knives, the homey smell of the scorched paper lamp shade, the unreadable eyes of her father, Rife and Ignacita.

Asa Putman himself carried out the trunk. There was already hay in the wagon, a gunny sack of oats, food in a canned-tomato box and utensils in another, a water keg, bed roll tied in a wagon sheet, an ax, a bridle and her own side-saddle made to order over a man's tree. Her eyes caught the gleam of a rifle leaning up against the seat in the lantern light. Tethered to the rear of the wagon stood her saddle mare, Fancy, with pricked ears. She was going to their new ranch home. Nancy Belle felt that she was still among intimate things, but outside the little circle of light lay darkness and the unknown.

When she said good-by to her father he kissed her—something he had not done for years.

"You haven't changed your mind, Nancy Belle?" he asked.

She climbed quickly up over the wheel to the spring seat of the wagon before he might see that she was crying. Rife swung up like a monkey on the other side and pushed the rifle into the crevice behind the seat cushion. The lines tautened and the wagon lurched.

"*Dios* go with you safe to your husband, Nancy Belle!' she heard Ignacita cry after her.

The morning star had set. They moved into a world of silent blackness. Nancy Belle could not see how the horses remained on the trail. When she looked back, the only light in all these square miles of black, unfriendly earth was the yellow window of her father's post.

It was almost a vision, golden and far away, like all beautiful things. She didn't trust herself to look again.

Two hours later the wagon was a lonely speck of boat rocking in an illimitable sage-green sea beneath the sun. The canvas wagon sheet fastened over the bows was a kind of sail, and eastward the sandy water did not stop rolling till it washed up at the foot of the faintly blue ramparts of the distant Espiritu Range.

Just before they turned west on the cross trail to the Rio Grande, a heavy wagon with a yoke of oxen in front and a cow behind toiled around the crumbling adobe walls of the old abandoned post house. A bearded man and a thin woman with a white face sat on the seat. She held a baby in her arms, and three black-eyed children peered from under the wagon sheet.

The bearded man saluted and stopped his willing team. Rife did likewise. The woman spoke first. Her tongue was swift and slightly acid.

"You better turn around and follow us if you want to save your hair!" she called. "Yesterday a sheep herder told us he saw—"

A sharp word from the bearded man caused her to relapse into sullen silence. He asked Rife where he might be going, then climbed down to the trail and said he wanted to talk to him a little. The boy followed reluctantly behind his wagon. Nancy Belle could hear the bearded man's tones coming slow and grave like her father's, while the woman made silent and horribly expressive lip language.

Rife came back, walking stiffly. The bearded man climbed up beside the woman.

"They got to go on," he told her in a low tone, then saluted with his whip. "Good luck, boy! And you, miss!"

Rife raised his whip in stiff acknowledgement. The wagons creaked apart. Nancy Belle saw in front of her the trail to the Rio Grande, little more than a pair of wheel tracks, that lost itself on the lonely plain. Rife seemed relieved that she did not ask what the bearded man had said. But it was enough for her not to be able to forget the woman's fearful signs and mouthings and the still horror in the curious eyes of the staring children.

Sister and brother talked very little. Nancy Belle saw her brother's eyes keep sweeping the country, scanning the horizons. Bunches of bear grass that might have been feathers pinioned his blue gaze, and clumps of cane cactus that seemed to hold pointing gun barrels. At arroyos thick with chamiso and Apache plume she could see his feet tighten on the footboard. Once he pulled out the rifle, but it was only a herd of antelopes moving across the desert page.

They camped for the night when the sun was still high. Nancy Belle asked no question as the boy drove far off the trail into a grassy *cañada*. She sang softly to herself as she fried the salt side bacon and put the black coffee-pot to boil.

Rife hobbled Anton Chico and the Bar X horse and staked out Fancy close to the wagon.

She pretended not to notice when, before dark, he poured earth on the fire till not a spark or wisp of smoke remained. Out of one eye she watched him climb the side of the *cañada* and stand long minutes sweeping the country from the ridge, a slight, tense figure against the sullen glow of the sunset.

"It's all right," he said when he came down. "You can go to bed."

"What's all right?" she asked him.

"The horses," he said, turning away, and Nancy Belle felt a stab of pain that so soon this boy must bear a man's responsibilities and tell a man's lies.

She prayed silently on her blankets spread on the hay in the wagon box, and lay down with her head on the side saddle, her unread Testament in her hand. She heard Rife unroll his camp bed on the ground beneath the wagon. It was all very strange and hushed without her father. Just to feel the Testament in her hand helped to calm her and to remember the day at the post when she had first met Stephen.

Her father had never let her come in contact with the men of the trail. Always, at the first sign of dust cloud on the horizon, he would tell both children to heap up the chip box, fill the water buckets and carry saddles and bridles into the house. But this day Asa Putman and Rife had gone to Fort Sumner. And to Nancy Bell, Uncle Gideon could seldom say no.

It had been a very hot day. She had been sitting in the shade of the earthen bank of the tank, moving her bare feet in the cool water, watching the ripples in the hot south wind. The leaves of the cottonwoods clashed overhead, and she heard nothing until she looked up, and there was a young man on a blue-gray horse with dust clinging to his hat brim and mustache. His eyes were direct as an eagle's. Firm lines modeled his lean face. But what she noticed most at the time was the little bow tie on his dark shirt.

Instantly she had tucked her bare, wet legs under her red dress. Her face burned with shame, but the young stranger talked to her about her father coolly, as if she, a girl of fifteen, had not been caught barefooted. Then he did what in her mind was a noble thing. When Uncle Gideon came out, he magnificently turned his back for her to run into the house and pull on shoes and stockings.

She thought of Stephen constantly next day and the next. She had grown a little used to the journey without her father now— the still, uncertain nights under the wagon sheet, sitting, lying, listening, waiting; the less uncertain days with the sun on the endless spaces; her never-quiet perch on the high spring seat under the slanted bow; the bumps, creaks and lumberings of the wagon; the sand sifting softly over the red, turning wheels; all afternoon the sun in their faces; ahead the far haze and heat waves in which were still lost Gunstock and the Rio Grande. Almost she had forgotten the bearded man with the oxen and the curious detached horror in the eyes of his children.

Since morning of the third day their progress had been slower. The trail seemed level, except for the heavy breathing of the horses. But when Nancy Belle glanced back she could see the steady grade they had been climbing. Abruptly, in mid-afternoon, she found that the long, blue Espiritu Range had disappeared, vanished behind a high pine-clad hill which was its southernmost beginning. It was like the lizard that swallowed itself, a very real lizard. At this moment they were climbing over the lizards tail.

"Cedars!" Rife said briefly, pointing with the whip to dark sprawling growths ahead.

"You breathe deep up here!" Nancy Belle drank in the light air.

Rife took a sniff, but his blue eyes never ceased to scan the high, black-thatched hill under whose frowning cliff they must pass.

"Soon we can see the Gunstock Mountains," Nancy Belle said.

"And Martin Cross' cabin," Rife nodded. "It's the last water to the Rio Grande."

"He's a nice old man," Nancy Belle ventured casually. "It would be nice to camp by his cabin tonight and talk."

The boy inclined his head. After a few moments he started to whistle softly. At the first cedar, Nancy Belle leaped off the moving wagon and climbed back with an evergreen branch. The twig, crushed in her hand, smelled like some store in Sante Fe.

They gained the summit. A breeze was sweeping here from the southwest, and the horses freshened. But Rife had suddenly stopped whistling and Nancy Bell's sprig of cedar lay on her lap. The growning cliff of the pine-clad hill was still there. But Martin Cross' cabin had turned to a desolate mound of ashes. As they stared, a gust of wind sent wisps of smoke scurrying from the mound, and a red eye opened to watch them from the embers. Nancy Belle felt an uncontrollable twitching in the hair roots at the base of her scalp.

Where Martin Cross' eastbound wheel tracks met the trail, Rife reluctantly halted the horses and wet his air-dried lips.

"The water keg's dry, and the horses. If papa was here, he'd drive over."

"I'm the oldest." Nancy Belle found her voice steady. I'll ride over. There might be something we can do."

The boy rose quickly. His eyes seemed to remember something his father had said.

"You can drive the wagon over if I wave."

He had thrown her the lines and slipped back through the canvass-covered tunnel of wagon box, picking up Fancy's bridle and the rifle. Barebacked he rode toward the smoldering ashes at the foot of that frowning hill. The chestnut mare's tail and mane streamed like something gold in the wind.

When she looked back to the trail, her eyes were pinioned by a light object in the wheel track ahead of the Bar X horse. It was a long gray feather.

Instantly she told herself that it had come from some wild turkey Martin Cross had shot, and yet never had air anywhere become so suddenly horrible and choking as in this canyon.

Rife did not signal her to drive over. She saw him come riding back at full speed. The mare was snorting. As he stopped her at the wagon, her chestnut head kept turning back toward what had once been a cabin. Rife slipped the lead rope about her neck and climbed into the seat with the rifle in his hands.

"The water—you wouldn't want it!" he said thickly. His cheeks she noticed, were the color of *yeso*.

"Rife"—Nancy Belle touched his arm when she had driven down the canyon—"what did you see at the cabin?"

The boy sat deaf and rigid beside her, eyes staring straight ahead. She saw that his young hands were still tortured around the barrel of his rifle.

Far down on the pitch-dark mesa she stopped the horses in the trail and listened. There were no stars, not a sound but the flapping of the wagon sheet in the wind and the clank of coffeepot and water bucket under the wagon. Half standing on the footboard, she guided the team off the trail in the intense blackness. Her swift hands helped the trembling boy stake out the mare and hobble the team. They did not light a lantern. Rife declined to eat. Nancy Belle chewed a few dry mouthfuls.

The wind came drawing out of the blackness with a great draft. It hissed through the grass, sucked and tore at the wagon sheet and whistled through the spokes and brake rigging. Rife did not take his bed roll under the wagon tonight. He drew the ends of the wagon sheet together and lay down in the wagon box near his sister. For a long time they were silent. When she heard his heavy breathing, she lifed the rifle from his chest.

The storm grew. Sand began pelting against the canvas and sifted into the wagon box. An invisible cloud of choking dust found its way into eyes, mouth, ears and lungs. Nancy Belle laid down the rifle a moment to pull a blanket over the face of he boy. He tossed and muttered pitifully, but he slept on.

Magically the rain, when it came, stopped the sand and dust. The girl drank in the clean-washed air. At daylight she slipped out to the ground. The mesa, stretching away in the early light, touched here and there with feathers of mist, would have been beautiful except for a sharp new loneliness. The horses were gone!

At her exclamation, Rife appeared from the wagon box. His shame at having slept through the night was quickly over-shadowed by their misfortune.

Together they found where Fancy's stake had been pulled out and dragged. Yards farther on they could tell by Anton Chico's tracks that his hobbles had parted.

Nancy Belle made her brother come back to the wagon and stuff his pockets with cold biscuits and antelope jerky. She said she would have a hot breakfast until he returned. The horses perhaps, were just down in some draw where they had drifted with the wind.

When he had gone with the rifle, she filled the coffeepot from a clearing water hole in the nearest arroyo. She fried potatoes and onions in the long-handled skillet. And when he did not come, she set fresh biscuits in the Dutch oven. Each biscuit held a square of salt side bacon in its top, and as it baked the fat oozed down and incased it in a kind of glazed tastiness.

At noon she thought she heard a shot. Nowhere could she see him on the endless sweep of mesa. By late afternoon she was still alone. She read her Testament and wondered how many women over the world had read it in hours like this. Sitting in the shadow of the wagon, facing the direction he had gone, she looked up every few minutes. But all her eyes could find were cloud shadows racing across the lonely face of the mesa. All she could hear were the desolate cries from the unseen lark sparrows.

Darkness, stillness settled down on the empty land. She climbed back into the wagon and sat on the chuck box, hands rigid on her knees. Again and again she convinced herself that the horses could not have been driven off or she would have seen the drivers' tracks. When wild, sharp barks shattered the still-ness and set wires jerking in her limbs, she talked to herself steadily, but a little meaninglessly, of the post—on and on as the darkness was filled with the ringing and counter-ringing of shrill, cracked yappings—not long tones like a dog's, but incredibly short syllables rising, rising in a mad eternal scale and discord.

"I wish papa had given me two of the chairs," she repeated. "Mamma said they were post oak from Texas. She said they had got white from scrubbing. I liked the laced rawhide seats with the hair left on. It made them soft to sit on. The seats in the parlor were black. And the ones in the kitchen were red. But I liked the brockle one in my room best."

The insane din around the wagon had become terrific. There were only two or three of the animals, Nancy Belle guessed, but they threw their voices and echoes together to make a score.

"When I was little I liked to go in the storage room," her voice went on, scarcely intelligible to her own ears. "It was dark and cool, and smelled of burlap and kerosene and whisky and sweetish with brown sugar. I can see the fat sacks of green coffee. And the round tins of kerosene had boards on the side. The flour sacks were printed Rough and Ready in red letters. Mamma once used to make our underwear out of the sacking. I can smell the salt side bacon in the gunny sacks."

She could tell from the sounds that one of the animals was running insanely back and forth near the wagon tongue. She had never noticed before that they yelped both when breathing in and out. Suddenly came silence. It warned her. Instinctively she felt for the ax.

"Nancy Belle!" a boy's far, anxious voice called from the darkness.

She hallooed and leaned out over the tailboard. Three shadowy forms were coming across the mesa in the starlight. Never had horses looked so good.

"Were you scared?" Rife greeted. "Anything bother you?"

"Nothing," Nancy Belle said. "Just coyotes."

"I had to give Fancy her head after it got dark." He slid wearily to the ground. "She brought us straight back to the wagon."

Nancy Belle had wanted to put her arms around her brother. Now she hugged the mare instead. Rife ate fresh biscuits and a tin plate piled with cold potatoes. He drank several tin cups of coffee. Nancy Belle had slipped the oats-laden gunny-sack morrals over the horses' heads.

"I had to walk halfway to the mountain," Rife said.

"Just help hitch up; then you can sleep all night," she promised.

It rained again heavily toward midnight. Flashes of lightning lit the drenched plain. For minutes at a time, quivering fingers of blue phosphorescence stood on the ears of the toiling horses. At dawn Nancy Belle still held the reins as the mud-splashed wagon crawled through a world bathed in early purple splendor.

Four days they had been crossing a hundred and seventy miles of desolate plain. Now the end waited in sight. To the west lay a land broken and tumbled by a mighty hand. Hill shouldered hill and range peered over range, all indescribably violet except where peaks tipped by the unseen sun were far-off flaming towers of copper.

It was a new land, her promised land, Stephen's land, Nancy Belle told herself, where nobody burned cow chips, but snapping cedar and pine, where cold water ran in the wooded canyons and the eye, weary of one flat circle the horizon round, had endless geometric designs to refresh the retina.

She sang softly as the wagon lumbered to the edge of a long, shallow valley, brown and uninhabited, running north and south, and desolate except for a winding ribbon that was white with sky and narrowly bordered with green.

"Rife!" Nancy Belle cried. "The Rio Grande!"

An hour afterward they pulled out of the sun into the shade of the long cottonwood *bosque.* Nancy Belle wasn't singing now. Where she remembered wide sand bars glistening with sky and tracked by water fowl, a chocolate-red flood rolled. Where had been the island, tops of tule and scrub willow swung to and fro with the current.

Anton Chico and the Bar X horse stopped of their own accord in the trail, ears pricked forward at the swirling brown wash. While Rife turned the three horses loose to graze, Nancy Belle silently fried bacon and made coffee. When she had washed skillet and tin dishes in the river, the boy had wired the wagon box to the brake rigging. Now he was tying securely one end of his rope to the center of the coupling pole under the wagon. The other end she knew he would fasten to the inadequate upper horn of the sidesaddle.

"I wouldn't mind the river if I just had my own saddle," he mourned.

They hitched up the team silently. Rife cinched the sidesaddle on Fancy and straddled it, the single stirrup useless to a man. Nancy Belle climbed into the wagon and picked up the lines. The other bank looked as far away as the Espiritu Range from the post. She wanted to say something to her brother— some last word, in case they didn't make it. But all she did was cluck her tongue to the horses.

Gingerly, one slow foot at a time, the team moved down the trail into the water.

"Give 'em their heads!" Rife called from the right rare.

Nancy Belle held a rein in each hand. The red channel water came to the wagon tongue, covered it, reached the horses' bellies.

The team wanted to stop. Nancy Belle swung her whip, a stick tipped with a long rawhide lash. The wagon went on. The collars of both horses kept dipping, but never entirely out of sight. Still barely wading, the slow team reached the firmer footing of the island.

Two-thirds of the river still rolled in front of the wagon. The west bank did not seem to have grown much closer, but the east bank behind them had moved far away. The team had to be whipped into the violent current. The water churned white through the wagon wheels. Suddenly both horses appeared to stumble and drop out of sight. Their heads came up wildly, spray blowing from their nostrils. The muddy water hid their legs, but by their bobbing motions Nancy Belle knew that they were swimming.

"Keep 'em pointed up the river!" Rife shouted.

Already she felt the wagon floating. It swung downstream with the current; then Rife's rope from Fancy's saddle snubbed it. The team was snorting with every breath. The Bar X horse swam high in the water, his withers and part of his back out of the chocolate current. But all she could see of Anton Chico were his nose and ears.

Down between her ankles she saw water in the wagon box. She thought of the hemstitched sheets at the bottom of her trunk, the towels and pillow cases crocheted with shell lace. Her blue velvet corduroy dress was probably wet already, and all the cunning print aprons with dust caps to match. River water couldn't hurt the little yellow creamer, sugar bowl and covered butter dish that had been her mother's. And the gingham dresses could be washed. What worried her were her wedding dress and the keepsake box, especially the tintypes, one of which was Rife in a child's suit edged with black braid, his brand-new hat on his knee.

An older Rife was shouting something behind her now. She couldn't catch the words. Then she found what it was. The neck and withers of Anton Chico raised suddenly out of the water and both horses were scrambling up the steep bank below the ford. Only quick work with the lines saved the wagon from turning over. Safe and blowing on the high bank, the dripping horses shook themselves like puppies.

Nancy Belle couldn't go on until she had opened the trunk and appraised the damage. Rife unsaddled Fancy and drove on with the refreshed team. Behind his light back in the wagon box, the girl changed to her blue-velvet corduroy, which was hardly wet at all. Then she combed her hair and rolled into a cranny of her trunk the old felt hat that had been too large for her father.

A half-dozen riders met the wagon some miles down the Gunstock Canyon. All of them Nancy Belle noticed, carried guns. Stephen wore a new white shirt and a gray hat with curled brim she had not seen before. He stood in his stirrups, and swung her down in front of him on the saddle, where he kissed her. She had never felt his lips press into such a straight line.

"Papa couldn't come," she said. "So Rife brought me."

She felt Stephen's rigid arm around her.

"We just got in from the Beaverhead ourselves."

"He means they never got any news out in the Beaverhead or he'd 'a' come further east to meet you!" Uncle Billy Williams put in. He had a lovable, squeaky voice. "The Apaches been breakin' loose again. Funny you didn't hear anything over in your country."

Nancy Belle gave him an inscrutable look with her gray eyes. Uncle Billy pulled out his bandanna and blew his nose.

"They got my old friend, Judge Hower, and his wife and kid in a buggy on the Upper Espiritu. The man that found what they did to 'em, they say, cried like a baby."

"That's all right, Uncle Billy," Stephen said in a gentle voice.

Nancy Belle glanced at Rife. Her brother's face looked gray and the eyes staring as when he had ridden in the late afternoon sunlight from the smoking ashes of Martin Cross' cabin.

Nearly fifty people, gathered in the big parlor upstairs at the hotel, greeted Nancy Belle. An old man whose young black eyes twinkled out of a bearded face said he was glad to see that she had her "Hair on straight." Rife stopped with the trunk before driving to the livery, and Stephen's mother showed Nancy Belle to a room to dress.

The guests stopped talking when she came into the parlor in her white wedding dress. Her basque came to a point in the front and back. It fitted like a glove. The silk underskirt came to her instep and the ruffled overskirt to her knees. She had parted her hair from side to side and brushed the bangs down on her forehead. She felt very light-headed. The wagon still seemed to be jerking under her.

She glimpsed Rife gazing at her, a rapt expression in his reticent blue eyes. She was glad to see that he had brushed his hair. The brass swinging lamp had been lighted and the dark woodwork of the parlor festooned with evergreen branches. White streamers from the wall met in a papier-mache bell in one corner. She noticed two children peering eagerly from the dark hall.

Stephen came to her, very straight in a long coat and stand-up collar with a black tie. He led her up beneath the papier-mache bell. In a sibilant, church-like whisper, the Gunstock preacher made sure of her full name. Then he coughed and began the ceremony. He had a deep voice, but Nancy Belle didn't hear all of the service. Her mind kept going back to a tall, grave man in a lonely adobe post on the wide Santa Ana plain. And after she had said "I do," her lips moved, but she was not praying for Stephen, her husband.

Discussion of "Early Marriage"

Conrad Richter (1890-   ) was born in Pennsylvania and was descended from a long line of ministers. At 15 he completed high school and went to work. After several years at such jobs as farm hand, bank teller, timberman and salesman, he became a newspaper reporter. In 1928 he moved his family west and he has spent the remainder of his life writing novels and stories which reflect an identification with the American southwest.

"Early Marriage" grew into a story out of the voluminous notes which Richter collected on early life in what is now New Mexico and Arizona. In our contemporary comfort it is easy to overemphasize the physical hardships of pioneer life. Yet the authentic pioneer story rarely stressed these. Those who are old enough to remember hearing accounts of pioneer life from those who actually experienced it, are often struck by the matter-of-fact rendition of incredible discomfort. Then, as now, the real drama of existence is not focused on the external. Physical situation is incidental to the internal questionings and resolutions out of which great character is formed.

"Early Marriage," by such criteria, is a story of significant growth. The setting is convincing, and the style is appropriate to its subject matter. But the real story here is one of two youngsters becoming adults. When Nancy Belle's father describes her as "pretty nigh a woman" and her brother, Rife, as "a good slice of a man," we are prepared for reaction and behavior that will suggest maturity, but the author skilfully allows us to participate in their final initiation into man and womanhood. We know from the first that Rife's apparent unconcern and Nancy Belle's calmness mask realistic awareness of the hazards they are undertaking. The effort it is costing young Rife to keep control of himself is hinted at repeatedly in the stiffness of his actions, and Nancy Belle's mature understanding of her plight is effectively suggested in her deliberately controlled emotions. She doesn't even hug her brother when he returns with the lost horses lest this break in the discipline she is imposing upon herself might weaken them both.

By the time they reach their destination, both Nancy Belle and Rife have demonstrated ability to adapt to the extraordinary demands of their journey, but it is worth noting that fear and danger have not blighted their appreciation of that which is still beautiful and worth-while. Growth need not be synonomous with disillusionment. If Rife has had to put away youthful concerns with brutal speed, the final picture we have of him is a brother who has purchased his manhood gladly. And if her wedding is marred by thought of what might have happened to her father, Nancy Belle tries her best to be the lovely bride Stephen is expecting.

This story breathes that controlled understatement that is the hallmark of the true pioneer tale, and it emphasizes how little years have to do with certain kinds of maturity. Part of the pleasure we receive from reading this work comes from the assurance we feel that Nancy Belle and Rife may increase in wisdom and experience as the years go by, but they are already prepared to be whatever circumstances demand of them.

My Kinsman, Major Molineux

by Nathaniel Hawthorne

After the Kings of Great Britain had assumed the right of appointing the colonial governors, the measures of the latter seldom met with the ready and generous approbation which had been paid to those of their predecessors, under the original charters. The people looked with most jealous scrutiny to the exercise of power which did not emanate from themselves, and they usually rewarded their rulers with slender gratitude for the compliances by which, in softening their instructions from beyond the sea, they had incurred the reprehension of those who gave them. The annals of Massachusetts Bay will inform us, that of six governors in the space of about forty years from the surrender of the old charter, under James II, two were imprisoned by a popular insurrection; a third, as Hutchinson inclines to believe, was driven from the province by the whizzing of a musket-ball; a fourth, in the opinion of the same historian, was hastened to his grave by continual bickerings with the House of Representatives; and the remaining two, as well as their successors till the Revolution, were favored with few and brief intervals of peaceful sway. The inferior members of the court party, in times of high political excitement, led scarcely a more desirable life. These remarks may serve as a preface to the following adventures, which chanced upon a summer night, not far from a hundred years ago. The reader, in order to avoid a long and dry detail of colonial affairs, is requested to dispense with an account of the train of circumstances that had caused much temporary inflamation of the popular mind.

It was near nine o'clock of a moonlight evening, when a boat crossed the ferry with a single passenger, who had obtained his conveyance at that unusual hour by the promise of an extra fare. While he stood on the landing-place, searching in either pocket for the means of fulfilling his agreement, the ferryman lifted a lantern, by the aid of which, and the newly risen moon, he took a very accurate survey of the stranger's figure. He was a youth of barely eighteen years, evidently country-bred, and now, as it should seem, upon his first visit to town. He was clad in a coarse gray coat, well worn, but in excellent repair; his under garments were durably constructed of leather, and fitted tight to a pair of serviceable and well-shaped limbs; his stockings of blue yarn were the incontrovertible work of a mother or a sister; and on his head was a three-cornered hat, which in its better days had perhaps sheltered the graver brow of the lad's father. Under his left arm was a heavy cudgel formed of an oak sapling, and retaining a part of the hardened root; and his equipment was completed by a wallet, not so abundantly stocked as to incommode the vigorous shoulders on which it hung. Brown, curly hair, well-shaped features, and bright cheerful eyes were nature's gifts, and worth all that art could have done for his adornment.

The youth, one of whose names was Robin, finally drew from his pocket the half of a little province bill of five shillings, which, in the depreciation in that sort of currency, did satisfy the ferryman's demand, with the surplus of a sexangular piece of parchment, valued at three pence. He then walked forward into the town, with as light a step as if his day's journey had not already exceeded thirty miles, and with as eager an eye as if he were entering London city, instead of a little metropolis of a New England colony. Before Robin had proceeded far, however, it occurred to him that he knew not whither to direct his step; so he paused, and looked up and down the narrow street, scrutinizing the small and mean wooden buildings that were scattered on either side.

"This low hovel cannot be my kinsman's dwelling," thought he, "nor yonder old house, where the moonlight enters at the broken casement; and truly I see none hereabouts that might be worthy of him. It would have been wise to inquire my way of the ferryman, and doubtless he would have gone with me, and earned a shilling from the Major for his pains. But the next man I meet will do as well."

He resumed his walk, and was glad to perceive that the street now became wider, and the houses more respectable in their appearance. He soon discerned a figure moving on moderately in advance, and hastened his steps to overtake it. As Robin drew nigh, he saw that the passenger was a man in years, with a periwig of gray hair, a wideskirted coat of dark cloth, and silk stockings rolled above his knees. He carried a long and polished cane, which he struck down perpendicularly before him at every step; and at regular intervals he uttered two successive hems, of a peculiarly solemn and sepulchral intonation. Having made these observations Robin laid hold of the skirt of the old man's coat, just when the light from the open door and windows of a barber's shop fell upon both their figures.

"Good evening to you, honored sir," said he, making a low bow, and still retaining his hold of the skirt. "I pray you tell me whereabouts is the dwelling of my kinsman, Major Molineux."

The youth's question was uttered very loudly; and one of the barbers, whose razor was descending on a well-soaped chin, and another who was dressing a Ramillies wig, left their occupations, and came to the door. The citizen, in the mean time, turned a long-favored countenance upon Robin, and answered him in a tone of excessive anger and annoyance. His two sepulchral hems, however, broke into the very centre of his rebuke, with most singular effect, like a thought of the cold grave obtruding among wrathful passions.

"Let go my garment, fellow! I tell you, I know not the man you speak of. What! I have authority, I have—hem, hem—authority; and if this be the respect you show for your betters, your feet shall be brought acquainted with the stocks by daylight, tomorrow morning!"

Robin released the old man's skirt, and hastened away, pursued by an ill-mannered roar of laughter from the barber's shop. He was at first considerably surprised by the result of his question, but, being a shrewd youth, soon thought himself able to account for the mystery.

"This is some country representative," was his conclusion, "who has never seen the inside of my kinsman's door, and lacks the breeding to answer a stranger civilly. The man is old, or verily—I might be tempted to turn back and smite him on the nose. Ah, Robin, Robin! even the barber's boys laugh at you for choosing such a guide! You will be wiser in time, friend Robin."

He now became entangled in a succession of crooked and narrow streets, which crossed each other, and meandered at no great distance from the waterside. The smell of tar was obvious to his nostrils, the masts of vessels pierced the moonlight above the tops of the buildings, and the numerous signs, which Robin paused to read, informed him that he was near the centre of business. But the streets were empty, the shops were closed, and lights were visible only in the second stories of a few dwelling-houses. At length, on the corner of a narrow lane, through which he was passing, he beheld the broad countenance of a British hero swinging before the door of an inn, whence proceeded the voices of many guests. The casement of one of the lower windows was thrown back, and a very thin curtain permitted Robin to distinguish a party at supper, round a well-furnished table. The fragrance of the good cheer steamed forth into the outer air, and the youth could not fail to recollect that the last remnant of his travelling stock of provision had yielded to his morning appetite, and that noon had found and left him dinnerless.

"Oh, that a parchment three-penny might give me a right to sit down at yonder table!" said Robin, with a sigh. "But the Major will make me welcome to the best victuals; so I will even step boldly in, and inquire my way to his dwelling."

He entered the tavern, and was guided by the murmur of voices and the fumes of tobacco to the public-room. It was a long and low apartment, with oaken walls, grown dark in the continual smoke, and a floor which was thickly sanded, but of no immaculate purity. A number of persons—the larger part of whom appeared to be mariners, or in some way connected with the sea— occupied the wooden benches, or leather-bottomed chairs, conversing on various matters, and occasionally lending their attention to some topic of general interest. Three or four little groups were draining as many bowls of punch, which the West India trade had long since made a familiar drink in the colony. Others, who had the appearance of men who lived by regular and laborious handicraft, preferred the insulated bliss of an unshared potation, and became more taciturn under its influence. Nearly all, in short, evinced a predilection for the Good Creature in some of its various shapes, for this is a vice to which, as Fast Day sermons of a hundred years ago will testify, we have a long hereditary claim. The only guests to whom Robin's sympathies inclined him were two or three sheepish countrymen, who were using the inn somewhat after the fashion of a Turkish caravansary; they had gotten themselves into the darkest corner of the room, and heedless of the Nicotian atmosphere, were supping on the bread of their own ovens, and the bacon cured in their own chimney-smoke. But though Robin felt a sort of brotherhood with these strangers, his eyes were attracted from them to a person who stood near the door, holding whispered conversation with a group of ill-dressed associates. His features were separately striking almost to grostesqueness, and the whole face left a deep impression on the memory. The forehead bulged out into a double prominence, with a vale between; the nose came boldly forth in an irregular curve, and its bridge was of more than a finger's breadth; the eyebrows were deep and shaggy, and the eyes glowed beneath them like fire in a cave.

While Robin deliberated of whom to inquire respecting his kinsman's dwelling, he was accosted by the innkeeper, a little man in a stained white apron, who had come to pay his professional welcome to the stranger. Being in the second generation from a French Protestant, he seemed to have inherited the courtesy of his parent nation; but no variety of circumstances was ever known to change his voice from the one shrill note in which he now addressed Robin.

"From the country, I presume, sir?" said he, with a profound bow. "Beg leave to congratulate you on your arrival, and trust you intend a long stay with us. Fine town here, sir, beautiful buildings, and much that may interest a stranger. May I hope for the honor of your commands in respect to supper?"

"The man sees a family likeness! the rogue has guessed that I am related to the Major!" thought Robin, who had hitherto experienced little superfluous civility.

All eyes were now turned on the country lad, standing at the door, in his worn three-cornered hat, gray coat, leather breeches, and blue yarn stockings, leaning on an oaken cudgel, and bearing a wallet on his back.

Robin replied to the courteous innkeeper, with such an assumption of confidence as befitted the Major's relative. "My honest friend," he said, "I shall make it a point to patronize your house on some occasion, when"—here he could not help lowering his voice—"when I may have more than a parchment three-pence in my pocket. My present business," continued he, speaking with lofty confidence, "is merely to inquire my way to the dwelling of my kinsman, Major Molineux."

There was a sudden and general movement in the room, which Robin interpreted as expressing the eagerness of each individual to become his guide. But the innkeeper turned his eyes to a written paper on the wall, which he read, or seemed to read, with occasional recurrences to the young man's figure.

"What have we here?" said he, breaking his speech into little dry fragments. "Left the house of the subscriber, bounden servant, Hezekiah Mudge,— had on, when he went away, gray coat, leather breeches, master's third-best hat.

One pound currency reward to whosoever shall lodge him in any jail of the providence.' Better trudge, boy; better trudge!"

Robin had begun to draw his hand towards the lighter end of the oak cudgel, but a strange hostility in every countenance induced him to relinquish his purpose of breaking the courteous innkeeper's head. As he turned to leave the room, he encountered a sneering glance from the bold-featured personage whom he had before noticed; and no sooner was he beyond the door, than he heard a general laugh, in which the innkeeper's voice might be distinguished, like the dropping of small stones into a kettle.

"Now, is it not strange," thought Robin, with his usual shrewdness,— "is it not strange that the confession of an empty pocket should outweigh the name of my kinsman, Major Molineux? Oh, if I had one of those grinning rascals in the woods, where I and my oak sapling grew up together, I would teach him that my arm is heavy though my purse be light!"

On turning the corner of the narrow lane, Robin found himself in a spacious street, with an unbroken line of lofty houses on each side, and a steepled building at the upper end, whence the ringing of a bell announced the hour of nine. The light of the moon, and the lamps from the numerous shop-windows, discovered people promenading on the pavement, and amongst them Robin had hoped to recognize his hitherto inscrutable relative. The result of his former inquiries made him unwilling to hazard another, in a scene of such publicity, and he determined to walk slowly and silently up the street, thrusting his face close to that of every elderly gentleman, in search of the Major's lineaments. In his progress, Robin encountered many gay and gallant figures. Embroidered garments of showy colors, enormous periwigs, gold-laced hats, and silver-hilted swords glided past him and dazzled his optics. Travelled youths, imitators of the European fine gentlemen of the period, trod jauntily along, half dancing to the fashionable tunes which they hummed, and making poor Robin ashamed of his quiet and natural gait. At length, after many pauses to examine the gorgeous display of goods in the shop-windows, and after suffering some rebukes for the impertinence of his scrutiny into people's faces, the Major's kinsman found himself near the steepled building, still unsuccessful in his search. As yet, however, he had seen only one side of the thronged street; so Robin crossed, and continued the same sort of inquisition down the opposite pavement, with stronger hopes than the philosopher seeking an honest man, but with no better fortune. He had arrived about midway towards the lower end, from which his course began, when he overheard the approach of some one who struck down a cane on the flag-stones at every step, uttering at regular intervals, two sephulchral hems.

"Mercy on us!" quoth Robin, recognizing the sound.

Turning a corner, which chanced to be close at his right hand, he hastened to pursue his researches in some other part of the town. His patience now was wearing low, and he seemed to feel more fatigue from his rambles since he

crossed the ferry, than from his journey of several days on the other side.
Hunger also pleaded loudly within him, and Robin began to balance the
propriety of demanding, violently, and with lifted cudgel, and necessary
guidance from the first solitary passenger whom he should meet.   While a
resolution to this effect was gaining strength, he entered a street of mean
appearance, on either side of which a row of ill-built houses was straggling
towards the harbor.   The moonlight fell upon no passenger along the whole
extent, but in the third domicile which Robin passed there was a half-opened
door, and his keen glance detected a woman's garment within.

"My luck may be better here," said he to himself.

Accordingly, he approached the door, and beheld it shut closer as he did
so; yet an open space remained, sufficing for the fair occupant to observe the
stranger, without a correspondingly display on her part.   All that Robin could
discern was a strip of scarlet petticoat, and the occasional sparkle of an eye, as
if the moonbeams were trembling on some bright thing.

"Pretty mistress," for I may call her so with a good conscience, thought
the shrewd youth, since I know nothing to the contrary,—"My sweet pretty
mistress, will you be kind enough to tell me whereabouts I must seek the
dwelling of my kinsman, Major Molineux?"

Robin's voice was plaintive and winning, and the female, seeing nothing
to be shunned in the handsome country youth, thrust open the door, and came
forth into the moonlight.   She was a dainty little figure, with a white neck,
round arms, and a slender waist, at the extremity of which her scarlet petticoat jutted out over a hoop, as if she were standing in a balloon.   Moreover,
her face was oval and pretty, her hair dark beneath the little cap, and her bright
eyes possessed a sly freedom, which triumphed over those of Robin.

"Major Molineux dwells here," said this fair woman.   Now, her voice was
the sweetest Robin had heard that night, yet he could not help doubting whether
that sweet voice spoke Gospel truth.   He looked up and down the main street,
and then surveyed the house before which they stood.   It was a small, dark
edifice of two stories, the second of which projected over the lower floor, and
the front apartment had the aspect of a shop for pretty commodities.

"Now, truly, I am in luck," replied Robin, cunningly, "and so indeed is
my kinsman, the Major, in having so pretty a housekeeper.   But I prithee trouble
him to step to the door; I will deliver him a message from his friends in the
country, and then go back to my lodgings at the inn."

"Nay, the Major has been abed this hour or more," said the lady of the
scarlet petticoat; "and it would be to little purpose to disturb him to-night,
seeing his evening draught was of the strongest.   But he is a kind-hearted man,
and it would be as much as my life's worth to let a kinsman of his turn away
from the door.   You are the good old gentleman's very picture, and I could
swear that was his rainy-weather hat.   Also he has garments very much re-

sembling those leather small-clothes. But come in, I pray, for I bid you hearty welcome in his name."

So saying, the fair and hospitable dame took her hero by the hand; and the touch was light, and the force was gentleness, and though Robin read in her eyes what he did not hear in her words, yet the slender-waisted woman in the scarlet petticoat proved stronger than the athletic country youth. She had drawn his half-willing footsteps nearly to the threshold, when the opening of a door in the neighborhood startled the Major's housekeeper, and leaving the Major's kinsman, she vanished speedily into her own domicile. A heavy yawn preceded the appearance of a man, who, like the Moonshine of Pyramus and Thisbe, carried a lantern, needlessly aiding his sister luminary in the heavens. As he walked sleepily up the street, he turned his broad, dull face on Robin, and displayed a long staff, spiked at the end.

"Home, vagabond, home!" said the watchman, in accents that seemed to fall asleep as soon as they were uttered. "Home, or we'll set you in the stocks by peep of day!"

"This is the second hint of the kind," thought Robin. "I wish they would end my difficulties, by setting me there to-night."

Nevertheless, the youth felt an instinctive antipathy towards the guardian of midnight order, which at first prevented him from asking his usual question. But just when the man was about to vanish behind the corner, Robin resolved not to lose the opportunity, and shouted lustily after him,—

"I say, friend! will you guide me to the house of my kinsman, Major Molineux?"

The watchman made no reply, but turned the corner and was gone; yet Robin seemed to hear the sound of drowsy laughter stealing along the solitary street. At that moment, also, a pleasant titter saluted him from the open window above his head; he looked up, and caught the sparkle of a saucy eye; a round arm beckoned to him, and next he heard light footsteps descending the staircase within. But Robin, being of the household of a New England clergyman, was a good youth, as well as a shrewd one; so he resisted temptation, and fled away.

He now roamed desperately, and at random, through the town, almost ready to believe that a spell was on him, like that by which a wizard of his country had once kept three pursuers wandering, a whole winter night, within twenty paces of the cottage which they sought. The streets lay before him, strange and desolate, and the lights were extinguished in almost every house. Twice, however, little parties of men, among whom Robin distinguished individuals in outlandish attire, came hurrying along; but, though on both occasions, they paused to address him, such intercourse did not at all enlighten his perplexity. They did but utter a few words in some language of which Robin knew nothing, and perceiving his inability to answer, bestowed a curse upon him in plain English and hastened away. Finally, the lad determined to knock at the door of every mansion that might appear worthy to be occupied by his kinsman, trusting that perseverance would overcome the fatality that had thwarted him. Firm in this resolve, he was passing beneath the walls of a church, which formed the corner of two streets, when, as he turned into the shade of its steeple, he encountered a bulky stranger, muffled in a cloak. The man was proceeding with the speed of earnest business, but Robin planted himself full before him, holding the oak cudgel with both hands across his body as a bar to further passage.

"Halt, honest man, and answer me a question," said he, very resolutely. "Tell me, this instant, whereabouts is the dwelling of my kinsman, Major Molineux!"

"Keep your tongue between your teeth, fool, and let me pass!" said a deep, gruff voice, which Robin partly remembered. "Let me pass, or I'll strike you to the earth!"

"No, no neighbor!" cried Robin, flourishing his cudgel, and then thrusting its larger end close to the man's muffled face. "No, no, I'm not the fool you take me for, nor do you pass till I have an answer to my question. Whereabouts is the dwelling of my kinsman, Major Molineux?"

The stranger, instead of attempting to force his passage, stepped back into the moonlight, unmuffled his face, and stared full into that of Robin.

"Watch here an hour, and Major Molineux will pass by," said he.

Robin gazed with dismay and astonishment on the unprecedented physiognomy of the speaker. The forehead with its double prominence, the broad hooked nose, the shaggy eyebrows, and fiery eyes were those which he had noticed at the inn, but the man's complexion had undergone a singular, or, more properly, a twofold change. One side of the face blazed an intense red, while the other was black as midnight, the division line being in the broad bridge of the nose; and a mouth which seemed to extend from ear to ear was black or red, in contrast to the color of the cheek. The effect was as if two individual devils, a fiend of fire and a fiend of darkness, had united themselves to form this infernal visage. The stranger grinned in Robin's face, muffled his party-colored features, and was out of sight in a moment.

"Strange things we travellers see!" ejaculated Robin.

He seated himself, however, upon the steps of the church-door, resolving to wait the appointed time for his kinsman. A few moments were consumed in philosophical speculations upon the species of man who had just left him; but having settled this point shrewdly, rationally, and satisfactorily, he was compelled to look elsewhere for his amusement. And first he threw his eyes along the street. It was of more respectable appearance than most of those into which he had wandered; and the moon, creating, like the imaginative power, a beautiful strangeness in familiar objects, gave something of romance to a scene that might not have possessed it in the light of day. The irregular and often quaint architecture of the houses, some of whose roofs were broken into numerous little peaks, while others ascended, steep and narrow, into a single point, and others again were square; the pure snow-white of some of their complexions, the aged darkness of others, and the thousand sparklings, reflected from bright substances in the walls of many; these matters engaged Robin's attention for a while, and then began to grow wearisome. Next he endeavored to define the forms of distant objects, starting away, with almost ghostly indistinctness, just as his eye appeared to grasp them; and finally he took a minute survey of an edifice which stood on the opposite side of the street, directly in front of the church-door, where he was stationed. It was a large, square mansion, distinguished from its neighbors by a balcony, which rested on tall pillars, and by an elaborate Gothic window, communicating therewith.

"Perhaps this is the very house I have been seeking," thought Robin.

Then he strove to speed away the time, by listening to a murmur which swept continually along the street, yet was scarcely audible, except to an unaccustomed ear like his; it was a low, dull, dreamy sound, compounded of many noises, each of which was at too great a distance to be separately heard. Robin marvelled at this snore of a sleeping town, and marvelled more whenever its continuity was broken by now and then a distant shout, apparently loud where it originated. But altogether it was a sleep-inspiring sound, and, to shake off its drowsy influence, Robin arose, and climbed a window-frame, that he might view the interior of the church. There the moonbeams came trembling in, and fell down upon the deserted pews, and extended along the quiet aisles. A fainter yet more awful radiance was hovering around the pulpit, and one solitary ray had dared to rest upon the open page of the great Bible. Had nature, in that deep hour, become a worshipper in the house which man had builded? Or was that heavenly light the visible sanctity of the place,— visible because no earthly and impure feet were within the walls? The scene made Robin's heart shiver with a sensation of loneliness stronger than he had ever felt in the remotest depths of his native woods; so he turned away and sat down again before the door. There were graves around the church, and now an uneasy thought obtruded into Robin's breast. What if the object of his search, which had been so often and so strangely thwarted, were all the time mouldering in his shroud? What if his kinsman should glide through yonder gate, and nod and smile to him in dimly passing by?

"Oh that any breathing thing were here with me!" said Robin.

Recalling his thoughts from this uncomfortable track, he sent them over forest, hill, and stream, and attempted to imagine how that evening of ambiguity and weariness had been spent by his father's household. He pictured them assembled at the door, beneath the tree, the great old tree, which had been spared for its huge twisted trunk and venerable shade, when a thousand leafy brethren fell. There, at the going down of the summer sun, it was his father's custom to perform domestic worship; that the neighbors might come and join with him like brothers of the family, and that the wayfaring man might pause to drink at that fountain, and keep his heart pure by freshening the memory of home. Robin distinguished the seat of every individual of the little audience, he saw the good man in the midst, holding the Scriptures in the golden light that fell from the western clouds; he beheld him close the book and all rise up to pray. He heard the old thanksgivings for daily mercies, the old supplications for their continuance, to which he had so often listened in weariness, but which were now among his dear remembrances. He perceived the slight inequality of his father's voice when he came to speak of the absent one; he noted his mother turned her face to the broad and knotted trunk; how his elder brother scorned, because the beard was rough upon his upper lip, to permit his features to be moved; how the younger sister drew down a low hanging branch before her eyes; and how the little one of all, whose sports had hitherto broken the decorum of the scene, understood the prayer for her playmate, and burst into clamorous grief. Then he saw them go in at the door; and when Robin would have entered also, the latch tinkled into its place, and he was excluded from his home.

"Am I here, or there?" cried Robin, starting; for all at once, when his thoughts had become visible and audible in a dream, the long, wide, solitary street shone out before him.

He aroused himself, and endeavored to fix his attention steadily upon the large edifice which he had surveyed before. But still his mind kept vibrating between fancy and reality; by turns, the pillars of the balcony lengthened into the tall, bare stems of pines, dwindled down to human figures, settled again into their true shape and size, and then commenced a new succession of changes. For a single moment when he deemed himself awake, he could have sworn that a visage—one which he seemed to remember, yet could not absolutely name as his kinsman's—was looking towards him from the Gothic window. A deeper sleep wrestled with and nearly overcame him, but fled at the sound of footsteps along the opposite pavement. Robin rubbed his eyes, discerned a man passing at the foot of the balcony, and addressed him in a loud, peevish, and lamentable cry.

"Hallo, friend! must I wait here all night for my kinsman, Major Molineux?"

The sleeping echoes awoke, and answered the voice; and the passenger, barely able to discern a figure sitting in the oblique shade of the steeple, traversed the street to obtain a nearer view. He was himself a gentleman in his prime, of open, intelligent, cheerful, and altogether prepossessing countenance. Perceiving a country youth, apparently homeless and without

friends, he accosted him in a tone of real kindness, which had become
strange to Robin's ears.

"Well, my good lad, why are you sitting here?" inquired he. "Can I
be of service to you in any way?"

"I'm afraid not, sir," replied Robin, despondingly; "yet I shall take
it kindly, if you'll answer me a single question. I've been searching, half
the night, for one Major Molineux; now, sir, is there really such a person
in these parts, or am I dreaming?"

"Major Molineux! The name is not altogether strange to me," said the
gentleman, smiling. "Have you any objection to telling me the nature of your
business with him?"

Then Robin briefly related that his father was a clergyman, settled on
a small salary, at a long distance back in the country, and that he and Major
Molineux were brothers' children. The Major, having inherited riches, and
acquired civil and military rank, had visited his cousin, in great pomp, a
year or two before; had manifested much interest in Robin and an elder brother,
and, being childless himself, had thrown out hints respecting the future
establishment of one of them in life. The elder brother was destined to succeed
to the farm which his father cultivated in the interval of sacred duties; it
was therefore determined that Robin should profit by his kinsman's generous
intentions, especially as he seemed to be rather the favorite, and was thought
to possess other necessary endowments.

"For I have the name of being a shrewd youth," observed Robin, in
this part of his story.

"I doubt not you deserve it," replied his new friend, good-naturedly;
"but pray proceed."

"Well, sir, being nearly eighteen years old, and well grown, as you see,"
continued Robin, drawing himself up to his full height, "I thought it high
time to begin in the world. So my mother and sister put me in handsome
trim, and my father gave me half the remnant of his last year's salary, and
five days ago I started for this place, to pay the Major a visit. But, would
you believe it, sir! I crossed the ferry a little after dark, and have yet found
nobody that would show me the way to his dwelling; only, an hour or two
since, I was told to wait here, and Major Molineux would pass by."

"Can you describe the man who told you this?" inquired the gentleman.

"Oh, he was a very ill-favored fellow, sir," replied Robin, "with two
great bumps on his forehead, a hook nose, fiery eyes; and, what struck me
as the strangest, his face was of two different colors. Do you happen to know
such a man, sir?"

"Not intimately," answered the stranger, "but I chanced to meet him
a little time previous to your stopping me. I believe you may trust his
word, and that the Major will very shortly pass through this street. In the

mean time, as I have a singular curiosity to witness your meeting, I will sit down here upon the steps and bear you company."

He seated himself accordingly, and soon engaged his companion in animated discourse. It was but of brief continuance, however, for a noise of shouting, which had long been remotely audible, drew so much nearer that Robin inquired its cause.

"What may be the meaning of this uproar?" asked he. "Truly, if your town be always as noisy, I shall find little sleep while I am an inhabitant."

"Why, indeed, friend Robin, there do appear to be three or four riotous fellows abroad to-night," replied the gentleman. "You must not expect all the stillness of your native woods here in our streets. But the watch will shortly be at the heels of these lads and" —

"Ay, and set them in the stocks by peep of day," interrupted Robin, recollecting his own encounter with the drowsy lantern-bearer. "But, dear sir, if I may trust my ears, an army of watchmen would never make head against such a multitude of rioters. There were at least a thousand voices went up to make that one shout."

"May not a man have several voices, Robin, as well as two complexions?" said his friend.

"Perhaps a man may; but Heaven forbid that a woman should!" responded the shrewd youth, thinking of the seductive tones of the Major's housekeeper.

The sounds of a trumpet in some neighboring street now became so evident and continual, that Robin's curiosity was strongly excited. In addition to the shouts, he heard frequent bursts from many instruments of discord, and a wild and confused laughter filled up the intervals. Robin rose from the steps, and looked wistfully towards a point whither people seemed to be hastening.

"Surely some prodigious merry-making is going on," exclaimed he. "I have laughed very little since I left home, sir, and should be sorry to lose an opportunity. Shall we step round the corner by that darkish house, and take our share of the fun?"

"Sit down again, sit down, good Robin," replied the gentleman, laying his hand on the skirt of the gray coat. "You forget that we must wait here for your kinsman; and there is reason to believe that he will pass by, in the course of a very few moments."

The near approach of the uproar had now disturbed the neighborhood; windows flew open on all sides; and many heads, in the attire of the pillow, and confused by sleep suddenly broken, were protruded to the gaze of whoever had leisure to observe them. Eager voices hailed each other from house to house, all demanding the explanation, which not a soul could give. Half-dressed men hurried towards the unknown commotion, stumbling as they went over the stone steps that thrust themselves into the narrow footwalk. The shouts, the laughter, and the tuneless bray, the antipodes of music, came onwards with increasing din, till scattered individuals, and then denser bodies, began to appear round a corner at the distance of a hundred yards.

"Will you recognize your kinsman, if he passes in this crowd?" inquired the gentleman.

"Indeed, I can't warrant it, sir; but I'll take my stand here, and keep a bright lookout," answered Robin, descending to the outer edge of the pavement.

A mighty stream of people now emptied into the street, and came rolling slowly towards the church. A single horseman wheeled the corner in the midst of them, and close behind him came a band of fearful wind-instruments, sending forth a fresher discord now that no intervening buildings kept it from the ear. Then a redder light disturbed the moonbeams, and a dense multitude of torches shone along the street, concealing, by their glare, whatever object they illuminated. The single horseman, clad in a military dress, and bearing a drawn sword, rode onward as the leader, and, by his fierce and variegated countenance, appeared like war personified; the red of one cheek was an emblem of fire and sword; the blackness of the other betokened the mourning that attends them. In his train were wild figures in the Indian dress, and many fantastic shapes without a model, giving the whole march a visionary air, as if a dream had broken forth from some feverish brain, and were sweeping visibly through the midnight streets. A mass of people, inactive, except as applauding spectators, hemmed the procession in; and several women ran along the sidewalk, piercing the confusion of heavier sounds with their shrill voices of mirth or terror.

"The double-faced fellow has his eye upon me," muttered Robin, with an indefinite but an uncomfortable idea that he was himself to bear a part in the pageantry.

The leader turned himself in the saddle, and fixed his glance full upon the country youth, as the steed went slowly by. When Robin had freed his eyes from those fiery ones, the musicians were passing before him, and the torches were close at hand; but the unsteady brightness of the latter formed a veil which he could not penetrate. The rattling of wheels over the stones sometimes found its way to his ear, and confused traces of a human form appeared at intervals, and then melted into the vivid light. A moment more, and the leader thundered a command to halt: the trumpets vomited a horrid breath, and then held their peace; the shouts and laughter of the people died away, and there remained only a universal hum, allied to silence. Right before Robin's eyes was an uncovered cart. There the torches blazed the brightest, there the moon shone out like day, and there, in tar-and-feathery dignity, sat his kinsman, Major Molineux!

He was an elderly man of large and majestic person, and strong, square features, betokening a steady soul; but steady as it was, his enemies had found means to shake it. His face was pale as death, and far more ghastly; the broad forehead was contracted in his agony, so that his eyebrows formed one grizzled line; his eyes were red and wild, and the foam hung white upon his quivering lip. His whole frame was agitated by a quick and continual tremor, which his pride strove to quell, even in those circumstances of overwhelming humiliation. But perhaps the bitterest pang of all was when his eyes met those of Robin; for he evidently knew him on the instant, as the youth stood witnessing the foul disgrace of a head grown gray in honor. They stared at each other in silence, and Robin's knees shook, and his hair bristled, with a mixture of pity and terror. Soon, however, a bewildering excitement began to seize upon his mind; the preceding adventures of the night, the unexpected appearance of the crowd, the torches, the confused din and the hush that followed, the spectre of his kinsman reviled by that great multitude,—all this, and, more than all, a perception of tremendous ridicule in the whole scene, affected him with a sort of mental inebriety. At that moment a voice of sluggish merriment saluted Robin's ears; he turned instinctively, and just behind the corner of the church stood the lantern-bearer, rubbing his eyes, and drowsily enjoying the lad's amazement. Then he heard a peal of laughter like the ringing of silvery bells; a woman twitched his arm, a saucy eye met his, and he saw the lady of the scarlet petticoat. A sharp, dry cachinnation appealed to his memory, and standing on tiptoe in the crowd, with his white apron over his head, he beheld the courteous little innkeeper. And lastly, there sailed over the heads of the multitude a great, broad laugh, broken in the midst by two sepulchral hems; thus, "Haw, haw, haw,—hem, hem,—haw, haw, haw, haw!"

The sound proceeded from the balcony of the opposite edifice, and thither Robin turned his eyes. In front of the Gothic window stood the old citizen, wrapped in a wide gown, his gray periwig exchanged for a nightcap, which was thrust back from his forehead, and his silk stockings hanging about his legs. He supported himself on his polished cane in a fit of convulsive merriment, which manifested itself on his solemn old features like a funny inscription on a tombstone. Then Robin seemed to hear the voices of the barbers, of the guests of the inn, and of all who had made sport of him that night. The contagion was spreading among the multitude, when all at once, it seized upon Robin, and he sent forth a shout of laughter that echoed through the street,—every man shook his sides, every man emptied his lungs, but Robin's shout was the loudest there. The cloud-spirits peeped from their silvery islands, as the congregated mirth went roaring up the sky! The Man in the Moon heard the far bellow. "Oho," quoth he, "the old earth is frolicsome tonight!"

When there was a momentary calm in that tempestuous sea of sound, the leader gave the sign, the procession resumed its march. On they went, like fiends that throng in mockery around some deak potentate, mighty no more, but majestic still in his agony. On they went, in counterfeited pomp, in senseless uproar, in frenzied merriment, tramping all on an old man's heart. On swept the tumult, and left a silent street behind.

"Well, Robin, are you dreaming?" inquired the gentleman, laying his hand on the youth's shoulder.

Robin started, and withdrew his arm from the stone post to which he had instinctively clung, as the living stream rolled by him. His cheek was somewhat pale, and his eye not quite as lively as in the earlier part of the evening.

"Will you be kind enough to show me the way to the ferry?" said he, after a moment's pause.

"You have, then, adopted a new subject of inquiry?" observed his companion, with a smile.

"Why, yes, sir," replied Robin, rather dryly. "Thanks to you, and to my other friends, I have at last met my kinsman, and he will scarce desire to see my face again. I begin to grow weary of a town life, sir. Will you show me the way to the ferry?"

"No, my good friend Robin,—not to-night, at least," said the gentleman. "Some few days hence, if you wish it, I will speed you on your journey. Or, if you prefer to remain with us, perhaps, as you are a shrewd youth, you may rise in the world without the help of your kinsman, Major Molineaux."

Discussion of "My Kinsman, Major Molineux"

Nathaniel Hawthorne (1804-1864) was descended from such differing ancestors as Justice Hawthorne who gained dubious fame as one of the judges in the Salem witchcraft trials and "Bold Hathorne," the hero of a Revolutionary War ballad. His own father, a sea captain, died when Nathaniel was only four years old, and his mother went into such complete mourning that her son and two daughters often did not see her for days. After his graduation from Bowdoin, young Hawthorne also became a recluse but was fortunate in meeting and marrying Sophia Peabody whom he idolized throughout a long and very happy marriage and who helped him "open an intercourse with the world."

"My Kinsman, Major Molineux" was among the earliest of Hawthorne's tales to appear in print, but its critical reception was mixed. Some thought this to be simply a tale of the necessary replacing of the old by the new.   Others felt that it was no more than the account of an ignorant country youth who was frustrated in his search for help from a prominent kinsman and, as a result, finally joined in public condemnation of him.

Recent critics have been more impressed.   They have usually recognized this as one of the great accounts of developing manhood. Note that even the young hero's name is suggestive of spring-like hope and anticipation.   As he innocently comes to town from the countryside in quest of his uncle, Robin cannot understand, at first, why he should be so tricked by the people he asks for information.   He is exposed to various kinds of evil, which fortunately do not touch him deeply, and possibly encounters Satan himself in the person of the gruesomely colored leader of the mob.   Yet Robin's major disappointment is his belated recognition that hope of advancement is futile; his famous uncle can do nothing for him.

Unlike the boy and girl of "Early Marriage" who are molded by their experience but not crushed by it, Robin seems to be in a state of almost complete disillusionment by the end of his story.   But we somehow feel that Robin will take the kindly stranger's advice and remain in the city to seek a fortune which is not dependent upon favor or chance.   Our confidence in this is built upon the hints we note that Robin has already profited by the experiences of the night.   If he has been in darkness, the dawn is about to break.

Hawthorne makes us smile at Robin's declared "shrewdness" which is everywhere shown to be little more than naiveté but the final description of him as "a shrewd youth" is meant to be taken seriously. For Robin's participation in the laughter of the brutal mob is directed more at himself than at anyone else.   As he reviews the frustrations and temptations of the night he suddenly puts his pretensions and asperations into focus—and they are merely laughable.   One suspects there is bitterness in his laughter as well as perspective.   Growing up can be excruciatingly painful.   There is also the loneliness of laughing in the crowd but not with it, for the "frenzied merriment" of the mob has little to do with his own self-ridicule.

The fact that Robin has come away from his contact with various manifestations of evil without succumbing to them is the truly encouraging note of this story's ending. His disillusionment has not resulted in cynicism. Perhaps he has never seen himself so clearly before. If the view is painful, it can be the prelude to positive change. His vision of home and family has made it clear to him that one only returns to the past in memory. Whether Robin stays or goes, he knows he is on his own and that further growth is inevitable.

SECTION FIVE

The Appreciation of Beauty

by Bruce B. Clark

"Snowstorm"

by Joseph Mallord William Turner (1775-1851) British (The National Gallery, London, England)

Commentary by
Floyd E. Brienholt, Associate Professor of Art, Brigham Young University

What is beauty?

"Beauty is truth—truth is beauty."

What is truth—that for which all search, that which, when discovered, strikes a harmonious chord within us, and we experience a spiritual or aesthetic thrill? Are the works of Joseph Turner beautiful? Are they true?

Joseph M. W. Turner, the London born artist, lover of the sea, world traveler, romanticist and innovator, was and still is a controversial figure. Important critics have differed intensely in their reaction to his works. Some acclaim him as a forerunner of our present expressionistic art and one who inspired the impressionists. John Ruskin, essayist, art critic and contemporary of Turner's, was greatly inspired by him. In the essay from *Modern Painters* printed in the lesson, Ruskin puts into words what he believed Turner was saying in paint. Implied in the essay is the idea that instead of painting the obvious, Turner chose an unusual moment and dramatized it forcefully, using an exaggerated splendor of light and movement to portray a truth. His great experience with the sea and as a sailor gave him a certain authority. It is said that at one time he asked the sailors to lash him to the mast during a terrific storm at sea so that he could experience the power and majesty of the elements. He was tied there for four hours before they could release him. This experience inspired "The Snowstorm."

Another writer, Julius Meier—Graefe in his book *Modern Art,* 1908, was less impressed with Turner's paintings and has this to say:

"To pile things up! This became Turner's principle more and more as the years passed by. To bring together as many things as a frame would hold, then to shake them up vigorously, and leave the rest to Ruskin!"

There is no doubt that Turner's paintings were different from any at his time and prior to it, that they radiate an emotional quality and an excitement of color and motion bathed in light not known before. They exclude use of realistic detail and one stands in awe at his concept of light.

Do his paintings strike a chord of harmony within you? Do you see what you sense to be true? We leave you to decide—what is truth? What is beauty? Is it in the eye of the beholder?

THE APPRECIATION OF BEAUTY

I pray Thee, oh God, that I may be beautiful within.

—Socrates

Introductory Comments

Like most of the other concepts that we are exploring in this volume, beauty (and its opposite, ugliness) is manifest abundantly both in the natural universe and in our human lives, to say nothing of the whole world of art (literature, music, painting, sculpturing, etc.), which is dedicated to the creation and sharing of beauty. In order to touch upon these several aspects of beauty, we are dividing this section into three sub-sections: first, a sub-section on beauty in man and woman; second, a sub-section on beauty in nature; and third, a sub-section on beauty in art.

Beauty in Man and Woman

Anyone who can appreciate beauty knows that there is visual beauty in the human form and face equalling whatever else of beauty the world has to offer. Painters and sculptors have spent more hours re-creating the beauty of the human face and figure than on all other things combined, and poets too have lavished their most eloquent words in praise of human beauty, usually female (most poets being male). Thus we find Edgar Allan Poe (1809-1849) writing a poem "To Helen" that glows with lovely phrasing as he describes Helen of Troy, ancient symbol of the idealization of pure beauty:

> Helen, thy beauty is to me
>   Like those Nicean barks of yore,
> That gently, o'er a perfumed sea,
>   The weary, way-worn wanderer bore
>   To his own native shore.
>
> On desperate seas long wont to roam,
>   Thy hyacinth hair, thy classic face,
> Thy Naiad airs have brought me home
>   To the glory that was Greece
> And the grandeur that was Rome.
>
> Lo! in yon brilliant window-niche
>   How statue-like I see thee stand!
>   The agate lamp within thy hand,
> Ah! Psyche, from the regions which
>   Are Holy Land!

The Elizabethan poet Thomas Campion (1567-1620) was even more extravagant in describing some unknown renaissance girl in his poem "There Is a Garden in Her Face." Indeed there is "a garden in her face" as with elaborate conceits, typical of the age, Campion has the girl's lips become, first cherries enclosing pearls, then rosebuds enclosing snow, while her eyes like guardian angels stand ready to protect her from any who might try to steal a kiss:

> There is a garden in her face,
> Where roses and white lilies grow;
>   A heavenly paradise is that place,

Wherein all pleasant fruits do flow.
There cherries grow which none may buy
Till cherry-ripe themselves do cry.

Those cherries fairly do enclose
Of orient pearl a double row.
Which when her lovely laughter shows,
They look like rosebuds filled with snow.
Yet them nor peer nor prince can buy
Till cherry-ripe themselves do cry.

Her eyes like angels watch them still;
Her brows like bended bows do stand,
Threat'ning with piercing frowns to kill
All that attempt with eye or hand
Those sacred cherries to come nigh.
Till cherry-ripe themselves do cry.

Fortunately, there has never been a woman who looked quite like this idealized "beauty" in Campion's poem. Fortunately, too, all mature people know that there is another kind of womanly beauty more beautiful than any that is merely physical. Indeed, physical beauty at its loveliest is radiant with the reflection of inward spirituality. And even when physical beauty seems altogether lacking, there can exist an integrity of character, a pleasantness of personality, and a conscious good grooming that are far more attractive than mere prettiness or handsomeness. We can't all be pretty or handsome, but we can all be friendly and genuine. It was something like this that George Eliot (1819-1880) had in mind when, in her novel *Adam Bede*, she argued for honesty and realism in literature:

These fellow-mortals, every one, must be accepted as they are: you can neither straighten their noses, nor brighten their wit, nor rectify their dispositions; and it is these people—amongst whom your life is passed—that it is needful you should tolerate, pity, and love. . . . So I am content to tell my simple story, without trying to make things seem better than they are; dreading nothing, indeed, but falsity. . . . All honour and reverence to the divine beauty of form! Let us cultivate it to the utmost in men, women, and children in our gardens and in our houses. But let us love that other beauty too, which lies in no secret of proportion, but in the secret of deep human sympathy. Paint us an angel, if you can, with a floating violet robe, and a face paled by the celestial

light. . . . But bless us, things may be lovable that are not altogether handsome. . . . Do not impose on us any aesthetic rules which shall banish from
the region of Art those old women scraping carrots with their work-worn
hands, . . . those rounded backs and weather-beaten faces that have bent over
the spade and done the rough work of the world—those homes with their tin
pans, their brown pitchers, their rough curs, and their clusters of onions. . . .
There are few prophets in the world; few sublimely beautiful women; few heroes.

Shakespeare also knew that surface beauty is a deceptive quality.
In one of his sonnets (#130) he openly satirizes the conventional
blonde beauty of the idealized renaissance heroine, mockingly stating
that he prefers a more earthly woman:

> My mistress' eyes are nothing like the sun;
> Coral is far more red than her lips' red:
> If snow be white, why then her breasts are dun:
> If hairs be wires, black wires grow on her head.
> I have seen roses damasked, red and white,
> But no such roses see I in her cheeks;
> And in some perfumes is there more delight
> Than in the breath that from my mistress reeks.
> I love to hear her speak, yet well I know
> That music hath a far more pleasing sound:
> I grant I never saw a goddess go, —
> My mistress, when she walks, treads on the ground:
>   And yet, by heaven, I think my love as rare
>   As any she belied with false compare.

Most readers will probably feel that Shakespeare here goes too far
in mocking ethereal beauty and treating women realistically, but he
certainly gets his point across.[1] More acceptable is "Stella's Birthday"
by Jonathan Swift (1667-1745), in which Swift shows his life-long
devotion to his beloved Stella (Hester Johnson). He makes her not
only a very believable woman, but also a very adored woman. The
poem is charming and lovely, not so much because Stella at 34 is
double her 16-year-old size as because Swift makes clear that he loves
her for her mind, her wit, her personality, her goodness rather than
for her mere physical beauty. Moreover, the tribute to Stella becomes
all the more appealing when one remembers that Swift was generally

---

[1]Generally Shakespeare idealizes women in his plays and poems. Here, for satiric
reasons, he goes to the other extreme.

acid-tongued and bitterly satirical in his writing, as all readers of
Gulliver's Travels will remember:

> Stella this day is thirty-four
> (We shan't dispute a year or more) —
> However, Stella, be not troubled,
> Although thy size and years are doubled,
> Since first I saw thee at sixteen,
> The brightest virgin on the green,
> So little is thy form declined;
> Made up so largely in thy mind.
>   Oh, would it please the gods, to split
> Thy beauty, size, and years, and wit;
> No age could furnish out a pair
> Of nymphs so graceful, wise, and fair;
> With half the lustre of your eyes,
> With half your wit, your years, and size.
> And then, before it grew too late,
> How should I beg of gentle Fate
> (That either nymph might have her swain)
> To split my worship too in twain.

In the preceding three volumes of this series we have again and
again presented portraits of admirable men and women—not perfect,
because they are human, but with admirable qualities: in Volume 1,
the leader in Wordsworth's "Character of the Happy Warrior," the
old shoemaker in Galsworthy's "Quality," Hunt's Abou Ben Adhem,
Wordsworth's Michael, Browning's Rabbi Ben Ezra; in Volume 2,
the parents in Ewald's "My Little Boy," Ruth in the Old Testament,
Elizabeth Barrett Browning and Robert Browning in their love poems
to each other, the mother in Kathleen Norris's "Mother," Mary in
"The Death of the Hired Man," Newman's ideal "gentleman," Sarah
Penn in "The Revolt of Mother," the wife in Zona Gale's "The
Woman," Abigail Adams in her letters to John Adams, Martin in
"Where Love Is, There God Is Also," Amy in "Bread and Milk," Fred
Roger in *Man to Man;* and in Volume 3, Mary in "A Courageous
Letter," Mrs. Kirby in "The Happy Journey to Trenton and Camden,"
Betsey Lane in "The Flight of Betsey Lane," Betsey Barton in "And
Now to Live Again," Tennyson's Dora, Maria in Joyce's "Clay,"

Thomas More in *A Man for All Seasons,* and the whole family in
"A Cotter's Saturday Night."

Because of this extensive coverage, another such portrait is perhaps not needed here. However, we did want to include at this point
one brief character sketch drawn from modern literature portraying
a twentieth-century woman beautiful because of her personality and
character—and we cannot find exactly what we want. We need a
sketch of a mature modern woman who is intelligent, but not intel-
lectually brittle, sophisticated, but not too sophisticated, spiritual,
yet still real, beautiful in personality and character, yet still believable.
In short, we need a typical high-quality modern wife and mother—
the kind all of us are acquainted with in real life. But in modern
literature we instead find mostly frustrated, neurotic, unfulfilled,
rebellious, unhappy women. These by the dozens, portrayed brilliantly. In their efforts to be realistic, the most talented of modern
writers concentrate on the massive frustrations of our age and ignore
the happy, well adjusted people. Hence, however brilliant and powerful
it is, there is a kind of unrealism in modern literature because it
doesn't present the whole picture of modern life. Implied in all of
this is, of course, a challenge to writers. If it is unrealistic to paint
the world too rosy, it is also unrealistic to paint it too black. Portraying the middle ground of normal, fairly well adjusted, imperfect, but
generally happy people—without sentimentalizing about them, without laughing at them, and without being superficial—is exceedingly
difficult. Such a literature, however, is needed if the whole picture
of modern life is to be portrayed.

Before concluding this first sub-section, we wish to include two
more brief selections. The first is a poem by the contemporary American poet John Frederick Nims (1914-   ). This delightful, insight-
ful, modern poem, written with extraordinary skill in word control,
comes very close to being the modern portrait we said we couldn't
find. The woman portrayed is imperfect enough to be believable
and yet has qualities that are truly beautiful. She is awkward with
her hands and careless with time, but in courtesy and love she is an
artist. The title is simply "Love Poem":

My clumsiest dear, whose hands shipwreck vases,
At whose quick touch all glasses chip and ring,
Whose palms are bulls in china, burs in linen,
And have no cunning with any soft thing

Except all ill-at-ease fidgeting people:
The refugee uncertain at the door
You make at home; deftly you steady
The drunk clambering on his undulant floor.

Unpredictable dear, the taxi drivers' terror,
Shrinking from far headlights pale as a dime
Yet leaping before red apoplectic streetcars—
Misfit in any space. And never on time.

A wrench in clocks and the solar system. Only
With words and people and love you move at ease.
In traffic of wit expertly maneuver
And keep us, all devotion, at your knees.

Be with me, darling, early and late. Smash glasses—
I will study wry music for your sake.
For should your hands drop white and empty
All the toys of the world would break.

The next and last item of this first sub-section is not so much a selection as a commentary. "I pray Thee, oh God, that I may be beautiful within" is the statement by Socrates with which this section on "The Appreciation of Beauty" begins. If ever a man had courage and integrity, which together make beauty of character, Socrates did. In ancient Greece, 2400 years ago, Socrates (469-399 B.C.) got into trouble with the state because he persisted in being a gadfly conversationalist endlessly asking questions that stung the people into probing self-examination. Accused of corrupting the youth and mocking the gods of the people, Socrates was condemned to death by the Athenian Senate. Rather than being a corrupter, Socrates was an idealist of the highest principles and one of the great men of all time, but he was still condemned to death. As the death-hour approached, Socrates was urged by friends to say the things necessary to save his life— to promise, for example, that he would stop asking questions, or to admit that he was wrong in his teachings. Socrates would neither lie nor promise to be silent—not even to save himself as a father for his children. Unflinching honesty compelled him to die rather than violate his integrity. Moreover, he said that, whatever the consequences, one should recognize the authority of the law. And so he drank hemlock poison, comforting his friends who had gathered round in his prison cell as the numbness of death crept upon him. All of this is recorded by the great philosopher Plato, who was Socrates' pupil, in the dialogues *Crito* and *Phaedo*. The following brief passage is from the *Crito*, as Socrates sort of talks to himself:

> Think not of life and children first, and of justice afterwards, but of justice first. . . . Depart in innocence, a sufferer and not a doer of evil; a victim, not of the laws, but of men. . . . Men of Athens, I honor and love you; but I shall obey God rather than you.

(Note: For further information about Socrates and his death, see pp. 45-49 earlier in this volume.)

Beauty in Nature

In "Fra Lippo Lippi," one of his great poems on art, Robert Browning says:

> You've seen the world—
> The beauty and the wonder and the power,
> The shapes of things, their colors, light and shades,
> Changes, surprises—and God made it all!—
> For what? . . . What's it all about?
> To be passed over, despised? or dwelt upon,
> Wondered at? oh, this last of course!—you say.
> But why not do as well as say—paint these
> Just as they are, careless what comes of it?
> God's works—paint any one, and count it crime
> To let a truth slip. . . .
> If you get simple beauty and naught else,
> You get about the best thing God invents—
>   . . . This world's no blot for us,
> Nor blank; it means intensely, and means good—
> To find its meaning is my meat and drink.

The speaker is Fra Lippo Lippi, one of the great renaissance painters of Florence, into whose mouth Browning puts his own philosophy of art—that God created a world of beauty, and it is the artist's opportunity to reproduce this beauty, isolating points of beauty for greater appreciation.

Many poets as well as painters share this philosophy of art, and hundreds of excellent poems are concerned primarily with describing the beauties of nature.[2] One of the most gifted of all nature lovers was Gerard Manley Hopkins (1844-1889), whose life we discussed along with two of his brilliant nature poems, "The Windhover" and "God's Grandeur," in Volume 1, pp. 96-104. Hopkins combines a love of nature with a worship of God, clearly seen in the following little poem called "Pied Beauty":

> Glory be to God for dappled things—
>   For skies of couple-color as a brinded cow;
>   For rose-moles all in stipple upon trout that swim;

---

[2]Many novels and stories are also impressive in their descriptions of nature—for example, the magnificent ocean scenes in the writings of Melville and Conrad, or the great description of Egdon Heath which forms the opening chapter of Hardy's *The Return of the Native.*

> Fresh-firecoal chestnut-falls; finches' wings;
>   Landscapes plotted and pieced—fold, fallow, and plow;
>   And all trades, their gear and tackle and trim.
> All things counter, original, spare, strange;
>   Whatever is fickle, freckled (who knows how?)
>   With swift, slow; sweet, sour; adazzle, dim;
> He fathers-forth whose beauty is past change:
>   Praise Him.

Stippling is a method of painting by dotting with the end of a brush, which is exactly the right way to describe the "rose-moles" dotting the sides of a certain kind of trout—one of the several multi-colored things that Hopkins draws attention to in this exciting little poem.

"Pied Beauty" is concerned with God and His world of beauty in nature. Hopkins always thought of God as the supreme creator of beauty, even when he makes no direct mention of God, as in the following poem, called "Moonrise." Here the moon is just rising, a mere fingernail fringe of a moon, still "clasped" and "fanged" by the peak (cusp or fluke) of the mountain. So enthralling was the scene to Hopkins that it startled him into full wakefulness, and as readers we will find the poem equally enchanting:

I awoke in the Midsummer not to call night, in the white and the walk of
   the morning:
The moon, dwindled and thinned to the fringe of a finger-nail held to the candle,
Or paring of paradisaical fruit, lovely in waning but lusterless,
Stepped from the stool, drew back from the barrow, of dark Maenefa the mountain;
A cusp still clasped him, a fluke yet fanged him, entangled him, not quit utterly.
This was the prized, the desirable sight, unsought, presented so easily,
Parted me leaf and leaf, divided me, eyelid and eyelid of slumber.

Equally superb as a nature poet who both described the beauties of nature and created beautiful poetry in the process is John Keats (1795-1821).[3] No poet was concerned about beauty more than Keats, who in *Endymion* said "A thing of beauty is a joy forever" and in "Ode on a Grecian Urn" said "Beauty is truth, truth beauty,—that is all / Ye know on earth, and all ye need to know."

_____

[3]For a discussion of Keats's life, and of "Ode on a Grecian Urn," see pp. 21-24 of Volume 1. See also Section 1 of this present volume for a discussion of Keats's "On First Looking into Chapman's Homer."

As examples of Keats's extraordinary power as a nature poet, we print two poems. The first is a sonnet, "On the Grasshopper and Cricket," which carefully follows the traditional Petrarchan form of abba abba cde cde rhymes. Conforming to so set a pattern and writing on so trivial a subject could be deadly dull for a lesser poet, but Keats injects the lines with a magic of sound, rhythm, and imagery which makes the poem come to life as a vivid little art piece:

> The poetry of earth is never dead:
>   When all the birds are faint with the hot sun,
>   And hide in cooling trees, a voice will run
> From hedge to hedge about the new-mown mead;
> That is the Grasshopper's—he takes the lead
>   In summer luxury,—he has never done
>   With his delights; for when tired out with fun
> He rests at ease beneath some pleasant weed.
> The poetry of earth is ceasing never:
>   On a lone winter evening, when the frost
>   Has wrought a silence, from the stove there shrills
> The Cricket's song, in warmth increasing ever,
>   And seems to one in drowsiness half lost,
>   The Grasshopper's among some grassy hills.

As a lover of nature, Keats was as much interested in the sounds of nature ("the poetry of earth") as in the sights. Both the poem just read, which describes the singing of the grasshopper and the cricket, and the poem to follow, which in its third stanza describes the sounds of autumn, give attention to the music of nature.

"To Autumn" is the name of this next poem. Its first stanza literally bursts with the plump richness of things ready for harvest. Note that emphasis in the first stanza is upon the verbs—"load," "bend," "fill," "swell," "plump"—suggesting this burstingly harvest-ready quality of the grains and fruits.

The second stanza slows down in tempo. The season is later. The harvest is mostly completed—the reaping, the threshing (winnowing), the cider-making. And everyone is weary and drowsy. The long, open vowels and the nasal consonants (l's, m's, n's) suggest this languorous weariness.

The third stanza, as already noted, describes the music of autumn —the wailful mourn of the gnats, the bleating of the lambs, the singing of the hedge-crickets, the treble-soft whistling of the red-breast, and the twittering swallows, who are "gathering," ominously suggesting that winter is close at hand.

The whole poem is mostly just a description; but again the sounds, rhythms, and images are so vivid and so richly musical that the poem is beautiful, both in what it describes and in what it creates:

Season of mists and mellow fruitfulness,
 Close bosom-friend of the maturing sun;
Conspiring with him how to load and bless
 With fruit the vines that round the thatch-eves run;
To bend with apples the moss'd cottage-trees,
 And fill all fruit with ripeness to the core;
  To swell the gourd, and plump the hazel shells
 With a sweet kernel; to set budding more,
And still more, later flowers for the bees,
Until they think warm days will never cease,
  For Summer has o'er-brimm'd their clammy cells.

Who hath not seen thee oft amid thy store?
 Sometimes whoever seeks abroad may find
Thee sitting careless on a granary floor,
 Thy hair soft-lifted by the winnowing wind;
Or on a half-reap'd furrow sound asleep,
 Drows'd with the fume of poppies, while thy hook
  Spares the next swath and all its twinèd flowers:
And sometimes like a gleaner thou dost keep
 Steady thy laden head across a brook;
 Or by a cyder-press, with patient look,
  Thou watchest the last oozings hours by hours.

Where are the songs of Spring? Ay, where are they?
 Think not of them, thou hast thy music too,—
While barred clouds bloom the soft-dying day,
 And touch the stubble-plains with rosy hue;
Then in a wailful choir the small gnats mourn
 Among the river sallows,[4] borne aloft
  Or sinking as the light wind lives or dies;
And full-grown lambs bleat from hilly bourn;
 Hedge-crickets sing; and now with treble soft
 The red-breast whistles from a garden-croft;
  And gathering swallows twitter in the skies.

_____

[4]Willows.

Another great nature lover, who found not only beauty in nature, but also sublime religious experiences, was William Wordsworth (1770-1850).[5] Of his many nature poems, one of the finest is a sonnet, "Composed upon Westminster Bridge," which describes the huge city of London asleep in early morning, bathed from all sides with the beauties and wonders of nature—the gliding river, the open fields, the streaming early-morning sun, and the pure smokeless air in the sky overhead. The sonnet provides us with at least two levels of appreciation. First of all, it is aesthetically beautiful—the liquid sound of rhyme and rhythm, the clean, clear images, the simple but dignified diction. Beyond this aesthetic appeal lies deeper meaning, however. The city is personified as a sleeping giant, wearing the beauty of the morning like a garment (lines 4-5), with a mighty heart beating as it sleeps (line 14), and with the pure world of nature all around. The "smokeless air," contrasting with the smoke and grime of normal city atmosphere, seems especially significant, apparently symbolizing the purity of nature's spirit which pervades the entire scene. The result is a poem enchanting in its loveliness as we feel the slumbering power of the great city of London almost transfigured in the beautiful full dawn of morning.[6]

> Earth has not anything to show more fair:
> Dull would he be of soul who could pass by
> A sight so touching in its majesty:
> This City now doth, like a garment, wear
> The beauty of the morning; silent, bare,
> Ships, towers, domes, theatres, and temples lie
> Open unto the fields, and to the sky;
> All bright and glittering in the smokeless air.
> Never did the sun more beautifully steep
> In his first splendour, valley, rock, or hill;
> Ne'er saw I, never felt, a calm so deep!
> The river glideth at his own sweet will:
> Dear God! the very houses seem asleep;
> And all that mighty heart is lying still!

----

[5]For a discussion of Wordsworth and his writings, see pp. 53-70 of Volume 1. For other poems by Wordsworth, see pp. 229-230 and 405-419 of Volume 1, pp. 360-364 of Volume 2, and pp. 4-7 and 229-230 of Volume 3.

[6]Two of the ideas used in the discussion of this sonnet were drawn from K. L. Knickerbocker and H. W. Reninger, *Interpreting Literature* (New York: Henry Holt and Co., 1955), pp. 378-379.

As a final poem portraying the beauty of nature we turn to the beginning lines of "Apology for Bad Dreams" by the modern American poet Robinson Jeffers (1887-1962).[7] In these lines Jeffers contrasts the ugly cruelty of the human race (represented by the woman and her son) with the magnificent beauty of the non-human universe. Certainly the beauty of nature is handled vividly—the redwood forest, the craggy shore-line, the vast ocean, the red sunset. Many readers, however, will feel that Jeffers goes too far in believing that humanity is this brutal:

In the purple light, heavy with redwood, the slopes drop seaward,
Headlong convexities of forest, drawn in together to the steep ravine. Below, on
    the sea-cliff,
A lonely clearing: a little field of corn by the streamside; a roof under spared
    trees. Then the ocean
Like a great stone someone has cut to a sharp edge and polished to shining.
    Beyond it, the fountain
And furnace of incredible light flowing up from the sunk sun. In the little
    clearing a woman
Was punishing a horse; she had tied the halter to a sapling at the edge of the
    wood; but when the great whip
Clung to the flanks the creature kicked so hard she feared he would snap the
    halter; she called from the house
The young man her son; who fetched a chain tie-rope, they working together
Noosed the small rusty links round the horse's tongue
And tied him by the swollen tongue to the tree.
Seen from this height they are shrunk to insect size,
Out of all human relation. You cannot distinguish
The blood dripping from where the chain is fastened,
The beast shuddering; but the thrust neck and the legs
Far apart. You can see the whip fall on the flanks . . .
The gesture of the arm. You cannot see the face of the woman.
The enormous light beats up out of the west across the cloud-bars of the
    trade-wind. The ocean
Darkens, the high clouds brighten, the hills darken together. Unbridled and
    unbelievable beauty
Covers the evening world. . . .

---

[7]For a previous discussion of Jeffers and several of his poems, see pp. 50-51, 448, and 452 of Volume 1.

Beauty in Art

In its concern for beauty, literature treats not only beauty in people and beauty in nature but also beauty in art. In this sense, literature both discusses and creates beauty. Already in this and previous volumes we have examined a number of great art poems that, in addition to whatever else they are doing, create unforgettable beauty in the music and imagery of their lines. Among these are such poems as Keats's "Ode on a Grecian Urn" (Vol. 1, pp. 21-24) and "The Eve of St. Agnes" (Vol. 2, pp. 74-90), Coleridge's "The Rime of the Ancient Mariner" (Vol. 1, pp. 304-328), Thompson's "The Hound of Heaven" (Vol. 1, pp. 343-351), Browning's "Andrea del Sarto" (Vol. 3, pp. 80-89), and Hopkins's "The Windhover" (Vol. 1, pp. 96-101), "God's Grandeur" (Vol. 1, pp. 102-104), and "The Leaden Echo and The Golden Echo" (Vol. 2, pp. 347-350).

As a further example of sheer artistic beauty in poetry we turn to another poem by Samuel Taylor Coleridge[8]—his famous "Kubla Khan: or, A Vision in a Dream":

In Xanadu did Kubla Khan
A stately pleasure-dome decree:
Where Alph, the sacred river, ran
Through caverns measureless to man
   Down to a sunless sea.   5
So twice five miles of fertile ground
With walls and towers were girdled round:
And there were gardens bright with sinuous rills,
Where blossomed many an incense-bearing tree;
And here were forests ancient as the hills,   10
Enfolding sunny spots of greenery.

But oh! that deep romantic chasm which slanted
Down the green hill athwart a cedarn cover!
A savage place! as holy and enchanted
As e'er beneath a waning moon was haunted   15
By woman wailing for her demon-lover!
And from this chasm, with ceaseless turmoil seething,
As if this earth in fast thick pants were breathing,
A mighty fountain momently was forced:
Amid whose swift half-intermitted burst   20

------

[8]For brief comments on Coleridge's work in general, see pp. 321-322 of Volume 1. See also "Work Without Hope" in Section 3 of this present volume.

Huge fragments vaulted like rebounding hail,
Or chaffy grain beneath the thresher's flail:
And 'mid these dancing rocks at once and ever
It flung up momently the sacred river.
Five miles meandering with a mazy motion   25
Through wood and dale the sacred river ran,
Then reached the caverns measureless to man,
And sank in tumult to a lifeless ocean:
And 'mid this tumult Kubla heard from far
Ancestral voices prophesying war!   30
　　The shadow of the dome of pleasure
　　Floated midway on the waves;
　　Where was heard the mingled measure
　　From the fountain and the caves.
It was a miracle of rare device,   35
A sunny pleasure-dome with caves of ice!

　　A damsel with a dulcimer
　　In a vision once I saw:
　　It was an Abyssinian maid,
　　And on her dulcimer she played,   40
　　Singing of Mount Abora.
　　Could I revive within me
　　Her symphony and song,
　　To such a deep delight 'twould win me,
That with music loud and long,   45
I would build that dome in air,
That sunny dome! those caves of ice!
And all who heard should see them there,
And all should cry, Beware! Beware!
His flashing eyes, his floating hair!   50
Weave a circle round him thrice,
And close your eyes with holy dread
For he on honey-dew hath fed,
And drunk the milk of Paradise.

Many readers feel that there is deep symbolic meaning in this poem, and perhaps there is. Various interpretations have been given, both philosophical and allegorical. Other readers argue that the poem contains no deep meanings but is simply the marvelous beginning of a verse narrative, such as "The Rime of the Ancient Mariner" or "Christabel." Still other readers feel that the poem is primarily descriptive, the description of a great pleasure palace built anciently in

Xanadu by Kubla Khan, a Mongol emperor of the thirteenth century, grandson of Genghis Khan, who founded the Mongol dynasty in China.

Our purpose in printing the poem is to illustrate artistic excellence, the sheer beauty of language in the creative hands of one of the great word masters. Whatever else "Kubla Khan" is, it is hauntingly beautiful poetry, "directionless melody" as one critic said, hovering over a dream landscape combining the extremes of beauty and terror. No matter which passage one examines, the word-handling is flawless—a magic interweaving of alliteration, assonance, rhyme, onomatopoeia, shimmering imagery, varying rhythms—all the devices that in the hands of a master give to poetry the beauty of music as well as the more obvious qualities of literature.

As examples of excellence, note the 17th line, which in its very movement suggests the "seething turmoil" of the threshing water; or the 18th line, built out of short, stubby, one-syllable words, suggesting the "panting" of the earth; or the 25th line, with the long, open vowels and alliterated m's, suggesting the slow meandering of the lazy river. This is onomatopoeia at its best—the suggestion of the meanings of words in their very sound.

So beautiful is this poetry that memorized passages can be recited as pure music, haunting the memory for years. And this is true whether one sees beneath-the-surface meaning in the lines or not, and whether one regards the poem as completed or not. Coleridge himself said that the poem came intact to him in a dream, several hundred lines long, but that he was interrupted for more than an hour after writing down only these 54 lines—and when he returned to complete the writing the remaining lines had all vanished from his memory, "like the images on the surface of a stream into which a stone had been cast." Whether fragmentary or completed, it is surely one of the most beautiful and most "finished" poems ever written.

Perhaps readers at this point will enjoy a comment on the language of poetry by the inimitable Gertrude Stein (1874-1946), American poet, novelist, critic, and famous expatriate resident of Paris. In her unique style Gertrude Stein points out what Coleridge's poem so beautifully illustrates, that whereas the key words of prose are verbs, the key words of poetry are nouns, for at its heart poetry is imagery and symbol. The passage is from Miss Stein's essay "What Is Poetry?":

> What is poetry.
> Poetry has to do with vocabulary as prose has not.
> So you see prose and poetry are not at all alike. They are completely different.
> Poetry is I say essentially a vocabulary just as prose is essentially not.
> And what is the vocabulary of which poetry absolutely is. It is a vocabulary entirely based on the noun as prose is essentially and determinately and vigorously not based on the noun.
> Poetry is concerned with using with abusing, with losing with wanting, with denying with avoiding with adoring with replacing the noun. It is doing that always doing that, doing that and doing nothing but that. Poetry is doing nothing but using losing refusing and pleasing and betraying and caressing nouns. That is what poetry does, that is what poetry has to do no matter what kind of poetry it is. And there are a great many kinds of poetry.
> When I said.
> A rose is a rose is a rose is a rose.
> And then later made that into a ring I made poetry and what did I do I caressed completely caressed and addressed a noun.

Pertinent at this point also is a little poem called "Ars Poetica" by Archibald MacLeish (1892-   ), contemporary American poet, dramatist, editor, and (since 1939) U. S. Librarian of Congress. MacLeish makes much the same point as Gertrude Stein: that the essence of a poem is not argument but existence, and that no restatement of the "meaning" of a poem is an adequate substitute for the poem itself as an artistic entity:

> A poem should be palpable and mute
> As a globed fruit
>
> Dumb
> As old medallions to the thumb
>
> Silent as the sleeve-worn stone
> Of casement ledges where the moss has grown—
>
> A poem should be wordless
> As the flight of birds

*

A poem should be motionless in time
As the moon climbs

Leaving, as the moon releases
Twig by twig the night-entangled trees,

Leaving, as the moon behind the winter leaves.
Memory by memory the mind—

A poem should be motionless in time
As the moon climbs.

*

A poem should be equal to:
Not true

For all the history of grief
An empty doorway and a maple leaf

For love
The leaning grasses and two lights above the sea—

A poem should not mean
But be.

As one further example of beauty in poetry we turn to a little poem entitled "Cargoes" by John Masefield (1878-1967), England's recent poet laureate, who just died this past year:

Quinquireme of Nineveh from distant Ophir
Rowing home to haven in sunny Palestine,
With a cargo of ivory,
And apes and peacocks,
Sandalwood, cedarwood, and sweet white wine.

Stately Spanish galleon coming from the Isthmus,
Dipping through the Tropics by the palm-green shores,
With a cargo of diamonds,
Emeralds, amethysts,
Topazes, and cinnamon, and gold moidores.

Dirty British coaster with salt-caked smoke-stack
Butting through the Channel in the mad March days,
With a cargo of Tyne coal,
Road-rail, pig-lead,
Firewood, iron-ware, and cheap tin trays.

The artistic beauty here especially derives from the carefully controlled *form* of the poem. Each stanza is five lines long, with the first, second, and fifth lines relatively long and the third and fourth lines relatively short. The second and fifth lines of each stanza rhyme, whereas the first, third, and fourth lines are unrhymed. The first two lines of each stanza identify a ship, its place of origin, and its voyage; and the last three lines describe the ship's cargo. All of this, of course, requires meticulous control. The careful control goes even further, however, reaching over into the implied *theme* of the poem. The first stanza describes an ancient ship with an exotic cargo, all presented in beautifully flowing words. The second stanza moves down through centuries to the renaissance, but the ship and its cargo are still romantically attractive, and the words describing them are still liquid-smooth and beautiful. The third stanza, however, comes to the present world. The ship is dirty, its cargo ugly, and the words describing them are choppy, stubby, and as ugly as the things they describe. The first two stanzas are consciously euphonious (attractive in sound); the third stanza is consciously cacophonous (unattractive in sound). Nothing is said explicitly about what Masefield thinks of the romantic past in relation to the present, but his attitude is clear enough, culminating in the phrase "cheap tin trays."

Up to this point we have been using selections concerned with creating or discussing beauty in literature. Writers are also concerned, of course, with beauty in the other arts. As one example, we turn to an essay by John Ruskin (1819-1900), one of England's great essayists and art critics, author of *Modern Painters* (from which this essay is taken), *The Seven Lamps of Architecture, The Stones of Venice, Sesame and Lilies, The Crown of Wild Olive,* and many other volumes of social and art criticism. Ruskin describes two sea paintings, *The Snow Storm* and *The Slave Ship,* by the English painter Joseph Mallord William Turner (1775-1851). As Ruskin describes the paintings, they come to vivid visual life before our eyes almost as if we were actually seeing them. In fact, Ruskin is so excellent an art critic that through him we see and appreciate many things in the paintings that would be overlooked by our untrained eyes, and the paintings are made so vivid for us that we are left almost breathless with the excitement of them:

Few people, comparatively, have ever seen the effect on the sea of a powerful gale continued without intermission for three or four days and nights; and to those who have not, I believe it must be unimaginable, not from the mere force or size of surge, but from the complete annihilation of the limit between sea and air. The water, from its prolonged agitation, is beaten, not into mere creaming foam, but into masses of accumulated yeast, which hang in ropes and wreaths from wave to wave, and, where one curls over to break, form a festoon like a drapery, from its edge; these are taken up by the wind, not in dissipating dust, but bodily, in writhing, hanging, coiling masses, which make the air white and thick as with snow, only the flakes are a foot or two long each; the surges themselves are full of foam in their very bodies, underneath, making them white all through, as the water is under a great cataract; and their masses, being thus half water and half air, are torn to pieces by the wind whenever they rise, and carried away in roaring smoke, which chokes and strangles like actual water. Add to this that, when the air has been exhausted of its moisture by long rain, the spray of the sea is caught by it and covers its surface, not merely with the smoke of finely divided water, but with boiling mist; imagine also the low rain-clouds brought down to the very level of the sea, as I have often seen them, whirling and flying in rags and fragments from wave to wave; and, finally, conceive the surges themselves in their utmost pitch of power, velocity, vastness, and madness, lifting themselves in precipices and peaks, furrowed with their whirl of ascent, through all this chaos; and you will understand that there is indeed no distinction left between the sea and air; that no object, nor horizon, nor any landmark or natural evidence of position is left; that the heaven is all spray, and the ocean all cloud, and that you can see no farther in any direction than you could see through a cataract. Suppose the effect of the first sunbeam sent from above to show this annihilation to itself, and you have the sea picture of the Academy, 1842—*The Snowstorm*—one of the very grandest statements of sea-motion, mist, and light that has ever been put on canvas, even by Turner. Of course it was not understood; his finest works never are; but there was some apology for the public's not comprehending this, for few people have had the opportunity of seeing the sea at such a time, and, when they have, cannot face it. To hold by a mast or a rock, and watch it, is a prolonged endurance of drowning which few people have courage to go through. To those who have, it is one of the noblest lessons of nature.

But I think the noblest sea that Turner has ever painted, and, if so, the noblest certainly ever painted by man, is that of *The Slave Ship*, the chief Academy picture of the exhibition of 1840. It is a sunset on the Atlantic after prolonged storm; but the storm is partially lulled, and the torn and streaming rain clouds are moving in scarlet lines to lose themselves in the hollow of the night. The whole surface of sea included in the picture is divided into two ridges of enormous swell, not high, nor local, but a low, broad heaving of the whole ocean, like the lifting of its bosom by deep-drawn breath after the torture of the storm. Between these two ridges the fire of the sunset falls along the trough of the sea, dyeing it with an awful but glorious light, the intense and lurid splendor which burns like gold and bathes like blood. Along this fiery path and valley the tossing waves by which the swell of the sea is restlessly divided, lift themselves in dark, indefinite, fantastic forms, each casting a faint and ghastly shadow behind it along the illumined foam. They do not rise everywhere, but three or four together in wild groups, fitfully and furiously, as the under strength of the swell compels or permits them; leaving between them treacherous spaces of level and whirling water, now lighted with green and lamplike fire, now flashing back the gold of the declining sun, now fearfully dyed from above with the indistinguishable images of the burning clouds, which fall upon them in flakes of crimson and scarlet and give to the reckless waves the added motion of their own fiery flying. Purple and blue, the lurid shadows of the hollow breakers are cast upon the mist of night, which gathers cold and low, advancing like the shadow of death upon the guilty ship as it labors amidst the lightning of the sea, its thin masts written upon the sky in lines of blood, girded with condemnation in that fearful hue which signs the sky with horror, and mixes its flaming blood with the sunlight, and, cast far along the desolate heave of the sepulchral waves, incarnadines the multitudinous sea.

I believe if I were reduced to rest Turner's immortality upon any single work, I should choose this. Its daring conception—ideal in the highest sense of the word—is based on the purest truth, and wrought out with the concentrated knowledge of a life; its color is absolutely perfect, not one false or morbid hue in any part or line, and so modulated that every square inch of canvas is a perfect composition; its drawing as accurate as fearless; the ship buoyant, bending, and full of motion; its tones as true as they are wonderful; and the whole picture dedicated to the most sublime of subjects and impressions—completing thus the perfect system of all truth, which we have shown to be formed by Turner's works—the power, majesty, and deathfulness of the open, deep, illimitable Sea.

If the paintings of Turner as described by Ruskin can evoke this much response in us, think how much more the even greater painters and sculptors of the world can give us—the glorious paintings by Michelangelo on the Sistine Chapel walls and ceiling in Rome; the equally glorious David, Moses, and Pieta statues of Michelangelo; Leonardo da Vinci's Last Supper painting, magnificent even though deteriorated with age; the acres of plump, rosy flesh painted by Rubens, with his babies looking like healthy, fat little piglets; El Greco's elongated human figures, impressively spiritual even though stretched like pulled taffy; Rembrandt's dark brown scenes streamed with light; Picasso's daring innovations—and on and on through the hundreds of works by dozens of other great artists.

The world of music is equally rich—Bach, Beethoven, Brahms, Tchaikovsky, Stravinsky, Wagner, Chopin, Debussy, Bartok, the Strausses, Handel, Haydn, Schumann, Liszt, Mendelssohn, Ravel, Bizet, Gershwin, Mozart, Schubert, Verdi, Gounod, Rimski-Korsakov, Puccini, Sibelius—and on and on. Music delights us when we are happy, comforts us when we mourn, gives courage when we are frightened, stirs us when we are apathetic, sustains us when we are soul-troubled,[9] and fills us with religious adoration when we worship. That music can do all these things, and more, is attested not only by the experience of humanity through centuries but by hundreds of stories, poems, and essays bearing record of the power, delight, and beauty of music.

As a sampling of all these we now print just one little poem—a sonnet by Edna St. Vincent Millay[10] entitled "On Hearing a Symphony of Beethoven." Miss Millay's poetry, ranging from ecstasy in her early poems to bitterness in her later verse, reflects the complexity of her years of struggle to find happiness. A lover of beauty wherever she could find it, she especially loved music, finding in it a temporary escape from the frustrations of her personal world. We feel this point of view in the poem that follows, a poem of intensity—in language, in thought, and in emotion:

> Sweet sounds, oh, beautiful music, do not cease!
> Reject me not into the world again.
> With you alone is excellence and peace,
> Mankind made plausible, his purpose plain.
> Enchanted in your air benign and shrewd,
> With limbs a-sprawl and empty faces pale,
> The spiteful and the stingy and the rude

---

[9]A Biblical incident showing the power of music to comfort the anguished mind is recorded in I Samuel 16:14-23. Saul is suffering from a terrible mental depression, tormented by an evil spirit, but is comforted and restored through listening to the music of a harp played by young David. Verse 23 reads: "And it came to pass, when the evil spirit from God was upon Saul, that David took an harp, and played with his hand: so Saul was refreshed, and was well, and the evil spirit departed from him." Browning wrote a great poem, "Saul," built around this incident and emphasizing the healing power of music.

[10]For earlier discussions of Miss Millay, see pp. 5-7 of Volume 2 and pp. 237-238 of Volume 3.

Sleep like the scullions in the fairy-tale.
This moment is the best the world can give:
The tranquil blossom on the tortured stem.
Reject me not, sweet sounds! oh, let me live,
Till Doom espy my towers and scatter them,
A city spell-bound under the aging sun.
Music my rampart, and my only one.

SECTION SIX

The Reward of Persistence

by Robert K. Thomas

"Two Self Portraits"

by Rembrant van Ryn (1606-1669) Dutch
Portrait of a Young Man—Taft Museum, Cincinnati, Ohio
Self Portrait—National Gallery of Art, Washington D.C.

Commentary by
Floyd E. Brienholt, Associate Professor of Art, Brigham Young University

Rembrandt van Ryn died in poverty in 1669. His only possessions were a few old clothes and his painting tools. He left no profound writings. Wise men do not quote him. No famous letters were
written by him for us to read. Yet from his time to the present men
have used such phrases as the following to describe him and his work:

The greatest of the Dutch Masters
One of the greatest painters who ever lived
The master of light
One true to himself
Possessed of integrity
Persistent
Followed his "star"
Made the ugly beautiful
No pose—no vanity
Searcher of truth
Dramatic but never theatrical
Valued truth and sincerity above harmony and beauty
Painter of the human soul

He was a successful portrait painter at the age of twenty-five.
He married a woman of wealth, bought a house, collected works of
art, and painted industriously. After the death of his wife his popu-
larity as a painter of portraits declined, primarily because he lost
interest in trying to please others and became more intent on his
search for truth and meaning in life and an understanding of self.
He lost his wealth and was saved from utter ruin by his second wife
and son who both preceded him in death. Throughout his lifetime
his fame as an artist stood high and has increased through the years,
but as one author states, "Fame alone does not suffice to make a
livelihood."

One reason we know him so well is because of the amazing record of his life he left in his many self portraits—about sixty in oil
alone. His face is the most familiar one in all art. From these we see
his physical and psychic evolution. The two portraits of him presented here not only are examples of his virtuosity as a master of
the brush, but more important, we see how he saw himself. First we
see a youth with vanity, beautifully costumed and full of pride. Second, we see an old man less concerned with worldly goods, saddened
by failures and suffering, with eyes reflecting humility and wisdom.
The persistence of his search for understanding of self and others

continued to the end of his life. His consistent drive to discover and paint the soul of man was an almost superhuman endeavor. Perhaps no one has come as close to capturing that "inner light" as Rembrandt van Ryn.

THE REWARD OF PERSISTENCE

"Persistent people begin their success where others end in failure."
—Edward Eggleston

Like many other potential virtues, persistence takes the moral coloring of its object. To the extent our faith is focused upon evil things our faith is degraded. Similarly, persistence in vice is hardly to be praised. Only if the object of our continuing effort is a worthy one can the fact of that effort deserve commendation. Yet persistence is such a rare attribute that we feel a grudging admiration for it wherever found. The unremitting effort which some animals display in storing food may only be instinctive, but it chides our inconsistency. The blade of grass, sprouting from a crack in the sidewalk, proclaims a determination to grow that shames our own lack of resolution.

Yet it is easier to commend tenacity than practice it. Perhaps we are not convinced that we must be persistent in the same sense that we acknowledge the necessity for being honest or accurate. The myth of the dramatic breakthrough betrays us into thinking that the rewards of persistence can be duplicated by a flash of inspiration or even a stroke of luck. Persistence tends to become that quality we strive for when we have run out of alternatives.

It also may be that we fail to recognize the part persistence plays in success. The applause we give to the runner who doggedly finishes his race a full lap behind the winner is seldom heartfelt. Our cheers are for the winner, and it seldom occurs to us that what the last place runner is demonstrating the man in first place has capitalized upon. Natural talents may vary widely, but in an encouraging number of instances diligent practice more than outstanding potential has distinguished the truly successful. The ancient scriptural injunction that the race belongs less to the swift than to the enduring is as fresh and practical today as it ever was.

In a provocative phrase Ralph Waldo Emerson insists that "practice is nine-tenths." This, at first reading, seems incomplete; but a little reflection suggests that Emerson is deliberately giving us a chance to finish this idea in terms of our own experience while recognizing the major contribution of sustained, repeated work.

The selections which follow touch upon circumstance and attitudes which compromise perseverance as well as those which foster it. In Arthur Hugh Clough's "Say Not the Struggle Naught Availeth," for instance, the forces which work in support of steadfast effort are dramatically recounted, but there is also a countering, negative shadow throughout the poem. Oliver Wendell Holmes' "The Chambered Nautilus" is consistently positive in presenting an image of developing vision and opportunity. "Learning the River" is one of the most appealing accounts ever written of how painful the maturing process can be, but these celebrated lines are also a comforting and inspiring testament to the value of unrelenting endeavor. With John Holmes' "Talk" we explore the relationship of growing skills to developing attitudes, and in S. Dilworth Young's "The March of Zion's Camp" we see how commitment gives significance to the harshest circumstance.

It is important that we finally understand the difference between persistence which is merely stubbornness and persistence which is steadfast perseverance. As Samuel tells the disobedient Saul, "Stubbornness is as iniquity and idolatry." It implies undiscriminating, self-centered obstinacy. Perseverance implies continuing effort toward a worthy goal. It is in such persistence that we enjoy earthly happiness and prepare for eternal exaltation.

Say Not the Struggle Nought Availeth

by Arthur Hugh Clough

Say not, the struggle nought availeth,
   The labour and the wounds are vain,
The enemy faints not, nor faileth,
   And as things have been they remain.

If hopes were dupes, fears may be liars;
   It may be, in yon smoke concealed,
Your comrades chase e'en now the fliers,
   And, but for you, possess the field.

For while the tired waves, vainly breaking,
   Seem here no painful inch to gain,
Far back, through creeks and inlets making,
   Comes silent, flooding in, the main.

And not by eastern windows only,
   When daylight comes, comes in the light,
In front, the sun climbs slow, how slowly,
   But westward, look, the land is bright.

Discussion of "Say Not the Struggle Nought Availeth"

Arthur Hugh Clough (1819-1861) was born abroad but spent the early part of his life in America where his father was a cotton merchant. Returning to England for his schooling, young Arthur attended Rugby and Oxford. While at Rugby he came under the influence of the famous school master, Thomas Arnold. Arnold's rigid orthodoxy made a deep impression upon his susceptible young student; but, by the time Clough had spent some years at Oxford, he found it increasingly difficult to subscribe to the Articles of the Church of England, and in 1848 he abruptly resigned his Oxford fellowship. He returned to America briefly, at the invitation of Ralph Waldo Emerson, but he did not remain long, and the rest of his short life was spent in rather aimless travel. He died at Florence, Italy, at the age of forty-two.

Not much of Clough's poetry has survived the critical sifting of modern taste, but "Say Not the Struggle Nought Availeth" answers a timeless question: How should one act when faced with apparent defeat? Clough believed that poetry should "touch some deep question, some vital feeling," and several generations of readers have found comfort and strength in the forthright declaration of this poem.

If Clough's own struggle was a theological one, his poem implies that defeatism need not have a major setting. Answers to problems are colored by the attitudes we bring to our efforts; if we are prepared to fail, we will fail. If we are determined to succeed, there is always some light in the darkness. Clough is quite aware of the continuing cost of trying—the poem is full of allusions to pain and frustration—but his opening line is a positive assertion, and his ending is alight with hope.

What makes this lyric memorable is its nice balance of the ideal and the real. The battle metaphor which is developed in the first two stanzas does not degenerate into superficial heroics. We don't meet a victor in this poem so much as a determined participant who refuses to give up. *For every negative assertion he has a positive counter. If his hopes have been blasted, his fears may be no more reliable. If the waves seem to be getting no place, the tide is flooding the shore.*

There is no attempt in this poem to suggest that the struggle makes difficulties easier to bear. At the conclusion, the sun is still not coming up very rapidly. But trying to find hope is in itself hope-producing. Refusal to accept defeat keeps us sensitive to every possibility of victory. In such sensitivity we are far more prepared to succeed than we would be if we let ourselves become so dulled by opposition that we couldn't recognize a positive opportunity when it appeared.

The Chambered Nautilus

by Oliver Wendell Holmes

This is the ship of pearl, which, poets feign,
  Sails the unshadowed main, —
  The venturous bark that flings
On the sweet summer wind its purpled wings
In gulfs enchanted, where the Siren sings,
  And coral reefs lie bare,
Where the cold sea-maids rise to sun their
  streaming hair.

Its webs of living gauze no more unfurl:
  Wrecked is the ship of pearl!
  And every chambered cell,
Where its dim dreaming life was wont to dwell,
As the frail tenant shaped his growing shell,
  Before thee lies revealed, —
Its irised ceiling rent, its sunless crypt unsealed!

Year after year beheld the silent toil
  That spread his lustrous coil;
  Still, as the spiral grew,
He left the past year's dwelling for the new,
Stole with soft step its shining archway through,
  Built up its idle door,
Stretched in his last-found home, and knew the
  old no more.

Thanks for the heavenly message brought by
  thee,
  Child of the wandering sea,
  Cast from her lap, forlorn!
From thy dead lips a clearer note is born
Than ever Triton blew from wreathed horn!
  While on mine ear it rings,
Through the deep caves of thought I hear a
  voice that sings: —

Build thee more stately mansions, O my soul,
  As the swift seasons roll!
  Leave thy low-vaulted past!
Let each new temple, nobler than the last,

Shut thee from heaven with a dome more vast,
Till thou at length art free,
Leaving thine outgrown shell by life's unresting
sea!

Discussion of "The Chambered Nautilus"

A great physician, Sir William Osler, once asked, a bit whimsically, whether Dr. Oliver Wendell Holmes (1808-1894) would rather be remembered as the man who saved the lives of many women through his research on infections incident to childbirth or as the author of "The Chambered Nautilus." Holmes heard of this question and wrote Sir William as follows:

> I think I will not answer the question you put to me . . . But in writing the poem I was filled with the highest state of mental exaltation and the most crystalline clairvoyance, as it seemed to me, that had ever been granted to me.

Holmes goes on to answer the question after all when he suggests that saving lives is a "nobler satisfaction" than the "selfish pleasure" to be gained from poetry, but he confesses that he has long cherished a special fondness for this poem with its "expression at once precise and musical."

Born of a distinguished family in New England, Holmes tried law before settling on medicine as a career. After a few years of general practice, he became an outstanding professor of anatomy and physiology at the Harvard Medical School. But the poems and essays which came regularly from his facile pen soon gave him an audience that reached far beyond his classrooms at Harvard.

"The Chambered Nautilus" was part of *The Autocrat of the Breakfast Table,* a book of informal essays and poems that has yet to be duplicated for its wit and charm. Among the light, familiar verse which is threaded throughout this work there is an occasional piece such as "The Chambered Nautilus." In introducing this poem, Holmes comments as follows:

> Did I not say to you a little while ago that the universe swam in an ocean of similitudes and analogies? I will

not quote Cowley, or Burns, or Wordsworth, just now
to show you what thoughts were suggested to them by the
simplest natural objects, such as a flower or a leaf; but
I will read you a few lines if you do not object, suggested by
looking at a section of one of those chambered shells to
which is given the name Pearly Nautilus. . . . If you will
look into Roget's Bridgewater Treatise, you will find
a figure of one of these shells and a section of it. The
last will show you the series of enlarging compartments
successively dwelt in by the animal that inhabits the shell,
which is built in a widening spiral. Can you find no lesson
in this?

Some modern commentators have complained that the "lesson"
of this lyric is too obvious, but such an attitude reflects only current
poetic prejudice. Holmes' contemporaries found no such objection
to it, and the final stanza is still so well known that allusions to it
are common.

The success of this poem grows out of its close following of
one idea—what Holmes called its "precise" quality—with unusually
melodic and artful movement. There is here a unique combination
of stately tread and light-footed ripple. The diction, too, combines
literal description and symbolic extension with conspicuous effec-
tiveness.

The facet of persistence which "The Chambered Nautilus"
illuminates is the inevitable growth which continuing endeavor
promises. As we fully live up to the opportunities we currently
enjoy, we become capable of still loftier and more rewarding experiences. We cannot be satisfied with present achievement lest we
make a prison out of our limited vision.

Learning the River

by Mark Twain

Samuel Langhorne Clemens, usually known by his pen name, Mark Twain, grew up in Hannibal, Missouri, on what he called "the great Mississippi, the majestic, the magnificent Mississippi." The following selection from his *Life on the Mississippi* (1883) tells of his youthful attempt to "learn the river" as an apprentice pilot.

The boat backed out from New Orleans at four in the afternoon, and it was "our watch" until eight. Mr. Bixby, my chief, "straightened her up," plowed her along past the sterns of the other boats that lay at the Levee, and then said, "Here, take her; shave those steamships as close as you'd peel an apple." I took the wheel, and my heartbeat fluttered up into the hundreds; for it seemed to me that we were about to scrape the side off every ship in the line, we were so close. I held my breath and began to claw the boat away from the danger; and I had my own opinion of the pilot who had known no better than to get us into such peril, but I was too wise to express it. In half a minute I had a wide margin of safety intervening between the Paul Jones and the ships; and within ten seconds more I was set aside in disgrace, and Mr. Bixby was going into danger again and flaying me alive with abuse of my cowardice. I was stung, but I was obliged to admire the easy confidence with which my chief loafed from side to side of his wheel, and trimmed the ships so closely that disaster seemed ceaselessly imminent. When he had cooled a little he told me that the easy water was close ashore and the current outside, and therefore we must hug the bank, up-stream, to get the benefits of the former, and stay well out, downstream, to take advantage of the latter. In my own mind I resolved to be a downstream pilot and leave the up-streaming to people dead to prudence.

Now and then Mr. Bixby called my attention to certain things. Said he, "This is Six-Mile Point." I assented. It was pleasant enough information, but I could not see the bearing of it. I was not conscious that it was a matter of any interest to me. Another time he said, "This is Nine-Mile Point." Later he said, "This is Twelve-Mile Point." They were all about level with the water's edge; they all looked about alike to me; they were monotonously unpicturesque. I hoped Mr. Bixby would change the subject. But no; he would crowd up around a point, hugging the shore with affection, and then say: "The slack water ends here, abreast this bunch of China trees; now we cross over." So he crossed over. He gave me the wheel once or twice, but I had no luck. I either came near chipping off the edge of a sugar-plantation, or I yawed too far from shore, and so dropped back into disgrace again and got abused.

The watch was ended at last, and we took supper and went to bed. At midnight the glare of a lantern shone in my eyes, and the night watchman said:

"Come, turn out!"

And then he left. I could not understand this extraordinary procedure; so I presently gave up trying to, and dozed off to sleep. Pretty soon the watchman was back again, and this time he was gruff. I was annoyed. I said:

"What do you want to come bothering around here in the middle of the night for? Now, as like as not, I'll not get sleep again tonight."

"Well, if this ain't good, I'm blessed."

The "off-watch" was just turning in, and I heard some brutal laughter from them, and such remarks as "Hello, watchman! ain't the new cub turned out yet? He's delicate, likely. Give him some sugar in a rag, and send for the chambermaid to sing 'Rock-a-by Baby,' to him."

About this time Mr. Bixby appeared on the scene. Something like a minute later I was climbing the pilot-house steps with some of my clothes on and the rest in my arms. Mr. Bixby was close behind, commenting. Here was something fresh—this thing of getting up in the middle of the night to go to work. It was a detail in piloting that had never occurred to me at all. I knew that boats ran all night, but somehow I had never happened to reflect that somebody had to get up out of a warm bed to run them. I began to fear that piloting was not quite so romantic as I had imagined it was; there was something very real and worklike about this new phase of it.

It was a rather dingy night, although a fair number of stars were out. The big mate was at the wheel, and he had the old tub pointed at a star and was holding her straight up the middle of the river. The shores on either hand were not much more than half a mile apart, but they seemed wonderfully far away and ever so vague and indistinct. The mate said:

"We've got to land at Jones' plantation, sir,"

The vengeful spirit in me exulted. I said to myself, "I wish you joy of your job, Mr. Bixby; you'll have a good time finding Mr. Jones' plantation such a night as this; and I hope you never will find it as long as you live."

Mr. Bixby said to the mate:

"Upper end of the plantation, or the lower?"

"Upper."

"I can't do it. The stumps there are out of water at this stage. It's no great distance to the lower, and you'll have to get along with that."

"All right, sir. If Jones don't like it, he'll have to lump it, I reckon."

And then the mate left. My exultation began to cool and my wonder to come up. Here was a man who not only proposed to find this plantation on such a night, but to find either end of it you preferred. I dreadfully wanted to ask a question, but I was carrying about as many short answers as my cargo-room would admit of, so I held my peace. All I desired to ask Mr. Bixby was the simple question whether he was silly enough to really imagine he was going to find that plantation on a night when all plantations were exactly alike and all of the same color. But I held in. I used to have fine inspirations of prudence in those days.

Mr. Bixby made for the shore and soon was scraping it, just the same as if it had been daylight. And not only that, but singing.

"Father in heaven, the day is declining," etc.

It seemed to me that I had put my life in the keeping of a peculiarly reckless outcast. Presently he turned on me and said:

"What's the name of the first point above New Orleans?"

I was gratified to be able to answer promptly, and I did. I said I didn't know.

"Don't know?"

His manner jolted me. I was down at the foot again, in a moment. But I had to say just what I had said before.

"Well, you're a smart one!" said Mr. Bixby.

"What's the name of the next point?"

Once more I didn't know.

"Well, this beats anything. Tell me the name of any point or place I told you."

I studied awhile and decided that I couldn't.

"Look here! What do you start out from, above Twelve-Mile Point, to cross over?"

"I—I—don't know."

"You—you—don't know?" mimicking my drawling manner of speech. "What do you know?"

"I—I—nothing, for certain."

"By the great Caesar's ghost, I believe you! You're the stupidest dunderhead I ever saw or ever heard of, so help me Moses! The idea of you being a pilot—you! Why, you don't know enough to pilot a cow down a lane."

Oh, but his wrath was up! He was a nervous man, and he shuffled from one side of his wheel to the other as if the floor was hot. He would boil awhile to himself, and then overflow and scald me again.

"Look here! What do you suppose I told you the names of those points for?"

I tremblingly considered a moment, and then the devil of temptation provoked me to say:

"Well to—to—be entertaining, I thought."

This was a red rag to the bull. He raged and stormed so (he was crossing the river at the time) that I judged it made him blind, because he ran over the steering-oar of a trading-scow. Of course the traders sent up a volley of red-hot profanity. Never was a man so grateful as Mr. Bixby was; because he was brimful, and here were subjects who could talk back. He threw open a window, thrust his head out, and such an eruption followed as I never had heard before. The fainter and farther away the scowmen's curses drifted, the higher Mr. Bixby lifted his voice and the weightier his adjectives grew. When he closed the window he was empty. You could have drawn a seine through his system and not caught curses enough to disturb your mother with. Presently he said to me in the gentlest way:

"My boy, you must get a little memorandum book; and every time I tell you a thing, put it down right away. There's only one way to be a pilot, and that is to get this entire river by heart. You have to know it just like A B C."

That was a dismal revelation to me; for my memory was never loaded with anything but blank cartridges. However, I did not feel discouraged long. I judged that it was best to make some allowance, for doubtless Mr. Bixby was "stretching." Presently he pulled a rope and struck a few strokes on the big bell. The stars were all gone now, and the night was as black as ink. I could hear the wheels churn along the bank, but I was not entirely certain that I could see the shore. The voice of the invisible watchman called up from the hurricane-deck:

"What's this, sir?"

"Jones' plantation."

I said to myself, "I wish I might venture to offer a small bet that it isn't." But I did not chirp. I only waited to see. Mr. Bixby handled the engine-bells, and in due time the boat's nose came to the land, a torch glowed from the forecastle, a man skipped ashore, a darkey's voice on the bank said: "Gimme de k'yarpetbag, Mass' Jones," and the next moment we were standing up the river again, all serene. I reflected deeply awhile, and then said—but not aloud—"Well, the finding of that plantation was the luckiest accident that ever happened; but it couldn't happen again in a hundred years." And I fully believed it was an accident, too.

By the time we had gone seven or eight hundred miles up the river, I had learned to be a tolerably plucky up-stream steersman, in daylight; and before we reached St. Louis I had made a trifle of progress in night work, but only a trifle. I had a note-book that fairly bristled with the names of towns, "points," bars, islands, bends, reaches, etc.; but the information was to be found only in the note-book—none of it was in my head. It made my heart ache to think I had only got half of the river set down; for as our watch was four hours off and four hours on, day and night, there was a long four-hour gap in my book for every time I had slept since the voyage began.

My chief was presently hired to go on a big New Orleans boat, and I packed my satchel and went with him. She was a grand affair. When I stood in her pilot-house I was so far above the water that I seemed perched on a mountain; and her decks stretched so far away, fore and aft, below me, that

I wondered how I could ever have considered the little Paul Jones a large craft. There were other differences, too. The Paul Jones's pilot-house was a cheap, dingy, battered rattle trap, cramped for room; but here was a sumptuous glass temple; room enough to have a dance in; showy red and gold window-curtains; an imposing sofa; leather cushions and a back to the high bench where visiting pilots sit, to spin yarns and "look at the river"; bright, fanciful "cuspidores," instead of a broad wooden box filled with sawdust; nice new oilcloth on the floor; a hospitable big stove for winter; a wheel as high as my head, costly with inlaid work, a wire tiller-rope; bright brass knobs for the bells; and a tidy, white-aproned, black "texas-tender," to bring up tarts and ices and coffee during mid-watch, day and night. Now this was "something like"; and so I began to take heart once more to believe that piloting was a romantic sort of occupation after all. The moment we were under way I began to prowl about the great steamer and fill myself with joy. She was as clean and as dainty as a drawing-room; when I looked down her long, gilded saloon, it was like gazing through a splendid tunnel; she had an oil-picture, by some gifted sign-painter, on every stateroom door; she glittered with no end of prism-fringed chandeliers; the clerk's office was elegant, the bar was marvelous, and the bar-keeper had been barbered and upholstered at incredible cost. The boiler-deck (i.e. the second story of the boat, so to speak) was as spacious as a church, it seemed to me; so with the forecastle; and there was no pitiful handful of deck-hands, firemen, and roustabouts down here, but a whole battalion of men. The fires were fiercely glaring from a long row of furnaces, and over them were eight huge boilers! This was unutterable pomp. The mighty engines—but enough of this. I had never felt so fine before. And when I found that the regiment of natty servants respectfully "sir'd" me, my satisfaction was complete.

At the end of what seemed a tedious while, I had managed to pack my head full of islands, towns, bars, "points," and bends; and a curiously inanimate mass of lumber it was, too. However, inasmuch as I could shut my eyes and reel off a good long string of these names without leaving out more than ten miles of river in every fifty, I began to feel that I could take a boat down to New Orleans if I could make her skip those little gaps. But of course my complacency could hardly get start enough to lift my nose a trifle into the air, before Mr. Bixby would think of something to fetch it down again. One day he turned on me suddenly with this settler:

"What is the shape of Walnut Bend?"

He might as well have asked me my grandmother's opinion of protoplasm. I reflected respectfully, and then said I didn't know it had any particular shape. My gun-powdery chief went off with a bang, of course, and then went on loading and firing until he was out of adjectives.

I had learned long ago that he only carried just so many rounds of ammunition, and was sure to subside into a very placable and even remorseful old smoothbore as soon as they were all gone. That word "old" is merely affectionate; he was not more than thirty-four. I waited. By and by he said:

"My boy, you've got to know the shape of the river perfectly. It is all there is left to steer by on a very dark night. Everything else is blotted out and gone. But mind you, it hasn't the same shape in the night that it has in the daytime."

"How on earth am I ever going to learn it, then?"

"How do you follow a hall at home in the dark? Because you know the shape of it. You can't see it."

"Do you mean to say that I've got to know all the million trifling variations of shape in the banks of this interminable river as well as I know the shape of the front hall at home?"

"On my honor, you've got to know them better than any man ever did know the shapes of the halls in his own house."

"I wish I was dead!"

"Now I don't want to discourage you, but—"

"Well, pile it on me; I might as well have it now as another time."

"You see, this has got to be learned; there isn't any getting around it. A clear starlight night throws such heavy shadows that, if you didn't know the shape of a shore perfectly, you would claw away from every bunch of timber, because you would take the black shadow of it for a solid cape; and you see you would be getting scared to death every fifteen minutes by the watch. You would be fifty yards from shore all the time when you ought to be within fifty feet of it. You can't see a snag in one of those shadows, but you know exactly where it is, and the shape of the river tells you when you are coming to it. Then there's your pitch-dark night; the river is a very different shape on a pitch-dark night from what it is on a star-light night. All shores seem to be straight lines, then, and mighty dim ones, too; and you'd run them for straight lines, only you know better. You boldly drive your boat right into what seems to be a solid, straight wall (you knowing very well that in reality there is a curve there), and that wall falls back and makes way for you. Then there's your gray mist. You take a night when there's one of these grisly, drizzly, gray mists, and then there isn't any particular shape to a shore. A gray mist would tangle the head of the oldest man that ever lived. Well, then, different kinds of moonlight change the shape of the river in different ways. You see—"

"Oh, don't say any more, please! Have I got to learn the shape of the river according to all these five hundred thousand different ways? If I tried to carry all that cargo in my head it would make me stoop-shouldered."

"No! you only learn the shape of the river; and you learn it with such absolute certainty that you can always steer by the shape that's in your head, and never mind the one that's before your eyes."

"Very well, I'll try it; but, after I have learned it, can I depend on it? Will it keep the same form and not go fooling around?"

Before Mr. Bixby could answer, Mr. W. came in to take the watch, and he said:

"Bixby, you'll have to look out for President's Island, and all that country clear away up above the Old Hen and Chickens. The banks are caving and the shape of the shores changing like everything. Why, you wouldn't know the point above 40. You can go up inside the old sycamore snag, now."

So that question was answered. Here were leagues of shore changing shape. My spirits were down in the mud again. Two things seemed pretty apparent to me. One was, that in order to be a pilot a man had got to learn more than any one man ought to be allowed to know; and the other was, that he must learn it all over again in a different way every twenty-four hours.

That night we had the watch until twelve. Now it was an ancient river custom for the two pilots to chat a bit when the watch changed. While the relieving pilot put on his gloves and lit his cigar, his partner, the retiring pilot would say something like this:

"I judge the upper bar is making down little at Hale's Point; had quarter twain with the lower head and mark twain with the other."

"Yes, I thought it was making down a little last trip. Meet any boats?"

"Met one abreast the head of 21, but she was away over hugging the bar, and I couldn't make her out entirely. I took her for the Sunny South — hadn't any skylights forward of the chimneys."

And so on. And as the relieving pilot took the wheel his partner would mention that we were in such-and-such a bend, and say we were abreast of such-and-such a man's woodyard or plantation. This was courtesy; I supposed it was necessity. But Mr. W. came on watch full twelve minutes late on this particular night — a tremendous breach of etiquette; in fact, it is the unpardonable sin among pilots. So Mr. Bixby gave him no greeting whatever, but simply surrendered the wheel and marched out of the pilot-house without a word. I was appalled; it was a villainous night for blackness, we were in a particularly wide and blind part of the river, where there was no shape or substance to anything, and it seemed incredible that Mr. Bixby should have left that poor fellow to kill the boat, trying to find out where he was. But I resolved that I would stand by him anyway. He should find that he was not wholly friendless. So I stood around, and waited to be asked where we were. But Mr. W. plunged on serenely through the solid firmament of black cats that stood for an atmosphere, and never opened his mouth. "Here is a proud devil!" thought I; "here is a limb of Satan that would rather send us all to destruction than put himself under obligations to me, because I am not yet one of the salt of the earth and privileged to snub captains and lord it over everything dead and alive in a steamboat." I presently climbed up on the bench; I did not think it was safe to go to sleep while this lunatic was on watch.

However, I must have gone to sleep in the course of time, because the next thing I was aware of was the fact that day was breaking, Mr. W. gone, and Mr. Bixby at the wheel again. So it was four o'clock and all well—but me: I felt like a skinful of dry bones, and all of them trying to ache at once.

Mr. Bixby asked me what I had stayed up there for. I confessed that it was to do Mr. W. a benevolence—tell him where he was. It took five minutes for the entire preposterousness of the thing to filter into Mr. Bixby's system, and then I judge it filled him nearly up to the chin; because he paid me a compliment—and not much of a one either. He said:

"Well, taking you by and large, you do seem to be more different kinds of a boob than any creature I ever saw before. What did you suppose he wanted to know for?"

I said I thought it might be a convenience to him.

"Convenience! Didn't I tell you that a man's got to know the river in the night the same as he'd know his own front hall?"

"Well, I can follow the front hall in the dark if I know it is the front hall; but suppose you set me down in the middle of it in the dark and not tell me which hall it is; how am I to know?"

"Well, you've got to, on the river!"

"All right. Then I'm glad I never said anything to Mr. W."

"I should say so! Why, he'd have slammed you through the window and utterly ruined a hundred dollars' worth of windowsash and stuff."

I was glad this damage had been saved, for it would have made me unpopular with the owners. They always hated anybody who had the name of being careless and injuring things.

I went to work now to learn the shape of the river; and of all the eluding and ungraspable objects that ever I tried to get mind or hands on, that was the chief. I would fasten my eyes upon a sharp, wooded point that projected far into the river some miles ahead of me, and go to laboriously photographing its shape upon my brain; and just as I was beginning to succeed to my satisfaction, we would draw up toward it and the exasperating thing would begin to melt away and fold back into the bank! If there had been a conspicuous dead tree standing upon the very point of the cape, I would find that tree inconspicuously merged into the general forest, and occupying the middle of a straight shore, when I got abreast of it! No prominent hill would stick to its shape long enough for me to make up my mind what its form really was, but it was as dissolving and changeful as if it had been a mountain of butter in the hottest corner of the tropics. Nothing ever had the same shape when I was coming down-stream that it had borne when I went up. I mentioned these little difficulties to Mr. Bixby. He said:

"That's the very main virtue of the thing. If the shapes didn't change every three seconds they wouldn't be of any use. Take this place where we are now, for instance. As long as that hill over yonder is only one hill, I can boom right along the way I'm going; but the moment it splits at the top and forms a V, I know I've got to scratch to starboard in a hurry, or I'll bang this boat's brains out against a rock; and then the moment one of the prongs of the V swings behind the other, I've got to waltz to larboard again, or I'll have a misunderstanding with a snag that would snatch the keelson out of this steamboat as neatly as if it were a sliver in your hand. If that hill didn't change its shape on bad nights there would be an awful steamboat graveyard around here inside of a year."

It was plain that I had got to learn the shape of the river in all the different ways that could be thought of—upside down, wrong end first, inside out, fore-and-aft, and "thort-ships"—and then know what to do on gray nights when it hadn't any shape at all. So I set about it. In the course of time I began to get the best of this knotty lesson, and my self-complacency moved to the front once more. Mr. Bixby was all fixed, and ready to start it to the rear again. He opened on me after this fashion:

"How much water did we have in the middle crossing at Hole-in-the-Wall, trip before last?"

I considered this an outrage. I said:

"Every trip, down and up, the leadsmen are singing through that tangled place for three-quarters of an hour on a stretch. How do you reckon I can remember such a mess as that?"

"My boy, you've got to remember it. You've got to remember the exact spot and the exact marks the boat lay in when we had the shoalest water, in every one of the five hundred shoal places between St. Louis and New Orleans; and you mustn't get the shoal soundings and marks of one trip mixed up with the shoal soundings and marks of another, either, for they're not often twice alike. You must keep them separate."

When I came to myself again, I said:

"When I get so that I can do that, I'll be able to raise the dead, and then I won't have to pilot a steamboat to make a living. I want to retire from this business. I want a slush bucket and a brush; I'm only fit for a roustabout. I haven't got brains enough to be a pilot; and if I had I wouldn't have strength enough to carry them around, unless I went on crutches."

"Now drop that! When I say I'll learn a man the river, I mean it. And you can depend on it, I'll learn him or kill him."

There was no use in arguing with a person like this. I promptly put such a strain on my memory that by and by even the shoal water and the countless crossing-marks began to stay with me. But the result was just the same. I never could more than get one knotty thing learned before another presented itself. Now I had often seen pilots gazing at the water and pretending to read it as if it were a book; but it was a book that told me nothing. A time came at last, however, when Mr. Bixby seemed to think me far enough advanced to bear a lesson on water-reading. So he began:

"Do you see that long, slanting line on the face of the water? Now that's a reef. More over, it's a bluff reef. There is a solid sand-bar under it that is nearly as straight up and down as the side of a house. There is plenty of water close up to it, but mighty little on top of it. If you were to hit it you would knock the boat's brains out. Do you see where the line fringes out at the upper end and begins to fade away?"

"Yes, sir."

"Well, that is a low place; that is the head of the reef. You can climb over there, and not hurt anything. Cross over, now, and follow along close under the reef—easy water there—not much current."

I followed the reef along till I approached the fringed end. Then Mr. Bixby said:

"Now get ready. Wait till I give the word. She won't want to mount the reef; a boat hates shoal water. Stand by—wait—wait—keep her well in hand. Now cramp her down! Snatch her! snatch her!"

He seized the other side of the wheel and helped to spin it around until it was hard down, and then we held it so. The boat resisted, and refused to answer for a while, and next she came surging to starboard, mounted the reef and sent a long, angry ridge of water foaming away from her bows.

"Now watch her; watch her like a cat, or she'll get away from you. When she fights strong and the tiller slips a little, in a jerky greasy sort of way, let up on her a trifle; it is the way she tells you at night that the water is too shoal; but keep edging her up, little by little, toward the point. You are well up on the bar now; there is a bar under every point, because the water that comes down around it forms an eddy and allows the sediment to sink. Do you see those fine lines on the face of the water that branch out like the ribs of a fan? Well, those are little reefs; you want to just miss the ends of them, but run them pretty close. Now look out—look out! Don't you crowd that slick, greasy-looking place; there ain't nine feet there; she won't stand it. She begins to smell it; look sharp, I tell you! Oh, blazes, there you go! Stop the starboard wheel! Quick! Ship up to back! Set her back!"

The engine bells jingled and the engines answered promptly, shooting white columns of steam far aloft out of the 'scape-pipes, but it was too late. The boat had "smelt" the bar in good earnest; the foamy ridges that radiated from her bows suddenly disappeared, a great dead swell came rolling forward, and swept ahead of her, she careened far over to larboard, and went tearing away toward the shore as if she were about scared to death. We were a good mile from where we ought to have been when we finally got the upper hand of her again.

During the afternoon watch the next day, Mr. Bixby asked me if I knew how to run the next few miles. I said:

"Go inside the first snag above the point, outside the next one, start out from the lower end of Higgins's woodyard, make a square crossing, and—"

"That's all right. I'll be back before you close up on the next point."

But he wasn't. He was still below when I rounded it and entered upon a piece of the river which I had some misgivings about. I did not know that he was hiding behind a chimney to see how I would perform. I went gaily along, getting prouder and prouder, for he had never left the boat in my sole charge such a length of time before. I even got to "setting" her and letting the wheel go entirely, while I vain-gloriously turned my back and inspected the stern marks and hummed a tune, a sort of easy indifference which I had prodigiously admired in Bixby and other great pilots. Once I inspected rather long, and when I faced to the front again my heart flew into my mouth so suddenly that if I hadn't clapped my teeth together I should have lost it. One of those frightful bluff reefs was stretching its deadly length right across our bows! My head was gone in a moment; I did not know which end I stood on; I gasped and could not get my breath; I spun the wheel down with such rapidity that it wove itself together like a spider's web; the boat answered and turned square away from the reef, but the reef followed her! I fled, but still it followed, still it kept—right across my bows! I never looked to see where I was going, I only fled. The awful crash was imminent. Why didn't that villain come? If I committed the crime of ringing a bell I might get thrown overboard. But better that than kill the boat. So in blind desperation, I started such a rattling "shivaree" down below as never had astounded an engineer in this world before, I fancy. Amidst the frenzy of the bells the engines began to back and fill in a curious way, and my reason forsook its throne—we were about to crash into the woods on the other side of the river. Just then Mr. Bixby stepped calmly into view on the hurricane-deck. My soul went out to him in gratitude. My distress vanished; I would have felt safe on the brink of Niagara with Mr. Bixby on the hurricane-deck. He blandly and sweetly took his toothpick out of his mouth between his fingers, as if it were a cigar—we were just in the act of climbing an overhangingg big tree, and the passengers were scudding astern like rats—and lifted up these commands to me ever so gently:

"Stop the starboard! Stop the larboard! Set her back on both!"

The boat hesitated, halted, pressed her nose among the boughs a critical instant, then reluctantly began to back away.

"Stop the larboard! Come ahead on it! Stop the starboard! Come ahead on it! Point her for the bar!"

I sailed away as serenely as a summer's morning. Mr. Bixby came in and said, with mock simplicity:

"When you have a hail, my boy, you ought to tap the big bell three times before you land, so that the engineers can get ready."

I blushed under the sarcasm, and said I hadn't had any hail.

"Ah! Then it was for wood, I suppose. The officer of the watch will tell you when he wants to wood up."

I went on consuming, and said I wasn't after wood.

"Indeed? Why, what could you want over here in the bend, then? Did you ever know of a boat following a bend up-stream at this stage of the river?"

"No, sir—and I wasn't trying to follow it. I was getting away from a bluff reef."

"No, it wasn't a bluff reef; there isn't one within three miles of where you were."

"But I saw it. It was as bluff as that one yonder."

"Just about. Run over it!"

"Do you give it as an order?"

"Yes. Run over it!"

"If I don't, I wish I may die."

"All right; I am taking the responsibility."

I was just as anxious to kill the boat now, as I had been to save it before. I impressed my orders upon my memory, to be used at the inquest, and made a straight break for the reef. As it disappeared under our bows I held my breath; but we slid over it like oil.

"Now, don't you see the difference? It wasn't anything but a wind reef. The wind does that."

"So I see. But it is exactly like a bluff reef. How am I ever going to tell them apart?"

"I can't tell you. It is an instinct. By and by you will just naturally know one from the other, but you never will be able to explain why or how you know them apart."

It turned out to be true. The face of the water, in time, became a wonderful book—a book that was a dead language to the uneducated passenger, but which told its mind to me without reserve, delivering its most cherished secrets as clearly as if it uttered them with a voice. And it was not a book to be read once and thrown aside, for it had a new story to tell every day. Throughout the long twelve hundred miles there was never a page that was void of interest, never one that you could leave unread without loss, never one that you would want to skip, thinking you could find higher enjoyment in some other thing. There never was so wonderful a book written by man; never one whose interest was so absorbing, so unflagging, so sparklingly renewed with every reperusal. The passenger who could not read it was charmed with a peculiar sort of faint dimple on its surface (on the rare occasions when he did not overlook it altogether); but to the pilot that was an italicized passage; indeed, it was

more than that, it was a legend of the largest capitals, with a string of
shouting exclamation-points at the top of it, for it meant that a wreck or a
rock was buried there that could tear the life out of the strongest vessel that
ever floated. It is the faintest and simplest expression the water ever makes,
and the most hideous to a pilot's eye. In truth, the passenger who could
not read this book saw nothing but all manner of pretty pictures in it, painted
by the sun and shaded by the clouds, whereas to the trained eye these were
not pictures at all, but the grimmest and most dead-earnest of reading matter.

Now when I had mastered the language of this water, and had come to
know every trifling feature that bordered the great river as familiarly as I
knew the letters of the alphabet, I had made a valuable acquisition. But
I had lost something, too. I had lost something which could never be restored
to me while I lived. All the grace, the beauty, the poetry, had gone out
of the majestic river! I still kept in mind a certain wonderful sunset which
I witnessed when steamboating was new to me. A broad expanse of the river
was turned to flood; in the middle distance the red hue brightened into gold,
through which a solitary log came floating, black and conspicuous, in one
place a long, slanting mark lay sparkling upon the water; in another the
surface was broken by boiling, tumbling rings, that were as many-tinted as an
opal; where the ruddy flush was faintest, was a smooth spot that was covered
with graceful circles and radiating lines, ever so delicately traced; the shore
on our left was densely wooded, and the somber shadow that fell from this
forest was broken in one place by a long, ruffled trail that shone like silver;
and high above the forest wall a clean-stemmed dead tree waved a single
leafy bough that glowed like a flame in the unobstructed splendor that was
flowing from the sun. There were graceful curves, reflected images, woody
heights, soft distances; and over the whole scene, far and near, the dissolving
lights drifted steadily, enriching it every passing moment with new marvels
of coloring.

I stood like one bewitched. I drank it in, in a speechless rapture. The
world was new to me, and I had never seen anything like this at home. But
as I have said, a day came when I began to cease from noting the glories and
the charms which the moon and the sun and the twilight wrought upon the
river's face; another day came when I ceased altogether to note them. Then,
if that sunset scene had been repeated, I should have looked upon it without
rapture, and should have commented upon it, inwardly, after this fashion:
"This sun means that we are going to have wind to-morrow; that floating log
means that the river is rising, small thanks to it; that slanting mark on the
water refers to a bluff-reef which is going to kill somebody's steamboat one
of these nights, if it keeps on stretching out like that; those tumbling 'boils'
show a dissolving bar and a changing channel there; the lines and circles in
the slick water over yonder are a warning that that troublesome place is shoaling
up dangerously; that silver streak in the shadow of the forest is the 'break'

from a new snag, and he has located himself in the very best place he could have found to fish for steamboats; that tall dead tree, with a single living branch, is not going to last long, and then how is a body ever going to get through this blind place at night without the friendly old landmark?"

No, the romance and beauty were all gone from the river. All the value any feature of it had for me now was the amount of usefulness it could furnish toward compassing the safe piloting of a steamboat. Since those days, I have pitied doctors from my heart. What does the lovely flush in a beauty's cheek mean to a doctor but a "break" that ripples above some deadly disease? Are not all her visible charms sown thick with what are to him the signs and symbols of hidden decay? Does he ever see her beauty at all, or doesn't he simply view her professionally, and comment upon her unwholesome condition all to himself? And doesn't he sometimes wonder whether he has gained most or lost most by learning his trade?

Discussion of "Learning the River"

Mark Twain (1835-1920) was born in Florida, Missouri, but moved to Hannibal at the age of four. During the next fourteen years he absorbed the atmosphere of this riverside village so thoroughly that it flavored his writing for years to come. Especially important was his feeling for the Mississippi River, that magical highway which brought the outer world to the doorstep of Hannibal.

When, in 1875, Twain was persuaded to write a series of papers entitled "Old Times on the Mississippi" for the *Atlantic Monthly,* the series was a little short to be a book; so he was asked to expand it. It was not until 1882, however, that Twain revisited the river and brought together the material we now know as *Life on the Mississippi.*

The first twenty chapters of this book (the selection in our text is taken from these chapters) evokes the great steamboating days before the Civil War, particularized and made personal through young Sam Clemens' apprenticeship as a pilot. This part of *Life on the Mississippi* has a simple dramatic unity; it is the Horatio Alger story of a poor boy making good despite obstacles. Conceived in even larger terms, it is an account of what it means to grow up, with both time and circumstance being of little consequence. Twain's recollections are convincingly specific, but they are not so personal that they cannot be shared. The problems young Clemens faces and overcomes are a summons to persevering effort on the part of any person who reads these fictionalized reminiscences.

The tone of this selection is often bantering, and some of the cleverest writing Mark Twain ever produced lies in these pages, but in the midst of our laughter we recognize unerring insight. Twain may be smiling, but he did not miss the point of his experience, and he sees to it that we do not. At the beginning of this account, quite naturally, we enter into the childish thought process of a youngster who has romantic notions of what a pilot does. We grow as he grows. By the end of our material, just as naturally, Twain is sharing with us his adult estimate of what he has gained—and lost—from his experience.

Since learning through experience is often painful, it is difficult to write a tale of trial and error that is not painful to read. The skillful ones, especially, may involve us so totally that we can't bear to finish them. "Learning the River" has an additional disadvantage. We not only undergo the frustration and despair of a cub pilot, but we are early told that the only way to learn the river is to absorb it totally, and nothing in this account deviates from this pedestrian task. How, then, does Twain keep our interest?

Above all else, Twain is a master of his language. His diction has such vitality that you almost expect the words to be warm to the touch. In the following lines, for instance note how gracefully and appropriately the image of the volatile Mr. Bixby as a muzzle loading rifle is developed:

> My gun-powdery chief went off with a bang, of course, and then went on loading and firing until he was out of adjectives. I had learned long ago that he only carried just so many rounds of ammunition, and was sure to subside into a very placable and even remorseful old smoothbore as soon as they were all gone.

The result of such skill is that this becomes one of the few accounts of persistent effort which is almost effortless reading.

Talk

by John Holmes

Some of the best talk I ever had
Was with a deaf old near-sighted wrestler who had been to sea,
And made ship-models for a living, and didn't say much.
I was a small boy, I stared. I hung around his shop after school.

He was very deaf, and it made a good silence for me to think in.
He spoke once or twice in an hour. He whittled out whaleboats, peering.
"Good," he would say, with a sharp knife and the wood near his nose.
When he held it to the window, I could see light through the boat's bows.

I'd be learning the shapes of ships from big slippery magazines,
Or I'd be turning crinkly blueprints and deck-plans, unrolling the rolls,
Using his tack-hammers and wood-scraps to make them lie flat.

Oh, and there once I saw
Alone with him one dim afternoon
The strict thin purposeful lines
On the flat plan, soar, live, sail,
Deck above deck, mast over deck, flag
Topping mast, and knew what he knew while he whittled.

What he said, he said with his hundreds of tools, sharp, meaningful,
Red-handled, a blade for every cut, a drill-size for everything.
He talked, I mean I knew what he was saying,
When he pushed the white pine planks into the power-saw
To cut out the rough curved layers he built up into hulls,
Then planed, whittled, sand-papered, rubbed with stub fingers into ships.
Then he painted them green under the waterline, or bronze;
Then he rigged them, he sewed sails for them finer than a handkerchief.
He could paint pictures, too,
Another way of talking; ships of the line, water-colors in red and blue,
Tacked on the shop walls above rubbish and bright tools and lumber.
He cast his own anchors, cannon, blocks; I fingered the moulds;
I breathed smells he made of hot metal, of oil, glue, sawdust, turpentine,
I smelled the color of the paint, I heard the shavings curl, a way of talking.
My pulse was the beat of the idle belts on the shafting, a way of talking.
I made believed I walked the decks, hung in the main-tops, rode
The piling swell of the green seas in the bowsprit chains.
I stared up from the afterdeck at the huge flowing balance, the color,
The riding cloud above me of sails, flags, rigging, masts, and sky.
"What are you doing now?" he would say, and I did not answer.

I've seen his ships sailing a glass cases in the great museums.
I still make believe. I still stare, I'm there
On the small perfect decks perfectly empty; up out of the crew's hatchway
I climb to take my turn at the night-watch in the bow.
He's there, too. That's why he built them, I think now.
It's a special thing, building them, collecting them, making believe.
But I understand why it's good. He told me.
I wouldn't have known that you throw work away
When you spoil it half-done. I guessed that he guessed
Like a cook with a cookbook sometimes, one look at the blueprints
And three at the wood. I wouldn't have known that.
I wouldn't have known that however you built it,
The ship must sail; you can't explain to the ocean.
But the pure grain of the wood achieving shape under tools,
The masts long like flower-stems, the spars tapered,
The blunt round of the bows of the finger-length whale-boats,
Smooth-dusty from sandpapering, no paint yet, the wood —
That was the best talk.
I remember the words of the wood, and his grimed quick fingers
Telling truth with a knife, reaching for the other tools,
Knowing his need, and the grain of the wood knowing.
Have you seen the most beautiful of all ships?
Not the clipper, the whaler, the yacht, the gray battle-cruiser,
It isn't the galley with banked oars, or the shouldering galleon.
It's the East Indiaman, four decks, and flaring with flags,
All the rails mahogany, the figurehead carven and colored, plunging,
The captain's gallery all windows at the great stern,
And the mountains of sail, the enormous lift of the long decks.
A castle, a country sailing, so proud, so golden and slow and proud.

He was an old man when I knew him, deaf and bad eyes.
He wore a gray sweater, and a very old cap, always.
"What have you been doing, John?" he would say, every day.
And I would say nothing. He couldn't hear.
"Do you know what this is I am making?"
I knew what he was making, even before it seemed to be.
I could hear. I could make believe. I could see.
He always had half a dozen ships on the bench, thinking them into shape.
He hummed, whittled, peered, studied blueprints.

It was some of the best talk I ever had.

Discussion of "Talk"

In commenting upon the truly great teachers who had helped shape his life and career, the well-known writer, John Ciardi, put John Holmes (1904-1962) at the top of his short list. Not only did Professor Holmes care deeply about the students he instructed at Tufts University, but he himself was such an able poet that he could display as well as discuss the techniques and insights of significant creative work.

In a rather informal tribute which Ciardi wrote at the time of Holmes' early death from cancer in 1962, it was suggested that Holmes' poems were often outside the main current of literary fashion but that they spoke truly of "the side streets of his own life and the house and furniture of its days."

"Talk" demonstrates how persuasively a local, personal situation can carry overtones of general truth when it is reported in its essence. The background given in the poem is quite scanty: a young boy loiters around the shop of a man who constructs minutely detailed ship models. Since the model builder is deaf, he rarely speaks. But what young John Holmes learns—and what we learn in sharing his reminiscence—are the inviolable rules of good craftsmanship. The facts of his experience speak to him as clearly as if they had been shouted aloud. In retrospect, they were part of the "best talk" he ever encountered.

Many of us can recall similar maturing experiences. Holmes is particularly successful in evoking how difficult it is for young people to understand that effort—no matter how persistent or sincere—must result in accomplishment if it is to have its full meaning. Persistence without development gives routine activity more than its due.

The boy in "Talk" does learn to appreciate the necessity for careful, continuing work, but he learns a good deal more than this in his watching and listening. He finally realizes that "however you built it, / The ship must sail; you can't explain to the ocean." Such an arresting comment gives labor its fulfillment. In an age given to explanation, which is often no more than justification for failure, we recognize how often we have tried to "explain to the ocean" while we were sinking.

As we develop the positive attitudes in which all skills must be based, we begin to understand that doggedness is a minor virtue until it is completed by real achievement. Habit may simply reinforce error unless it supports a worthy goal.

The March of Zions Camp

by S. Dilworth Young

The word to start was given;
The twenty drivers snapped their whips;
The twenty teams leaned into their collars,
Their haunches straining,
Their feet digging
At the resisting earth;
The wagons rolled.
Then followed men;
One hundred twenty-five,
(Later increased by a hundred men, or so)
Some laughing, cheerfully joking,
Others sober, surveying the task ahead
With judgment, cool and calculating,
Measuring in their minds
The day by day strength it takes
To walk twelve hundred miles.
At first it was thought that all could ride,
But soon gifts of succor and relief came in
With such generosity the twenty wagons
Scarce contained it all.
And so the trek began.

Within two days the prophet
Told them how to organize.
The men were given place in groups of twelve,
Electing their own captains,
Who, in turn, appointed to each man his daily task:
Two to cook the meager food;
Two to fetch and cut the wood;
Two to pitch and strike the tent;
One a runner, errand bent;
Two to fill the water pails;
Two to grease the wagon wheels
And to give the horses care;
One to find and purchase food.
Each day they walked, the distance varied
As the weather.
Not disciplined marching,
Not by cadences.

Each man chose
His own stride,
Side-stepping chuck and hole,
Lending a hand here, or there,
As need arose,
Laughing often at the difficulties
And the hazards of the march;
Discipline, not of body
But of soul!

This will be the order of the day,
Said Joseph Smith:
Arise at four a.m.;
Then morning prayer,
Each group in its own tent,
Then breakfast
(Such as men prepare,
More crude than good);
March then until noon.
The horses fed and rested.
The men should
Have a cold light lunch;
Travel far as possible
Before the evening comes;
Then make camp
In an open place,
On a hill, if one can be found,
Where sentinels can see oncoming foes.
Then at the close of day,
With supper fed,
Let each group pray
And seek an early bed.

Each day they marched,
Walking as the summer's heat
Bore down. Their hot feet blistered badly
In their leather boots.
A few, those hurting most,
Could ride an hour or two
In turn.
How welcome was the evening!
They bathed their feet in cooling, flowing stream.
The cooks prepared the food

Over cooking fires which pierced the dark,
The smell of hot salt pork
And corn pone on the coals
Rising on the lazy air.
Scanty fare to men
Who had traveled
Twenty sweating miles,
Sometimes hitched to a wagon
In the mud, or sand.
At last they prayed and slept,
Slept on the warming earth
Where warmth of summer's sun
Still lingered through the night.
Thus they walked on through
Each sweating day,
Until they had traversed
Twelve hundred miles.

Joseph Smith walked on among his men,
Their leader and their prophet,
Not asking any odds.
One saw him pull his boots,
Glimpsed raw and bleeding feet,
But no complaining word
Escaped his lips.
He pulled more than his share
Of wagons from the mire,
And shared his crusts
With those more hungry
Than himself.
He practiced them in warlike acts,
Yet led them to be men of peace,
Taught to kill no living thing
Except from stark necessity.
He did not know just how
He was to redeem Zion,
But each day led the camp
In that day's work
With perfect trust,
The spirit whispering
Each day's task;
One step at a time,
No more.

And each day led their hearts
Away from thoughts
Of violence and war.

Do not forget Fishing River,
You saints of latter days.
Between its forks,
Beyond the ford,
The camp paused for the night.
They had intended to go on through to Liberty,
But delay piled on delay:
Wheels continually came off,
And time was lost replacing them
And looking for the nuts which
Held them on;
A tire worked loose and
Time was taken to heat and shrink
The iron; a horse went lame.
Thus more delay
Consumed the hours of the day.
Until, by nightfall, miles short
Of their goal,
They camped on the high ground
Between the Fishing River forks.

Five armed, snarling, hateful men
Rode into camp
And promised that the
Jackson County mob,
Assisted by like-minded
Men from Clay,
Was gathering to wipe
Them out next day.
Then, even as they rode away,
Their curses hanging heavy
On the evening air,
A cloud appeared,
No larger than a hand
In the darkening sky,
And swiftly grew
Until the western heaven
Was a swirling mass
Of black, forbidding clouds,

Which spilled their load
Of wind and hail upon the
Mobbers' heads.
Hail fell, large as eggs.
Driven by a wind
Which laid crops flat.
Uprooted trees, and
Devastated the countryside.
All night the storm raged.
Lightning flashed incessantly;
Thunder boomed without ceasing:
The water in
The forks of Fishing River
Rose full thirty feet,
Effective bar to those who had
Not beat a fast retreat before
The storm.
Next day not a mobber was in sight
Who had sworn death to them
The previous night.
The mobbers afterwards
Were heard to say
They fought against God
On that dark day.
The word of the Lord
Came to Joseph Smith:
For behold, I do not
Require at their hands
To fight the battles of Zion;
For, as I said in
A former commandment,
Even so will I fulfill—
I will fight your battles.

Discussion of "The March of Zions Camp"

S. Dilworth Young (1897-   ) was born in Salt Lake City shortly after the Semi-Centennial Jubilee of the entrance of the Mormon pioneers in the Salt Lake valley under the leadership of his great-grandfather, Brigham Young. After service in the first World War, he spent two years as a missionary before being named a Boy Scout Executive. In 1945 he was called to serve as a member of the First Council of Seventy.

The author of several books, President Young has long written skillfully upon Church themes. In *The Long Road* he gives poetic expression to incidents in the life of the Prophet Joseph Smith. "The March of Zions Camp" is taken from a section in this work entitled "Zion."

To those who have read the history of the march which is here commemorated, this poem speaks with special poignance. Few commandments in early Church history seemed more capable of testing faith and commitment than the order to march to the relief of their brothers and sisters in Missouri. Although five hundred men were called for, only about one hundred left Kirtland in May, 1834. Along the way an additional hundred joined the group. Despite warning from the Prophet against disunity, some members of the company expressed dissatisfaction with the purpose and results of the expedition, and an epidemic of cholera left more than a score dead.

The incident which is the dramatic center of President Young's account—the miraculous deliverance at Fishing River—helped many who were in the group to understand that the Lord requires our best efforts but is not dependent upon them.

The form of this poem, with its apparently casual lines, is an interesting example of the loose but real organization which characterized Zions Camp. Line lengths may vary but none really gets out of hand. Rhythm shifts with idea as the actual cadence of informally marching men adapts itself to terrain and circumstance. Although there is a clear narrative tone to this work, there is such tension in most of the lines that they are at least as much exhortation as they are part of a story.

"The March of Zions Camp" seems appropriate conclusion for our section on persistence, for it aids us in seeing that the reward of sustained effort may not be the expected one. Those who left Ohio in this determined band thought they were going to "redeem" Zion. When the Camp was disbanded, the saints in Missouri were still undergoing trial, and there were those who felt that the whole effort was unsuccessful. In retrospect, however, those who were to assume major positions in the Church had their faith tested under fire. In addition, the Lord was preparing men through this experience for the responsibility of moving the entire Latter-day Saint people west in the even more difficult days to come.

SECTION SEVEN

The Achievement of Serenity

by Bruce B. Clark

THE ACHIEVEMENT OF SERENITY

Nothing can bring you peace but the triumph of principles
—Emerson

Introductory Comments

Serenity, one of our most beautiful words, describes the tranquil strength of great men and women who live by unyielding integrity. Serenity is the outward calm of an inner conscience at peace with itself. Serenity is the reward of never compromising one's principles no matter how great the temptation or how fearsome the danger. Serenity is the deep inward peace of mind that results from always doing what one believes is right. Serenity is the combination of quiet courage linked with undeviating standards.

The fruits of righteous living may at times be material but at all times will be spiritual, and one of the greatest of these is peace of mind; just as the punishments for unrighteous living may at times be physical but at all times will be spiritual—the anguish of a guilty conscience, the torment of a troubled mind. Moreover, as the joy and serenity are greater for one who does right knowingly rather than accidentally or in ignorance, so the anguish and torment are greater for one who does wrong knowingly rather than accidentally or in ignorance. Serenity, then, is the ultimate earthly reward for one who lives always by high principle and who both lives and dies with a clear conscience.[1]

Unfortunately no man or woman ever achieves complete serenity in this life because we are all imperfect. Christ alone was perfect. Even so, serenity still stands as a beautiful ideal to work towards, and one that can in considerable measure be reached if the total of good things in our lives heavily outweighs the total of contrary things.

Edna St. Vincent Millay in her poem "Conversations at Midnight" had something like this in mind when she wrote:

---

[1]For an earlier discussion of these matters and some comments by Lowell Bennion, see Volume 1, pp. 394-396.

> There is no peace on earth today save the peace in the heart
> At home with God. From that sure habitation
> The heart looks forth upon the sorrows of the savage world
> And pities them, and ministers to them; but is not implicated.
> All else has failed, as it must always fail.
> No man can be at peace with his neighbor who is not at peace
> With himself; the troubled mind is a trouble maker.
> There is no freedom like the freedom of a man who sees his duty plain
> And does it without demur; . . .

Perhaps we may wish to question the meaning of "implicated" in the fourth line and debate the accuracy of "the troubled mind is a trouble maker" in the seventh line, but the over-all message seems beautifully clear and to the point.

In previous selections we have already seen examples of quiet courage and faith approaching serenity. For example, the leader of men in Wordsworth's "Character of the Happy Warrior" (volume 1), Lazarus in Browning's "An Epistle of Karshish" (volume 1), the old bootmaker in Galsworthy's "Quality" (volume 1), the grieving father in Wordsworth's "Michael" (volume 1), the old Rabbi in Browning's "Rabbi Ben Ezra" (volume 1), Sir Thomas More in Robert Bolt's *A Man for All Seasons* (volume 3), and the dying Socrates earlier in this present volume. Now to further illustrate serenity, or at least to illustrate courageous integrity in the face of great adversity, we turn, not to the standard forms of literature, but to some dramatic moments lifted from history. Carlyle once wrote, "The history of the world is the biography of great men." Familiar to all of us are incidents of great moral courage in the lives of the Savior and such religious prophets as Joseph Smith in Carthage Jail and Nephi and Abinadi in the Book of Mormon. Less familiar to Latter-day Saint readers, but equally courageous, are the incidents we now present through excerpts from some great speeches made by some extraordinary men.[2]

In printing these speeches it is not our intent to assess the rightness or wrongness of the position each man held. Some of these

----

[2]For some of the information regarding these speeches, I am indebted to *A Treasury of the World's Great Speeches*, edited by Houston Peterson (New York: Simon and Schuster, 1965).

matters are still controversial and must await the judgment of history. Rather, our purpose is to portray moments in the lives of a few great men when they spoke with a combination of deep courage and earnest sincerity, speaking the convictions of their heart no matter what the consequences.

Martin Luther

Martin Luther (1483-1546) began life as the son of a miner in Saxony, Germany; studied law briefly as a young man; then at the age of 21 became an Augustinian monk. After the necessary period of study and training in the monastery, he became a teacher, first at Erfurt, and later at the new university at Wittenberg. For several years he suffered from a heavy sense of sin, not so much for himself as for the sins of humanity, and pondered the possibilities of salvation versus damnation. While preparing some lectures he was especially struck by Paul's statement in the epistle to the Romans: "The just shall live by faith." So important did this sentence seem to him that he began to question whether the sacraments and ornate ritualism of the Catholic Church had any meaning in helping a person towards salvation. Even "good works" seemed of little significance. Faith was all-important. The sale of indulgences as a means to avoid punishment for sin seemed especially evil to him, and he began to denounce this practice.

On 31 October 1517, at the age of 34, Luther nailed on the door of the church at Wittenberg his 95 theses challenging the uses and abuses of indulgences. Violent debate followed, with warnings from Rome, and with Luther vigorously defending his position in a series of pamphlets. Finally a "papal bull" (official declaration of the Pope) was issued condemning 41 of Luther's statements. Luther defiantly burned the bull at Wittenberg, and he was thereupon excommunicated for heresy. He was also ordered to stand trial before the Diet of Worms, an assembly of noblemen presided over by Charles V, who was both King of Spain and the new Emperor of the Holy Roman Empire. When asked if he had written certain books and if he would recant the "heresies" they contained, Luther requested time to prepare an answer. He was given just one day, then responded with the following speech, delivered on 18 April 1521:

Most Serene Emperor, Illustrious Princes, Gracious Lords: In obedience to your commands given me yesterday, I stand here, beseeching you, as God is merciful, so to deign mercifully to listen to this cause, which is, as I believe, the cause of justice and of truth. And if through inexperience I should fail to apply to any his proper title, or offend in any way against the manners of courts, I entreat you to pardon me as one not conversant with courts, but rather with the cells of monks, and claiming no other merit than that of having spoken and written with that simplicity of mind which regards nothing but the glory of God and the pure instruction of the people of Christ.

Two questions have been proposed to me: whether I acknowledge the books that are published in my name, and whether I am determined to defend or disposed to recall them. To the first of these I have given a direct answer, in which I shall ever persist that those books are mine and published by me, except so far as they may have been altered or interpolated by the craft or officiousness of rivals. To the other I am now about to reply; and I must first entreat your Majesty and your Highnesses to deign to consider that my books are not all of the same description. For there are some in which I have treated the piety of faith and morals with simplicity so evangelical that my very adversaries confess them to be profitable and harmless and deserving the perusal of a Christian. Even the Pope's bull, fierce and cruel as it is, admits some of my books to be innocent, though even these, with a monstrous perversity of judgment, it includes in the same sentence. If, then, I should think of retracting these, should I not stand alone in my condemnation of that truth which is acknowledged by the unanimous confession of all, whether friends or foes?

The second species of my publications is that in which I have inveighed against the papacy and the doctrine of the papists, as of men who by their iniquitous tenets and examples have desolated the Christian world, both with spiritual and temporal calamities. No man can deny or dissemble this. The sufferings and complaints of all mankind are my witnesses that, through the laws of the Pope and the doctrines of men, the consciences of the faithful have been ensnared, tortured, and torn in pieces, while, at the same time, their property and substance have been devoured by an incredible tyranny, and are still devoured without end and by degrading means, and that too, most of all, in this noble nation of Germany. Yet it is with them a perpetual statute that the laws and doctrines of the Pope be held erroneous and reprobate when they are contrary to the Gospel and the opinions of the Fathers.

If, then, I shall retract these books, I shall do no other than add strength to tyranny and throw open doors to this great impiety, which will then stride forth more widely and licentiously than it has dared hitherto; so that the reign of iniquity will proceed with entire impunity, and, notwithstanding its intolerable oppression upon the suffering vulgar, be still further fortified and established; especially when it shall be proclaimed that I have been driven to this act by the authority of your serene Majesty and the whole Roman Empire. What a cloak, blessed Lord, should I then become for wickedness and despotism!

In a third description of my writings are those which I have published against individuals, against the defenders of the Roman tyranny and the subverters of the piety taught by men. Against these I do freely confess that

I have written with more bitterness than was becoming either my religion or my profession; for, indeed, I lay no claim to any especial sanctity, and argue not respecting my own life, but respecting the doctrine of Christ. Yet even these writings it is impossible for me to retract, seeing that through such retraction despotism and impiety would reign under my patronage, and rage with more than their former ferocity against the people of God.

Yet since I am but man and not God, it would not become me to go further in defense of my tracts than my Lord Jesus went in defense of His doctrine; who, when He was interrogated before Annas, and received a blow from one of the officers, answered: "If I have spoken evil, bear witness of the evil; but if well, why smitest thou me?" If then the Lord Himself, who knew His own infallibility, did not disdain to require arguments against His doctrine even from a person of low condition, how much rather ought I, who am the dregs of the earth and the very slave of error, to inquire and search if there be any to bear witness against my doctrine! Wherefore, I entreat you, by the mercies of God, that if there be anyone of any condition who has that ability, let him overpower me by the sacred writings, prophetical and evangelical. And for my own part, as soon as I shall be better instructed I will retract my errors and be the first to cast my books into the flames.

It must now, I think, be manifest that I have sufficiently examined and weighed, not only the dangers, but the parties and dissensions excited in the world by means of my doctrine, of which I was yesterday so gravely admonished. . . . And thus I commend myself to your serene Majesty and all the princes, humbly beseeching you not to allow the malice of my enemies to render me odious to you without a cause. I have done.

Upon completion of his speech, Luther was challenged to answer one simple question, "Will you recant?"—to which he responded as follows:

Since your most serene Majesty and the princes require a simple answer, I will give it thus: Unless I shall be convinced by proofs from Scripture or by evident reason—for I believe neither in popes nor councils, since they have frequently both erred and contradicted themselves—I cannot choose but adhere to the word of God, which has possession of my conscience; nor can I possibly, nor will I ever make any recantation, since it is neither safe nor honest to act contrary to conscience! Here I stand; I cannot do otherwise, so help me God! Amen.

Luther knew full well that he might be executed for his defiance of both the Pope and the Emperor. Instead he was protected by the German members of the Diet until he could withdraw from the hostility of the Spanish nobles. Thus began the split of the empire and of Christianity. Luther lived another 25 years, but the massive division of Christianity which was to follow, known by Protestants as the Great Reformation and by Catholics as the Great Rebellion, began with this momentous incident. Whether Luther was the restorer of Christianity or the destroyer of Christian unity is still a matter of violent world debate. But there is little debate about Luther's deep sincerity and great courage.

Robert Emmet

Robert Emmet (1778-1803) may not be known to most readers of this book, but his life shines out of the pages of history as a courageous example of youthful sincerity. A brilliant student at Trinity College in Dublin, he also was a dedicated young Irish patriot who struggled to free the Irish from British rule. It is not our intent here to take sides on this centuries-old conflict but rather to present a young man who lived and died bravely for his convictions. Eloquent as a speaker, he stirred fellow students with fiery talks about the glories of Irish history in earlier years and the evils of present-day tyranny. Because of his activities and speeches, he was expelled in 1798 from Trinity, after which he lived several years as an exile in continental Europe. In July of 1803 he returned secretly to Ireland to lead a brief uprising in behalf of Irish independence. The uprising failed, and Emmet was condemned to death for treason. His last words, spoken on 19 September 1803 to the court, were addressed to listeners in future generations:

My Lords: I am asked what have I to say why sentence of death should not be pronounced on me, according to law. I have nothing to say that can alter your predetermination, nor that it will become me to say, with any view to the mitigation of that sentence which you are to pronounce and I must abide by. But I have that to say which interests me more than life, and which you have labored to destroy. I have much to say why my reputation should be rescued from the load of false accusation and calumny which has been cast upon it. I do not imagine that, seated where you are, your mind can be so free from prejudice as to receive the least impression from what I am going to utter. I have no hopes that I can anchor my character in the breast of a court constituted and trammeled as this is. I only wish, and that is the utmost that I expect, that your lordships may suffer it to float down your memories untainted by the foul breath of prejudice, until it finds some more hospitable harbor to shelter it from the storms by which it is buffeted. . . . The man dies but his memory lives. That mine may not perish, that it may live in the respect of my countrymen, I seize upon this opportunity to vindicate myself from some of the charges alleged against me. When my spirit shall be wafted to a more friendly port—when my shade shall have joined the bands of those martyred heroes who have shed their blood on the scaffold and in the field, in the defense of their country and of virtue—this is my hope: I wish that my memory and my name may animate those who survive me, . . .

I appeal to the immaculate God—I swear by the throne of heaven, before which I must shortly appear—by the blood of the murdered patriots who have gone before me—that my conduct has been, through all this peril, and through all my purposes, governed only by the conviction which I have uttered, and by no other view than that of the emancipation of my country from the superinhuman oppression under which she has so long and too patiently travailed; and I confidently hope that, wild and chimerical as it may appear, there is still union and strength in Ireland to accomplish this noblest of enterprises. Of this I speak with the confidence of intimate knowledge, and with the consolation that appertains to that confidence. Think not, my lords, I say this for the petty gratification of giving you a transitory uneasiness. A man who never yet raised his voice to assert a lie will not hazard his character with posterity by asserting a falsehood on a subject so important to his country and on an occasion like this. . . .

My lords, it may be a part of the system of angry justice to bow a man's mind by humiliation to the purposed ignominy of the scaffold; but worse to me than the purposed shame or the scaffold's terrors would be the shame of such foul and unfounded imputations as have been laid against me in this court. You, my lord, are a judge; I am the supposed culprit. I am a man; you are a man also. By a revolution of power we might change places, though we never could change characters. If I stand at the bar of this court and dare not vindicate my character, what a farce is your justice! If I stand at this bar and dare not vindicate my character, how dare you calumniate it? Does the sentence of death, which your unhallowed policy inflicts on my body, condemn my tongue to silence and my reputation to reproach? Your executioner may abridge the period of my existence; but while I exist, I shall not forbear to vindicate my character and motives from your aspersions; and, as a man, to whom fame is dearer than life, I will make the last use of that life in doing justice to that reputation which is to live after me, and which is the only legacy I can leave to those I honor and love, and for whom I am proud to perish. . . . My country was my idol! To it I sacrificed every selfish, every endearing sentiment; and for it I now offer up myself, . . . I do not fear to approach the Omnipotent Judge to answer for the conduct of my whole life; . . .

Let no man dare, when I am dead, to charge me with dishonor; let no man attaint my memory by believing that I could have engaged in any cause but that of my country's liberty and independence; or that I could have become the pliant minion of power in the oppression and misery of my country. The proclamation of the provisional government speaks for our views; no inference can be tortured from it to countenance barbarity or debasement at home, or subjection, humiliation, or treachery from abroad. I would not have submitted to a foreign oppressor, for the same reason that I would resist the foreign and domestic oppressor. In the dignity of freedom, I would have fought upon the threshold of my country, and its enemy should enter only by passing over my lifeless corpse. And am I, who lived but for my country, and who have subjected myself to the dangers of the jealous and watchfull oppressor, and the bondage of the grave, only to give my countrymen their rights, and my country her independence—am I to be loaded with calumny, and not suffered to resent it? No; God forbid!

Here the judge interrupted to tell Emmet that he had disgraced his family and his education, but especially his father, an eminent doctor, who, if alive, would not have tolerated such opinions. Young Emmet responded:

If the spirits of the illustrious dead participate in the concerns and cares of those who were dear to them in this transitory life, oh, ever dear and venerated shade of my departed father! look down with scrutiny upon the conduct of your suffering son, and see if I have, even for a moment, deviated from those principles of morality and patriotism which it was your care to instill into my youthful mind, and for which I am now about to offer up my life. My lords, you are impatient for the sacrifice. The blood which you seek is not congealed by the artificial terrors which surround your victim—it circulates warmly and unruffled through the channels which God created for noble purposes, but which you are now bent to destroy for purposes so grievous that they cry to heaven. Be yet patient! I have but a few more words to say—I am going to my cold and silent grave—my lamp of life is nearly extinguished—my race is run —the grave opens to receive me, and I sink into its bosom. I have but one request to ask at my departure from this world: it is—the charity of its silence. Let no man write my epitaph; for, as no man who knows my motives dares now vindicate them, let not prejudice or ignorance asperse them. Let them and me rest in obscurity and peace, and my tomb remain uninscribed, and my memory in oblivion, until other times and other men can do justice to my character. When my country takes her place among the nations of the earth, then, and not till then, let my epitaph be written. I have done.

Robert Emmet's speech was much longer than the brief excerpts printed here, defending both the principles he believed in and his personal integrity. Historians now generally agree that Lord Norbury, the trial judge, was terribly prejudiced and harsh. No amount of pleading could persuade him to lessen the death sentence, and Emmet was executed at the age of twenty-five. As he had requested, no epitaph was written for his grave, and even its site is now unknown. But his name lives on, especially among Irish people the world over, as a symbol of all young idealists who have died for the principles they espoused.

Abraham Lincoln

Once Abraham Lincoln belonged to America. Now he belongs to the world. Many strong leaders have grown up in America, and among them Lincoln stands tallest of all. There was something about this homely, good, great man that made people trust him and turn to him for strength. This was true while he lived, and it is even more true now that he has been dead for over a hundred years.

The facts of Lincoln's life are well known. He was born to uneducated parents in a log cabin in Kentucky in 1809. The family, always moving in search of better opportunities along the frontier, shifted in 1816 to Indiana, where Lincoln spent his youth, and where his mother died in 1818. When he was twenty-one the family moved to Illinois, and here Lincoln lived in one town or another for the next thirty years, until he was elected President in 1860. While in Illinois he had a mixed career as riverboatman, railsplitter, storekeeper, hired hand, postmaster, surveyor, and member of the state legislature (from 1834 to 1842) before marrying Mary Todd in 1842 and beginning a private law practice. In 1847 he was elected to the U.S. Congress, but his opposition to the extension of slavery lost him the election of 1849. After several more years as a private lawyer, he returned in 1854 to the Illinois State Legislature. Then came the famous debates with Stephen A. Douglas during the race for the U.S. Senate in 1858. Lincoln lost the election but gained great political stature and was subsequently elected President of the United States in 1860. His first term of office was filled with all the troubles and agonies of the Civil War, but he was more than equal to the challenge and grew with each new crisis. In 1864 he was elected for a second term, but was shot to death by John Wilkes Booth in Ford's Theater in Washington, D.C., a little more than a month after the second term began in the spring of 1865.

There are many aspects to Lincoln's greatness, including extraordinary power as a speaker and writer. From his many writings space permits us to print only a few samples, but these will be sufficient to show both his deep human understanding and his deceptively simple prose style with its rhythmical balance, high dignity, and perfect clarity.

We begin with a letter written 2 January 1851 to John D. Johnston, showing Lincoln's rich earthy wisdom:

Dear Johnston: Your request for eighty dollars I do not think it best to comply with now. At the various times when I have helped you a little you have said to me, "We can get along very well now"; but in a very short time I find you in the same difficulty again. Now this can only happen by some defect in your conduct. What that defect is, I think I know. You are not lazy, and still you are an idler. I doubt whether, since I saw you, you have done a good whole day's work in any one day. You do not very much dislike to work, and still you do not work much, merely because it does not seem to you that you could get much for it. This habit of uselessly wasting time is the whole difficulty; it is vastly important to you, and still more so to your children, that you should break the habit. It is more important to them, because they have longer to live, and can keep out of an idle habit before they are in it, easier than they can get out after they are in.

You are now in need of some money; and what I propose is, that you shall go to work, "tooth and nail," for somebody who will give you money for it. Let father and your boys take charge of your things at home, prepare for a crop, and make the crop, and you go to work for the best money wages, or in discharge of any debt you owe, that you can get; and to secure you a fair reward for your labor, I now promise you, that for every dollar that you will, between this and the first of May, get for your own labor, either in money or as your own indebtedness, I will then give you one other dollar. By this, if you hire yourself at ten dollars a month, from me you will get ten more, making twenty dollars a month for your work. In this I do not mean you shall go off to St. Louis, or the lead mines, or the gold mines in California, but I mean for you to go at it for the best wages you can get close to home in Coles County. Now, if you will do this, you will be soon out of debt, and, what is better, you will have a habit that will keep you from getting in debt again. But if I should now clear you out of debt, next year you would be just as deep in as ever. You say you would almost give your place in heaven for seventy or eighty dollars. Then you value your place in heaven very cheap, for I am sure you can, with the offer I make, get the seventy or eighty dollars for four or five months' work. You say if I will furnish you the money you will deed me the land, and, if you don't pay the money back, you will deliver possession. Nonsense! If you can't now live with the land, how will you then live without it? You have always been kind to me, and I do not mean to be unkind to you. On the contrary, if you will but follow my advice, you will find it worth more than eighty times eighty dollars to you.

Affectionately your brother,

(signed) Abraham Lincoln

Next we turn to Lincoln's farewell remarks at Springfield on 11 February 1861, as he left Illinois to become President—surely as poignant a farewell as has ever been spoken from the rear platform of a railroad train:

> My Friends: No one, not in my situation, can appreciate my feeling of sadness at this parting. To this place, and the kindness of these people, I owe everything. Here I have lived a quarter of a century, and have passed from a young to an old man. Here my children have been born, and one is buried. I now leave, not knowing when or whether ever I may return, with a task before me greater than that which rested upon Washington. Without the assistance of that Divine Being who ever attended him, I cannot succeed. With that assistance, I cannot fail. Trusting in Him, who can go with me, and remain with you, and be everywhere for good, let us confidently hope that all will yet be well. To His care commending you, as I hope in your prayers you will commend me, I bid you an affectionate farewell.

A letter written by Lincoln to General Ulysses S. Grant on 13 July 1863 is a beautiful illustration of Lincoln's frankness, honesty, and wonderful brevity with words:

> My Dear General: I do not remember that you and I ever met personally. I write this now as a grateful acknowledgment for the almost inestimable service you have done the country. I wish to say a word further. When you first reached the vicinity of Vicksburg, I thought you should do what you finally did—march the troops across the neck, run the batteries with the transports, and thus go below; and I never had any faith, except a general hope that you knew better than I, that the Yazoo Pass expedition and the like could succeed. When you got below and took Port Gibson, Grand Gulf and vicinity, I thought you should go down the river and join General Banks, and when you turned northward, east of the Big Black, I feared it was a mistake. I now wish to make the personal acknowledgment that you were right and I was wrong.

About 50,000 men were killed, wounded, or missing in three days of battle at Gettysburg, Pennsylvania, in July 1863. The dead were buried first in makeshift shallow graves, then re-buried in a new cemetery on a nearby hill, now the Gettysburg National Cemetery. For the dedication on 19 November 1863 one of the most eloquent orators of the day, Edward Everett, was invited to give the main address. He talked for two hours in top rhetorical form. When it was learned that President Lincoln would also be there, courtesy demanded that he be invited to make "a few appropriate remarks." The response of the audience of 15,000 was less than enthusiastic, but the world now agrees with Edward Everett when the next day he wrote the President: "I should be glad if I could flatter myself that I came as near the central idea of the occasion in two hours as you did in two minutes." The Gettysburg Address lives for all time as a model of excellence in speaking and writing:

Four score and seven years ago our fathers brought forth on this continent a new nation, conceived in liberty, and dedicated to the proposition that all men are created equal.

Now we are engaged in a great civil war; testing whether that nation, or any nation so conceived and so dedicated, can long endure. We are met on a great battlefield of that war. We have come to dedicate a portion of that field as a final resting-place for those who here gave their lives that that nation might live. It is altogether fitting and proper that we should do this.

But, in a larger sense, we cannot dedicate—we cannot consecrate—we cannot hallow—this ground. The brave men, living and dead, who struggled here have consecrated it, far above our poor power to add or detract. The world will little note, nor long remember, what we say here, but it can never forget what they did here. It is for us the living, rather, to be dedicated here to the unfinished work which they who fought here have thus far so nobly advanced. It is rather for us to be here dedicated to the great task remaining before us—that from these honored dead we take increased devotion to that cause for which they gave the last full measure of devotion; that we here highly resolve that these dead shall not have died in vain; that this nation, under God, shall have a new birth of freedom; and that government of the people, by the people, for the people, shall not perish from the earth.

When Lincoln learned that a Mrs. Bixby had lost five sons in the Civil War, he took time on 21 November 1864 to write her a personal letter—another masterpiece of simplicity, sympathy, humanity, and dignity. One of Lincoln's skills as both speaker and writer was that he was wise enough to say the essentials and not waste time on the unnecessary:

Dear Madam: I have been shown in the files of the War Department a statement of the Adjutant-General of Massachusetts that you are the mother of five sons who have died gloriously on the field of battle. I feel how weak and fruitless must be any words of mine which should attempt to beguile you from the grief of a loss so overwhelming. But I cannot refrain from tendering to you the consolation that may be found in the thanks of the Republic they died to save. I pray that our heavenly Father may assuage the anguish of your bereavement, and leave you only the cherished memory of the loved and lost, and the solemn pride that must be yours to have laid so costly a sacrifice upon the altar of freedom.

(signed) Abraham Lincoln

As a final selection from Lincoln's writings we would like to print the great Second Inaugural Address, delivered 4 March 1865, just a month before he was assassinated—but the speech is a little too long. So we print only the closing paragraph, one of the most beautiful passages Lincoln ever wrote. The references in it are, of course, to the wounds of the Civil War, still in progress:

> With malice toward none; with charity for all; with firmness in the right, as God gives us to see the right, let us strive on to finish the work we are in; to bind up the nation's wounds; to care for him who shall have borne the battle, and for his widow, and his orphan—to do all which may achieve and cherish a just and lasting peace among ourselves, and with all nations.

During the hundred years since Lincoln's death, many books have been written about him, including a ten-volume biography by J. G. Nicolay and John Hay called *Abraham Lincoln: A History,* and more recently including Carl Sandburg's two great studies: *Abraham Lincoln: The Prairie Years* (two volumes) and *Abraham Lincoln: The War Years* (four volumes). Several excellent dramas have also been based on Lincoln's life, including Robert Sherwood's moving three-act play, *Abe Lincoln in Illinois.* And there have been an especially large number of poems on Lincoln,[3] including Walt Whitman's little "O Captain! My Captain" and his much greater "When Lilacs Last in the Dooryard Bloom'd," Edwin Markham's excellent "Lincoln, The Man of the People," James Oppenheim's "The Lincoln Child," Witter Bynner's "A Farmer Remembers Lincoln," Edgar Lee Masters's "Anne Rutledge," and three poems by Vachel Lindsay—"When Lincoln Came to Springfield," "Nancy Hanks, Mother of Abraham Lincoln," and "Abraham Lincoln Walks at Midnight" with its fine descriptive third stanza:

> A bronzed, lank man! His suit of ancient black,
> A famous high top-hat and plain worn shawl

---

[3] Also some first-quality musical compositions, including Aaron Copland's "Lincoln Portrait."

> Make him the quaint great figure that men love,
> The prairie-lawyer, master of us all.

As examples of the many poems on Lincoln, we will print just two, and one of these only in part. First we print the opening lines of John Gould Fletcher's great elegy called simply "Lincoln," which remind us that what Bruce Catton once said is true, "There is a dignity in the human spirit which can become most clearly visible in the moment of defeat and disaster." Here are the first 26 lines of Fletcher's 64-line poem:

I

Like a gaunt, scraggly pine
Which lifts its head above the mournful sandhills;
And patiently, through dull years of bitter silence,
Untended and uncared for, begins to grow.

Ungainly, laboring, huge,
The wind of the north has twisted and gnarled its branches;
Yet in the heat of midsummer days, when thunder-clouds ring the horizon,
A nation of men shall rest beneath its shade.

And it shall protect them all,
Hold everyone safe there, watching aloof in silence;
Until at last one mad stray bolt from the zenith
Shall strike it in an instant down to earth.

II

There was a darkness in this man; an immense and hollow darkness,
Of which we may not speak, nor share with him, nor enter;
A darkness through which strong roots stretched downwards into the earth
    towards old things;
Towards the herdman-kings who walked the earth and spoke with God,
Towards the wanderers who sought for they knew not what, and found
    their goal at last;
Towards the men who waited, only waited patiently when all seemed lost,
Many bitter winters of defeat;
Down to the granite of patience
These roots swept, knotted fibrous roots, prying, piercing, seeking,
And drew from the living rock and the living waters about it
The red sap to carry upwards to the sun.

Not proud, but humble,
Only to serve and pass on, to endure to the end through service. . . .

The other poem is a delightful piece by Rosemary Benét called "Nancy Hanks." Nancy was Lincoln's mother who died when he was a little boy.

If Nancy Hanks
Came back as a ghost
Seeking news
Of what she loved most,
She'd ask first
"Where's my son?
What's happened to Abe?
What's he done?

"Poor little Abe,
Left all alone
Except for Tom,
Who's a rolling stone;
He was only nine
The year I died.
I remember still
How hard he cried.

"Scraping along
In a little shack,
With hardly a shirt
To cover his back,
And a prairie wind
To blow him down
Or pinching times
If he went to town.

"You wouldn't know
About my son?
Did he grow tall?
Did he have fun?
Did he learn to read?
Did he get to town?
Do you know his name?
Did he get on?"

As a final selection in this section on Lincoln, who was surely a man of quiet, courageous integrity if ever a man was, we print one of the most extraordinary advertisements ever appearing in a magazine. I have no idea who wrote this great tribute to Lincoln, but he was obviously a skilled writer. This appeared some years ago as an advertisement of the John Hancock Mutual Life Insurance Company of Boston. It is, however, no mere advertisement. It is first-quality literature!

Let's skip all the things you've read about him, all the things you heard too often or too young.

Forget the face on the penny, the statue in Washington, the Emancipation Proclamation, the speech at Gettysburg. Forget the official things and look at the big thing.

Why do we love this man, dead long before our time, yet dear to us as a father? What was there about Abraham Lincoln?

He came out of nowhere special—a cabin like any other out West. His folks were nobody special—pleasant, hardworking people like many others. Abe was a smart boy, but not too smart. He could do a good day's work on the farm, though he'd just as soon stand around and talk. He told funny stories. He was strong and kind. He'd never try to hurt you, or cheat you, or fool you.

Young Abe worked at odd jobs and read law books at night. Eventually he found his way into local politics. And it was then that people, listening to his speeches, began to know there was something special about Abe Lincoln.

Abe talked about running a country as if it were something you could do. It was just a matter of people getting along.

He had nothing against anybody, rich or poor, who went his own way and let the other fellow go his. No matter how mixed up things got, Abe made you feel that the answer was somewhere among those old rules that everybody knows: no hurting, no cheating, no fooling.

Abe had a way of growing without changing. So it seemed perfectly natural to find him in the White House one day, padding around in his slippers, putting his feet on a chair when he had a deep one to think about—the same Abe Lincoln he'd always been, and yet the most dignified and the strongest and the steadiest man anybody had ever known. And when that terrible war came that might have torn his country apart, no one doubted what Abe would do. He was a family man; he resolved to keep the American family together.

Abe Lincoln always did what most people would have done, said what most people wanted said, thought what most people thought when they stopped to think about it. He was everybody, grown a little taller—the warm and living proof of our American faith that greatness comes out of everywhere when it is free to come.

Emile Zola

Emile Zola (1840-1902) was already a distinguished French novelist famed throughout the world long before he became involved in the celebrated Dreyfus case. Captain Alfred Dreyfus, a relatively unknown Jewish member of the French army's General Staff, had been sentenced in 1894 to life imprisonment on Devil's Island for supposedly selling military secrets to the German General Staff. Frenchmen generally believed that Dreyfus was guilty, a traitor to his country; but a stalwart few, including Zola, were convinced that he was innocent, a victim of anti-Jewish prejudice and a scapegoat for some spots of corruption in the army. Zola's participation in the investigation came to a climax in late 1897 when he published three vigorous articles containing some explosive accusations. This was followed in January 1898 by an open letter from Zola to the President of the French Republic, which Clemenceau published in his newspaper under the heading of Zola's opening words, "J'accuse." In this letter the outraged Zola fearlessly made charges against a number of people in places of high authority, both in the army and out, exposing what he was convinced were evidences of dishonesty and corruption. Zola knew that he would probably be prosecuted, and he was. He also knew that he was standing before a hostile court and a nation massed against him. He knew even that his life was in danger. Nevertheless, with great courage, and brilliant eloquence, he reviewed the facts of the case as he understood them, including the following comments and conclusion in his great speech of 21 February 1898:

I am thus excused, gentlemen, for having brought you here from your private affairs without being able to inundate you with the full flood of light of which I dreamed. The light, the whole light—this was my sole, my passionate desire! And this trial has just proved it. We have had to fight step by step against an extraordinarily obstinate desire for darkness. A battle has been necessary to obtain every atom of truth. Everything has been refused us. Our witnesses have been terrorized in the hope of preventing us from proving our case. And it is on your behalf alone that we have fought, that this proof might be put before you in its entirety, so that you might give your opinion on your consciences without remorse. I am certain, therefore, that you will give us credit for our efforts, and I feel sure too that sufficient light has been thrown upon the affair.

You have heard the witnesses; you are about to hear my counsel, who will tell you the true story, the story that maddens everybody and that everybody knows. I am, therefore, at my ease. You have the truth at last, and it will do its work. . . .

I am not defending myself, moreover. I leave history to judge my act, which was a necessary one; . . . Do me the honor of believing that I am not defending my liberty. By punishing me you would only magnify me. Whoever suffers for truth and justice becomes august and sacred. Look at me. Have I the look of a hireling, of a liar, and a traitor? Why should I be playing a part? I have behind me neither political ambition nor sectarian passion. I am a free writer, who has given his life to labor; who tomorrow will go back to the ranks and resume his interrupted task. . . .

So I do not defend myself. But what a blunder would be yours if you were convinced that by striking me you would re-establish order in our unfortunate country! Do you not understand now that what the nation is dying of is the darkness in which there is such an obstinate determination to leave her? The blunders of those in authority are being heaped upon those of others; one lie necessitates another, so that the mass is becoming formidable. A judicial blunder was committed, and then to hide it, it has been necessary to commit every day fresh crimes against good sense and equity! The condemnation of an innocent man has involved the acquittal of a guilty man, and now today you are asked in turn to condemn me because I have cried out in my anguish on beholding our country embarked on this terrible course. Condemn me, then! But it will be one more error added to the others—a fault the burden of which you will hear in history. And my condemnation, instead of restoring the peace for which you long, and which we all of us desire, will be only a fresh seed of passion and disorder. The cup, I tell you, is full; do not make it run over! . . .

The Dreyfus case, gentlemen, has now become a very small affair. It is lost in view of the formidable questions to which it has given rise. There is no longer a Dreyfus case. The question now is whether France is still the France of the rights of man, the France that gave freedom to the world, and ought to give it justice. Are we still the most noble, the most fraternal, the most generous of nations? Shall we preserve our reputation in Europe for justice and humanity? Are not all the victories that we have won called in question? Open your eyes, and understand that, to be in such confusion, the French soul must have been stirred to its depths in face of a terrible danger. A nation cannot be thus moved without imperiling its moral existence. This is an exceptionally serious hour; the safety of the nation is at stake.

When you have understood that, gentlemen, you will feel that but one remedy is possible—to tell the truth, to do justice. Anything that keeps back the light, anything that adds darkness to darkness, will only prolong and aggravate the crisis. The duty of good citizens, of all who feel it to be imperatively necessary to put an end to this matter, is to demand broad daylight. There are already many who think so. The men of literature, philosophy, and science are rising in the name of intelligence and reason. And I do not speak of the foreigner, of the shudder that has run through all Europe. Yet the foreigner is not necessarily the enemy. Let us not speak of the nations that may be our opponents tomorrow. But great Russia, our ally; little and generous Holland; all the sympathetic nations of the north; those countries of the French language, Switzerland and Belgium—why are their hearts so heavy, so overflowing with sympathetic suffering? Do you dream, then, of an isolated France? Do you prefer, when you pass the frontier, not to meet the smile of approval for your historic reputation for equity and humanity?

Alas! gentlemen, like so many others, you expect the thunderbolt to descend from heaven in proof of the innocence of Dreyfus. Truth does not come thus. It requires research and knowledge. We know well where the truth is, . . .

Dreyfus is innocent. I swear it! I stake my life on it—my honor! At this solemn moment, in the presence of this tribunal which is the representative of human justice, before you, gentlemen, who are the very incarnation of the country, before the whole of France, before the whole world, I swear that Dreyfus is innocent. By my forty years of work, by the authority that this toil may have given me, I swear that Dreyfus is innocent. By all I have now, by the name I have made for myself, by my works, which have helped for the expansion of French literature, I swear that Dreyfus is innocent. May all that melt away, may my works perish, if Dreyfus be not innocent! He is innocent. All seems against me—the two Chambers, the civil authority, the most widely circulated journals, the public opinion they have poisoned. And I have for me only an ideal of truth and justice. But I am quite calm; I shall conquer. I was determined that my country should not remain the victim of lies and injustice. I may be condemned here. The day will come when France will thank me for having helped to save her honor.

It would be hard to find a passage in literature more eloquently simple, more dramatically sincere than this last paragraph; but the court remained hostile and Zola was sentenced to a year's imprisonment, plus a fine of three thousand francs. Appeals delayed his imprisonment until new evidence re-opened the Dreyfus case and both Dreyfus and Zola were partly exonerated. By the time Zola died in 1902 he was regarded as one of the great heroes of France, a champion of truth, "a moment in the conscience of man" as Anatole France said. Not until after Zola's death was Dreyfus's name completely cleared, when in 1906 the French Supreme Court of Appeals declared that he was totally innocent of all charges that had been made against him. He returned to military duty and served as a general during World War I. The case has now faded into history, but Zola's speech remains as an eloquent and brave stand in defense of principle.

Mahatma Gandhi

Perhaps the world has never known another man who carried so much strength of will-power and character in so small a body as Mohandas K. Gandhi (1869-1948). Shriveled and fragile in appearance, gentle and humble in manner, he nevertheless drew upon seemingly inexhaustible inner resources of energy and power.

Gandhi was born into a middle-class, middle-caste family in India. Educated in his native land and in London, he went in 1893 as a young lawyer to South Africa, where he remained most of the time for the next twenty years, gradually becoming more and more recognized as a leader of his people in their struggle for freedom and dignity. In 1914 Gandhi returned to India, where he soon rose to leadership as a dedicated crusader in behalf of human rights for all the peoples of India, whatever their caste, and where through his vast program of non-violent non-cooperation he worked towards the independence of India from British rule. By 1920 he was the recognized leader of the India National Congress, under whose auspices he traveled far and wide over the country making hundreds of speeches to frenzied crowds of tens of thousands of people. In 1922 he was arrested and charged with sedition for several articles published in his magazine, *Young India*. As his trial drew to a close in the crowded little courtroom of Ahmadabad, Gandhi was permitted to make a statement before receiving sentence. He had a written statement which he was prepared to read but first made some impromptu comments as follows:

Before I read this statement, I would like to state that I entirely endorse the learned Advocate General's remarks in connection with my humble self. I think that he was entirely fair to me in all the statements that he has made, because it is very true and I have no desire whatsoever to conceal from this court the fact that to preach disaffection toward the existing system of government has become almost a passion with me; and the learned Advocate General is also entirely in the right when he says that my preaching of disaffection did not commence with my connection with *Young India*, but that it commenced much earlier; and in the statement that I am about to read, it will be my painful duty to admit before this court that it commenced much earlier than the period stated by the Advocate General. It is the most painful duty with me, but I have to discharge that duty knowing the responsibility that rests upon my shoulders, and I wish to endorse all the blame that the learned

Advocate General has thrown on my shoulders, in connection with the Bombay occurrences, Madras occurrences, and the Chauri Chaura occurrences. Thinking over these deeply and sleeping over them night after night, it is impossible for me to dissociate myself from the diabolical crimes of Chauri Chaura or the mad outrages of Bombay. He is quite right when he says that as a man of responsibility, a man having received a fair share of education, having had a fair share of experience of this world, I should have known the consequences of every one of my acts. I know that I was playing with fire. I ran the risk, and if I was set free, I would still do the same. I have felt it this morning that I would have failed in my duty, if I did not say what I said here just now.

I wanted to avoid violence, I want to avoid violence. Nonviolence is the first article of my faith. It is also the last article of my creed. But I had to make my choice. I had either to submit to a system which I considered had done an irreparable harm to my country, or incur the risk of the mad fury of my people bursting forth, when they understood the truth from my lips. I know that my people have sometimes gone mad. I am deeply sorry for it and I am therefore here to submit not to a light penalty but to the highest penalty. I do not ask for mercy. I do not plead any extenuating act. I am here, therefore, to invite and cheerfully submit to the highest penalty that can be inflicted upon me for what in law is a deliberate crime and what appears to me to be the highest duty of a citizen. The only course open to you, the judge, is, as I am just going to say in my statement, either to resign your post or inflict on me the severest penalty, if you believe that the system and law you are assisting to administer are good for the people. I do not expect that kind of conversion, but by the time I have finished with my statement, you will perhaps have a glimpse of what is raging within my breast to run this maddest risk which a sane man can run.

Gandhi then read his prepared statement, reviewing in detail the many events that through the years had turned him from a "staunch loyalist and co-operator" to an "uncompromising disaffectionist and non-co-operator." To support a government and a system that allow terrible injustices to millions of people is evil, Gandhi explained, and therefore conscience compelled him to withdraw his support and advocate non-violent non-cooperation. He concluded his long written speech with the following comments, re-stating his hatred of violence and his advocacy of non-violence as a political tool and admitting his guilt according to the law:

I believe that I have rendered a service to India and England by showing in non-co-operation the way out of the unnatural state in which both are living. In my humble opinion, non-co-operation with evil is as much a duty as is co-operation with good. But in the past, non-co-operation has been deliberately expressed in violence to the evildoer. I am endeavoring to show to my country-men that violent non-co-operation only multiplies evil and that as evil can only be sustained by violence, withdrawal of support of evil requires complete abstention from violence. Nonviolence implies voluntary submission to the penalty for non-co-operation with evil. I am here, therefore, to invite and submit cheerfully to the highest penalty that can be inflicted upon me for what in law is a deliberate crime and what appears to me to be the highest duty of a citizen. The only course open to you, the judge, is either to resign your post, and thus dissociate yourself from evil if you feel that the law you are called upon to administer is an evil and that in reality I am innocent, or to inflict on me the severest penalty if you believe that the system and the law you are assisting to administer are good for the people of this country and that my activity is therefore injurious to the public weal.

Passing sentence on Gandhi, the judge confessed, was one of the most difficult judgments he had ever had to make. Clearly Gandhi was a cultured, educated, even saintly man, but clearly he also had defied the law of the land and must, said the judge, be treated as a criminal. Consequently he sentenced Gandhi to six years' imprison-ment. Gandhi said the sentence was as light as any judge could give under the circumstances—and thanked the court for being courteous to him. The people then came forward and fell sobbing at his feet, worshiping their hero. Gandhi comforted and encouraged them, calm and smiling, and then allowed himself to be led quietly to jail.

For twenty-five years Gandhi lived on to give countless speeches all over India, submitting again and again to imprisonment and self-imposed fasting in the long struggle to establish India and her millions of starving people as an independent nation. Finally his voice was stopped by an assassin's bullet fired from the gun of a Hindu nationalist 30 January 1948. Not everyone had agreed with Gandhi's policies and views, but all the world knew that it had lost one of the most quietly courageous men who ever lived. A few hours after Gandhi's death, Jawaharlal Nehru, then Prime Minister of India, spoke by radio to the grieving nation:

Friends and comrades, the light has gone out of our lives and there is darkness everywhere. I do not know what to tell you and how to say it. Our beloved leader, Bapu as we called him, the father of the nation, is no more. Perhaps I am wrong to say that. Nevertheless, we will not see him again as we have seen him for these many years. We will not run to him for advice and seek solace from him, and that is a terrible blow, not to me only, but to millions and millions in this country, and it is a little difficult to soften the blow by any other advice that I or anyone else can give you.

The light has gone out, I said, and yet I was wrong. For the light that shone in this country was no ordinary light. The light that has illumined this country for these many years will illumine this country for many more years, and a thousand years later that light will still be seen in this country and the world will see it and it will give solace to innumerable hearts. For that light represented the living truth . . . the eternal truths, reminding us of the right path, drawing us from error, taking this ancient country to freedom.

All this has happened when there was so much more for him to do. We could never think that he was unnecessary or that he had done his task. But now, particularly, when we are faced with so many difficulties, his not being with us is a blow most terrible to bear.

A madman has put an end to his life, for I can only call him mad who did it, and yet there has been enough of poison spread in this country during the past years and months, and this poison has had effect on people's minds. We must face this poison, we must root out this poison, and we must face all the perils that encompass us and face them not madly or badly but rather in the way that our beloved teacher taught us to face them. The first thing to remember now is that no one of us dare misbehave because we are angry. We have to behave like strong and determined people, determined to face all the perils that surround us, determined to carry out the mandate that our great teacher and our great leader has given us, remembering always that if, as I believe, his spirit looks upon us and sees us, nothing would displease his soul so much as to see that we have indulged in any small behavior or any violence.

So we must not do that. But that does not mean that we should be weak, but rather that we should in strength and in unity face all the troubles that are in front of us. We must hold together, and all our petty troubles and difficulties and conflicts must be ended in the face of this great disaster. A great disaster is a symbol to us to remember all the big things of life and forget the small things, of which we have thought too much. . . .

Tomorrow should be a day of fasting and prayer for all of us. . . . And while we pray, the greatest prayer that we can offer is to take a pledge to dedicate ourselves to the truth and to the cause for which this great countryman of ours lived and for which he has died.

Winston Churchill

Perhaps the greatest orator of the twentieth century, and surely one of the greatest world statesmen, was Winston Churchill, England's Prime Minister during World War II. After years of brilliant service, Churchill, then 66, was named Prime Minister in May 1940 and asked to form a new government, just as Hitler's massive troops were beginning to smash across the countries of Europe. His speeches during those first months as Prime Minister were so eloquent, so powerful that they electrified not only despairing, beleagured Britain but also the whole allied world. Here is his first speech as Prime Minister (13 May 1940), displaying not only his masterful control of words but also his magnetic energy and courage:

On Friday evening last I received His Majesty's commission to form a new administration. It was the evident wish and will of Parliament and the nation that this should include all parties, both those who supported the late Government and also the parties of the Opposition. I have completed the most important part of this task. A War Cabinet has been formed of five Members, representing, with the Opposition Liberals, the unity of the nation. The three party leaders have agreed to serve, either in the War Cabinet or in high executive office. The three fighting services have been filled. It was necessary that this should be done in one single day, on account of the extreme urgency and rigor of events. A number of other key positions were filled yesterday, and I am submitting a further list to His Majesty tonight. I hope to complete the appointment of the principal Ministers during tomorrow. The appointment of the other Ministers usually takes a little longer, but I trust that, when Parliament meets again, this part of my task will be completed, and that the administration will be complete in all respects.

I considered it in the public interest to suggest that the House should be summoned to meet today. Mr. Speaker agreed, and took the necessary steps, in accordance with the powers conferred upon him by the Resolution of the House. At the end of the proceedings today, the adjournment of the House will be proposed until Tuesday, May 21, with, of course, provision for earlier meeting if need be. The business to be considered during that week will be notified to Members at the earliest opportunity. I now invite the House, by the Resolution which stands in my name, to record its approval of the steps taken and to declare its confidence in the new Government.

To form an administration of this scale and complexity is a serious undertaking in itself, but it must be remembered that we are in the preliminary stage of one of the greatest battles in history, that we are in action at many points in Norway and in Holland, that we have to be prepared in the Mediterranean, that the air battle is continuous and that many preparations have to be made here at home. In this crisis I hope I may be pardoned if I do not address the House at any length today. I hope that any of my friends and colleagues, or former colleagues, who are affected by the political reconstruction, will make all allowance for any lack of ceremony with which it has been necessary to act. I would say to the House, as I said to those who have joined this Government: "I have nothing to offer but blood, toil, tears and sweat."

We have before us an ordeal of the most grievous kind. We have before us many, many long months of struggle and of suffering. You ask what is our policy? I will say: It is to wage war, by sea, land and air, with all our might and with all the strength that God can give us: to wage war against a monstrous tyranny, never surpassed in the dark, lamentable catalogue of human crime. That is our policy. You ask, What is our aim? I can answer in one word: Victory—victory at all costs, victory in spite of all terror, victory, however long and hard the road may be; for without victory, there is no survival. Let that be realized; no survival for the British Empire; no survival for all that the British Empire has stood for, no survival for the urge and impulse of the ages, that mankind will move forward towards its goal. But I take up my task with buoyancy and hope. I feel sure that our cause will not be suffered to fail among men. At this time I feel entitled to claim the aid of all, and I say, "Come, then, let us go forward together with our united strength."

Three weeks later (4 June 1940) Churchill gave another great speech, reporting the miracle of the Dunkirk evacuation, which rescued 335,000 French and British soldiers "out of the jaws of death and shame." Although eloquent in his praise of the heroism of the navy, army, and air force, he was quick to point out that "We must be very careful not to assign to this deliverance the attributes of victory," for "wars are not won by evacuations." Most of the speech outlines the relentless advance of the Nazi armies across the lands of Continental Europe, crushing whatever resistance stood in their path, and making necessary the evacuation at Dunkirk. Much of the speech is also concerned with strengthening the will of the British and French peoples to continue the fight. Churchill knew that an invasion of the British Isles was imminent, and his principal purpose as he closed the speech was to stir the people to unyielding courage:

I have, myself, full confidence that if all do their duty, if nothing is neglected, and if the best arrangements are made, as they are being made, we shall prove ourselves once again able to defend our island home, to ride out the storm of war, and to outlive the menace of tyranny, if necessary for years, if necessary alone. At any rate, that is what we are going to try to do. That is the resolve of His Majesty's Government—every man of them. That is the will of Parliament and the nation. The British Empire and the French Republic, linked together in their cause and in their need, will defend to the death their native soil, aiding each other like good comrades to the utmost of their strength. Even though large tracts of Europe and many old and famous states have fallen or may fall into the grip of the Gestapo and all the odious apparatus of Nazi rule, we shall not flag or fail. We shall go on to the end, we shall fight in France, we shall fight on the seas and oceans, we shall fight with growing confidence and growing strength in the air, we shall defend our island, whatever the cost may be, we shall fight on the beaches, we shall fight on the landing grounds, we shall fight in the fields and in the streets, we shall fight in the hills; we shall never surrender, and even if, which I do not for a moment believe, this island or a large part of it were subjugated and starving, then our Empire beyond the seas, armed and guarded by the British fleet, would carry on the struggle, until, in God's good time, the New World, with all its power and might, steps forth to the rescue and the liberation of the old.

One after another in those early months of the war the great speeches rolled off Churchill's golden tongue. America had not yet entered the conflict, France and the other countries of the Continent were already smashed, and Britain stood virtually alone. Worse still, her own defenses were far weaker than Churchill would admit publicly. The one thing Britain did have was Churchill's marvelous courage and eloquence which continued to stir bravery in all who listened. As a final example of the magnetic strength and eloquence of this amazing man, we print his speech of 18 June 1940:

During the first four years of the last war [World War I] the Allies experienced nothing but disaster and disappointment. . . . We repeatedly asked ourselves the question, "How are we going to win?" and no one was ever able to answer it with much precision, until at the end, quite suddenly, quite unexpectedly, our terrible foe collapsed before us, and we were so glutted with victory that in our folly we threw it away.

However. matters may go in France or with the French government or other French governments, we in this island and in the British Empire will never lose our sense of comradeship with the French people. . . . If final victory rewards our toils they shall share the gains—aye, and freedom shall be restored to all. We abate nothing of our just demands; not one jot or tittle do we recede. . . . Czechs, Poles, Norwegians, Dutch, Belgians, have joined their causes to our own. All these shall be restored.

What General Weygand called the Battle of France is over. I expect that the Battle of Britain is about to begin. Upon this battle depends the survival of Christian civilization. Upon it depends our own British life, and the long continuity of our institutions and our Empire. The whole fury and might of the enemy must very soon be turned on us. Hitler knows that he will have to break us in this island or lose the war. If we can stand up to him, all Europe may be free and the life of the world may move forward into broad, sunlit uplands. But if we fail, then the whole world, including the United States, including all that we have known and cared for, will sink into the abyss of a new Dark Age, made more sinister, and perhaps more protracted, by the lights of perverted science. Let us therefore brace ourselves to our duties, and so bear ourselves that, if the British Empire and its Commonwealth last for a thousand years, men will say, "This was their finest hour."

John F. Kennedy

During this century the world has known many eloquent, courageous leaders in addition to those already quoted. If we had space we could print speeches by President Woodrow Wilson, President Franklin D. Roosevelt, General Douglas MacArthur, General Charles De Gaulle, Chancellor Konrad Adenauer, Governor Adlai Stevenson and a number of other world leaders to illustrate further the power of words and the strength of character. Because these men and their views are still close to us, readers would undoubtedly disagree about their philosophies, but most would agree that in them were men of strength, courage, and sincerity.

As one final example we print the inaugural address of President John Fitzgerald Kennedy delivered 20 January 1961. President Kennedy also is still a controversial figure, but this speech has been recognized by almost everyone as both brilliant in phrase and rich in humanity. By personal affiliation I am politically a Republican and President Kennedy was a Democrat, but I am happy to pay tribute to the eloquence of this stirring speech, sealed less than two years later by the testimony of his own blood:

> We observe today not a victory of party but a celebration of freedom, symbolizing an end as well as a beginning, signifying renewal as well as change. For I have sworn before you and Almighty God the same solemn oath our forebears prescribed nearly a century and three-quarters ago.
>
> The world is very different now. For man holds in his mortal hands the power to abolish all forms of human poverty and all forms of human life. And yet the same revolutionary belief for which our forebears fought is still at issue around the globe, the belief that the rights of man come not from the generosity of the state but from the hand of God.
>
> We dare not forget today that we are the heirs of that first revolution. Let the word go forth from this time and place, to friend and foe alike, that the torch has been passed to a new generation of Americans, born in this century, tempered by war, disciplined by a hard and bitter peace, proud of our ancient heritage, and unwilling to witness or permit the slow undoing of these human rights to which this nation has always been committed, and to which we are committed today at home and around the world.
>
> Let every nation know, whether it wishes us well or ill, that we shall pay any price, bear any burden, meet any hardship, support any friend, oppose any foe to assure the survival and the success of liberty.

This much we pledge—and more.

To those old allies whose cultural and spiritual origins we share, we pledge the loyalty of faithful friends. United, there is little we cannot do in a host of co-operative ventures. Divided, there is little we can do, for we dare not meet a powerful challenge at odds and split asunder.

To those new states whom we welcome to the ranks of the free, we pledge our word that one form of colonial control shall not have passed away merely to be replaced by a far more iron tyranny. We shall not always expect to find them supporting our view. But we shall always hope to find them strongly supporting their own freedom, and to remember that, in the past, those who foolishly sought power by riding the back of the tiger ended up inside.

To those peoples in the huts and villages of half the globe struggling to break the bonds of mass misery, we pledge our best efforts to help them help themselves, for whatever period is required, not because the Communists may be doing it, not because we seek their votes, but because it is right. If a free society cannot help the many who are poor, it cannot save the few who are rich.

To our sister republics south of the border, we offer a special pledge: to convert our good words into good deeds, in a new alliance for progress, to assist free men and free governments in casting off the chains of poverty. But this peaceful revolution of hope cannot become the prey of hostile powers. Let all our neighbors know that we shall join with them to oppose aggression or subversion anywhere in the Americas. And let every other power know that this hemisphere intends to remain the master of its own house.

To that world assembly of sovereign states, the United Nations, our last best hope in an age where the instruments of war have far outpaced the instruments of peace, we renew our pledge of support: to prevent it from becoming merely a forum for invective, to strengthen its shield of the new and the weak, and to enlarge the area in which its writ may run.

Finally, to those nations who would make themselves our adversary, we offer not a pledge but a request: that both sides begin anew the quest for peace, before the dark powers of destruction unleashed by science engulf all humanity in planned or accidental self-destruction.

We dare not tempt them with weakness. For only when our arms are sufficient beyond doubt can we be certain beyond doubt that they will never be employed.

But neither can two great and powerful groups of nations take comfort from our present course—both sides overburdened by the cost of modern weapons, both rightly alarmed by the steady spread of the deadly atom, yet both racing to alter that uncertain balance of terror that stays the hand of mankind's final war.

So let us begin anew, remembering on both sides that civility is not a sign of weakness, and sincerity is always subject to proof. Let us never negotiate out of fear, but let us never fear to negotiate.

Let both sides explore what problems unite us instead of belaboring those problems which divide us.

Let both sides, for the first time, formulate serious and precise proposals for the inspection and control of arms, and bring the absolute power to destroy other nations under the absolute control of all nations.

Let both sides seek to invoke the wonders of science instead of its terrors. Together let us explore the stars, conquer the deserts, eradicate disease, tap the ocean depths and encourage the arts and commerce.

Let both sides unite to heed in all corners of the earth the command of Isaiah to "undo the heavy burdens . . . [and] let the oppressed go free."

And if a beachhead of co-operation may push back the jungle of suspicion, let both sides join in creating a new endeavor, not a new balance of power, but a new world of law, where the strong are just and the weak secure and the peace preserved.

All this will not be finished in the first one hundred days. Nor will it be finished in the first one thousand days, nor in the life of this Administration, nor even perhaps in our lifetime on this planet. But let us begin.

In your hands, my fellow citizens, more than mine, will rest the final success or failure of our course. Since this country was founded, each generation of Americans has been summoned to give testimony to its national loyalty. The graves of young Americans who answered the call to service surround the globe.

Now the trumpet summons us again—not as a call to bear arms, though arms we need; not as a call to battle, though embattled we are; but a call to bear the burden of a long twilight struggle, year in and year out, "rejoicing in hope, patient in tribulation," a struggle against the common enemies of man: tyranny, poverty, disease and war itself.

Can we forge against these enemies a grand and global alliance, North and South, East and West, that can assure a more fruitful life for all mankind? Will you join in that historic effort?

In the long history of the world, only a few generations have been granted the role of defending freedom in its hour of maximum danger. I do not shrink from this responsibility; I welcome it. I do not believe that any of us would exchange places with any other people or any other generation. The energy, the faith, the devotion which we bring to this endeavor will light our country and all who serve it, and the glow from that fire can truly light the world.

And so, my fellow Americans, ask not what your country can do for you; ask what you can do for your country.

My fellow citizens of the world, ask not what America will do for you, but what together we can do for the freedom of man.

Finally, whether you are citizens of America or citizens of the world, ask of us here the same high standards of strength and sacrifice which we ask of you. With a good conscience our only sure reward, with history the final judge of our deeds, let us go forth to lead the land we love, asking His blessing and His help, but knowing that here on earth God's work must truly be our own.

Eliza R. Snow

All of the preceding selections are excellent examples of that kind of serenity which results from courage combined with deep inner conviction and integrity—but all depict experiences in the lives of men. Because this book is intended especially for women readers, it seems desirable that at least one of the selections on serenity should explore the life and writings of a woman. This is not to suggest that the selections already used are inapplicable to women. Serenity, courage, integrity, peace of mind—these are qualities that may be shared equally by men and women. There is a special kind of serenity, however, which is probably best illustrated through the life of a woman.

Although women have not been in the forefront of history as dramatically as men, there are many noble, courageous, high-principled, faith-abiding women, both in and out of the Church, whose lives might be used to illustrate serenity. We have chosen for consideration one of our own LDS pioneer women, probably the most poetically gifted of all the pioneer women, and one of the great women leaders of all time in the Church—Eliza R. Snow.

The following information on Eliza R. Snow is excerpted from a booklet published at Brigham Young University several years ago for the dedication of the Eliza R. Snow Hall, one of the beautiful Heritage Halls for women students:

"From the age of twenty-nine when Eliza Roxey Snow was baptized into the Church, until the end of her long life in 1887, this practical daughter of Puritan forebears was concerned with furthering the cause of the Gospel by helping members of the Church to live more abundant lives. As organizer and executive, as writer and speaker, and as the first woman schoolteacher in the Church, she devoted her unusual energy and talents to stimulating active understanding of Gospel principles.

"Her marked intellectual ability was early recognized by her family, and she was given the best education available in her home state of Massachusetts. It was she who was selected by the Prophet Joseph to teach his 'family school'—both in Kirtland and Nauvoo. Her 'select school for young ladies' in Kirtland presented an opportunity for the education of girls not generally available at that time. But Sister Snow's ideas on education were never narrowly academic. She encouraged her students to become proficient in the domestic arts and was herself a skilled needlewoman. Most of all, however, she wanted the young people of the Church to recognize the need for schooling in the Gospel. In a poem addressed to 'parents in Zion' she states that education 'wisely given'—that is, education in eternal as well as earthly principles—is the 'richest fortune' which parents can leave their children.

"Eliza R. Snow had that rare understanding of young people which only great teachers possess. Only someone of such rare insight into youth could reach and inspire them, and yet carefully avoid the preaching which young people suspect or the pleading which embarrasses them.

"Apparently severe and uncompromising with herself, she showed no lack of tenderness and sympathy for the many who were less strong and who came to rely on her for spiritual and temporal sustenance. During the persecution in Missouri she was constantly engaged in caring for the sick and encouraging the weak. Even in the trying days following the martyrdom of Joseph and Hyrum, although almost an invalid herself, she again acted as nurse and counselor to those less fortunate. . . .

"She drove a team of oxen part way across the continent yet, despite her recurring illness, did not neglect to keep a detailed—and often sprightly—account of her journey. True to her trust as secretary of the first Relief Society in Nauvoo, she brought its 'Book of Records' with her to the Salt Lake Valley. In 1866 President Brigham Young called her to aid the bishops in organizing a Relief Society in every ward and branch of the Church. During the ensuing twenty-one years, as the General President of Relief Society, she faithfully performed this mission. In addition to presiding over the Relief Society, Eliza R. Snow stood at the head of the Young Women's MIA and the Primary Association until the year 1880. She was also in charge of the women's work in the Endowment House, superintendent of the Women's Store, and president of the Deseret Hospital.

"Born January 21, 1804, in Becket, Massachusetts—the second

girl in a family of seven children—young Eliza combined a fervent love of country with deep religious sensibility. . . .

"Today in the Church Eliza R. Snow is probably best remembered as the author of the poem 'O My Father,' which preaches the uniquely Mormon doctrine that we have a Mother as well as a Father in Heaven. Composed in 1843 while she was living with the Stephen Markhams, this poem was written out on a wooden chest—the only piece of furniture resembling a table which her room afforded. Such a setting seems appropriate for this hymn of practical aspiration, and it is typical of 'Aunt Eliza'—as she was affectionately known to thousands. She never lost herself in theological abstraction but viewed this life, serenely accepted and well-lived, as a foretaste of Heaven.

"Perhaps no other woman in the history of the Church had such a profound effect on so many of its leaders. She was sealed, that is married for time and eternity, to the Prophet Joseph Smith in June of 1842 and was a constant inspiration to him until his martyrdom. She was later married for time to Brigham Young, who relied on her to organize and integrate the women's activities for the entire Church. Her relationship to her brother, Lorenzo, the fifth president of the Church, was one of rare affection and tenderness. . . .

"Eliza R. Snow's vision of the role of women in the Church has left its imprint on all the auxiliary organizations in which women take a directing part. No poem which she has left us pleads so eloquently her love for the truth of the restored Gospel as does her life. To the women of the Church she is a symbol of selflessness— of complete devotion to the role which the Lord assigned her. At her funeral no word was used so often as 'Mother' to describe this childless woman. Apostle John W. Taylor suggested that if George Washington, who died without children, was entitled to be known as the Father of his Country, 'Aunt Eliza' deserved to be called the Mother of the Church. . . ."

As we study the poetry of Eliza R. Snow a century after it was written, it will probably seem somewhat old-fashioned to many readers today. The language tends to be flowery and a little stilted, and the poems lack the rich imagery and other artistic subtleties that appeal to contemporary poetic tastes. She was writing in the fashion of her day, and many of her poems were primarily sermons in verse.

But this is not to say that she is not an important writer. She wrote hundreds of poems, which considered as a group form an impressive body of writing.[4] The poems may be lacking in artistic sophistication, but they are rich in both human wisdom and religious faith, and through them we see the personality and character of a truly great woman—diligent, courageous, spiritual, idealistic, but also sensible, practical, realistic, forgiving, and, above all else, serene in the confidence of her faith in God.

Today Eliza R. Snow is best known as a poet through her hymns. In addition to "O My Father," our standard LDS Hymnbook contains twelve other hymns[5] by Sister Snow, including such favorites as "How Great the Wisdom and the Love," "Truth Reflects Upon Our Senses," "Behold the Great Redeemer Die," and the beautiful "Though Deepening Trials."[6]

Because these hymns are readily available, we will turn instead to Eliza R. Snow's hundreds of other poems for a sampling of her poetry. Altogether she published two full volumes of poems (in 1856 and 1877), plus dozens of other poems spread through lectures, journals, etc.

We shall examine first a small poem called "Some Good Things" which expresses the serenity of her faith. No matter what obstacles or disappointments one may encounter, no matter what other people may do or say, life can be filled with peace of mind if we will "lean upon the Lord" with a "steadfast, firm, decided mind":

---

[4]She also wrote many lectures, journals, etc., in addition to poems, including a beautifully simple *Story of Jesus.*

[5]These thirteen hymns may be found on the following pages in the hymnbook: "Think Not When You Gather to Zion," p. 21; "How Great the Wisdom and the Love," pp. 68, 316, and 358; "O My Father," pp. 138, 139, 270, and 336; "Thou Dost Not Weep Alone," p. 181; "The Time Is Far Spent," p. 184; "Truth Reflects Upon Our Senses," p. 188; "Awake, Ye Saints of God," p. 229; "Behold the Great Redeemer Die," p. 230; "Great Is the Lord, 'Tis Good to Praise," p. 234; "Again We Meet around the Board," p. 242; "O Awake! My Slumbering Minstrel," p. 268; "Though Deepening Trials," p. 285; "The Lord Imparted from Above," p. 298.

[6]There is also considerable evidence that Eliza R. Snow is the author of that beautifully stirring hymn "Praise to the Man Who Communed with Jehovah," which is listed in the hymnbook (pp. 147 and 326) as having been written by William W. Phelps. For evidence that Sister Snow is the correct author see pp. 234-238 of *Eliza R. Snow: An Immortal,* published in 1957 by the Nicholas G. Morgan Foundation.

Some Good Things

When from injustice' bitter cup
We're forc'd to drink the portion up,
And wait in silence heaven's reward,
'Tis *good* to lean upon the Lord.

When haplessly we're plac'd among
The venom of a lying tongue,
'Tis *good* to feel our spirits pure,
And our inheritance secure.

'Tis *good*, 'tis soothing to the mind,
If friends we cherish prove unkind,
And meet us with an angry mood,
To know we sought to do them good.

When pale-fac'd Envy seeks to fling
Across our path its envious sting,
'Tis *good* to know we never aim'd
To gain a prize that others claim'd.

When by unmerited demand
We bow beneath oppression's hand,
'Tis *good* within ourselves to know
That tides of fortune ebb and flow.

When persecution aims to blind
The judgment and pervert the mind,
'Tis *good* to know the path we've trod
Is sanction'd and approv'd of God.

When superstition's meagre form
Goes forth and stirs the wrathful storm,
'Tis *good* amid the blast to find
A steadfast, firm, decided mind.

When we are tossing to and fro
Amid the varying scenes below,
'Tis *good* to hope through Jesus' love
To share his glorious rest above.

'Tis *good* to live by every word
Proceeding from the mouth of God:
'Tis *good* His faithfulness to trust,
And freely own His precepts just.

This serene faith in God which was the main source of Eliza R. Snow's unceasing strength is further shown in several "psalms" which she wrote, including the following:

The Lord Is My Trust

Thou that didst create the heavens and the earth, the seas and the fountains of water, thou art my God.

Thou art the same—thou changest not, therefore I will not fear; for thy word will endure, and thy promises will surely be verified.

In thee have I put my trust; and I know in whom I have confided, and I shall not be confounded.

Though difficulties rise before me higher than the Himmaleh mountains, I will go forward; for thou, Lord, wilt open the way before me, and make straight paths for my feet.

When the billows of Change encompass me—when its surges dash furiously, and the foam thereof is nigh unto overwhelming, thy power will sustain me: I will smile at the rage of the tempest, and ride fearlessly and triumphantly across the boisterous ocean of circumstance.

Thy Spirit is better than the juice of the grape, thy approbation is preferable to the smiles of earthly friends, thy favor is richer than the finest gold, and thy wisdom transcendeth all human understanding.

Thy power is supreme, thy plans are founded in wisdom, thou wilt perform thy purposes and none can prevent.

The principles of thy kingdom are principles of truth, and truth is everlasting as thyself, therefore thy kingdom will stand, and those that abide its laws will come up before thee to dwell in thy presence.

I will adhere to thy statutes, I will abide the New and Everlasting Covenant, not counting my life dear unto me.

When the clouds of uncertainty gather upon the horizon, darker than the shades of midnight, when distrust is raising its standard over the broad field of expectation, thy word will dissipate every obstruction, and the *"testimony of Jesus"* will light up a lamp that will guide my vision through the portals of immortality, and communicate to my understanding the glories of the Celestial kingdom.

In another poem, called "Immortality," Sister Snow develops still further the theme that her faith derives above all else from the knowledge that life is eternal and that some day we may dwell again with those loved ones who have preceded us in death. Wealth, she explains in a poem called "My Bankrupt Bill," is not a matter of having money but of having the riches of the Gospel, just as poverty is not being without money but being without faith. Listen to a few lines from the middle of the poem:

'Tis true, we all may many wants endure.
But then, a saint of God is never poor;
One in whose soul the holy fire of God,
The light of truth, is richly shed abroad.
    What though he cannot claim one foot of land,
Nor yet one dime of currency command?
Altho' no gold and silver—he has got
A costly pearl, the purse-proud world has not,
    The peace of God abiding in the breast—

.   .   .   .

    Show me a saint that's poor and, once for all,
I'll show you one that is no saint at all;
He may be moneyless—Who has not been?
That, here, is neither poverty nor sin.
Leanness of soul and meagerness of thought—
A cherish'd barrenness of mind, is what
I should call poverty. . . .

In another poem, called "Contentment," Eliza R. Snow describes a peace of mind that is close to what we have called serenity— not contentment resulting from laziness or stupor or insensitivity or passive unawareness—but contentment that flows from a soul at peace with itself and with God:

Contentment

Contentment is wealth that I would not resign
For all the gold dust, ever found in the mine:
'Tis a boon so unearthly—a jewel so fair
That with crowns, thrones, and empires will never compare.
And I would not exchange it for beauty's fine grace
Nor all fickle attractions that time will erase:
Boasted honors and titles I freely despise,
When contrasted with this incomparable prize.

Would you feel in your bosom a music of soul,
Like the soft gliding stream's imperceptible roll?—
Clothe your mind with a sweetness surpassing the rose?
Fondly cherish the fortune, Contentment bestows.

What! that passive contentment that laziness screens,
Which recoils at the use of appropriate means?
That inactive content which can carelessly wait,
And leave objects adrift on the ocean of fate,
And not hazard an effort, nor reach forth a hand,
By the dint of exertion to bring them to land?
The cold stupor that reigns when the heart-strings are mute,
And which fills the warm bosom with feelings acute?

No; no: but the charm which spontaneously springs
From a view of the nature and order of things.
Not a torpid inertia, with pulses confin'd;
But a principle in, and controlling the mind—
That sweet placid compliance, which virtue inspires,
And which rigid necessity often requires.

Yes, that cheerful concurrence that heaves not a sigh
O'er the change-woven sceneries that time ushers by:
Which performs as a limner, when prospects grow pale,
And creates a bright lamp in obscurity's vale:
Which can smile at misfortune, and sport amid toil—
The dark-omen'd predictions of poverty foil:
Which extracts the rough poison from malice and hate—
That which draws from oppression its heaviest weight—
Wakes up speech in retirement and sportively sings,
In the midst of life's storms, inexpressible things:
Which presides over feeling, with power so strange,
That oft varying condition's divested of change.

If contentment's true impulse benignly imparts
Submission's sweet influence over our hearts,
Nine-tenths of the varied discomfitures here,
Recede in the distance, and rarely appear;
And whate'er of life's comforts are graciously given,
Are used with thanksgiving as blessings from heaven.

Harmonious communication and trust-filled understanding—
these meant a great deal to Eliza R. Snow. "Sweeter to me than
honey in the comb is the communion of congenial minds," she wrote
in a poem called "Confidence." Not very often does she speak
harshly of anyone, but occasionally she lashes out against those
who deceive and betray, "who pray like Abel and perform like Cain,"

who use "creamy words" to hide dishonesty. Note for example the opening lines of her poem "The Hypocrite and the Traitor":

> I hate hypocrisy—that velvet thing
> With silken lips, whence oily words flow out.
> 'Tis like a mildew in the social cup
> Of life—'tis worse than mould—'tis poison—'tis
> A worm disguised, that eats asunder the
> Most holy cords of confidence that bind
> In cordial fellowship the hearts of men.
> Kind words, with falsehood in them? Yes, how strange!
> Designed to please—and yet, they do not please,
> But sting, like vipers, into friendship's core.

In much this same indignant vein she harshly criticizes a type of woman, hopefully rare, whom she finds especially destructive:

The Tattler

> It has been said by some, that woman's heart
> Should never hate.
>   I know, the placid wreath
> Of gentleness, is beautiful upon
> The female brow; and that the pure, white wand
> Of innocence, by women wielded, has
> A salutary potency, that's far
> Superior to arbitrary power—
> That in her bosom, love's sweet mellow tones
> Are more congenial to the sphere which heav'n
> Design'd for her; than hatred's bitterness.
>
> I know the worth of woman's rectitude:
> It is the fairest gem upon the crest
> Of social life: and I would not presume
> To step beyond the sacred halo of
> Propriety. But there's *one character*
> I even *dare to hate.* And e'en in this
> Age of effeminacy, is there who
> Would *say*—would *think* it is a crime to hate
> The Tattler, whose unhallow'd business seems,
> To wake up nonsense and to stir up strife?
>
> And after all, I feel my heart relax,
> And pity is preponderating in

My breast. I pity ev'ry human form,
Degraded with that most detestable,
And most ignoble trait. Whose head is but
A vacuum where vanity presides,
And sits enthron'd o'er pompous nothingness:
Where, if reflection chance to come, she finds
No seat—no resting place—no lamp to shine
Upon her path: but like a traveler,
When lost in some dark spacious catacomb,
Amid the mould'ring heaps, to stumble o'er
Unconscious matter, without path or guide;
She's lost in everlasting hopelessness.

Wretched propensity—and wretched the
Possessor of this bane of social life!
Whose soul, if soul is there at all, must be
Unto non-entity so near allied,
As to require a microscopic pow'r
To swell it into visibility.

But while I pity the *possessor*, if
I should not *hate*, I surely may *despise*
The *character*, the mean propensity,
'Tis falsehood's vehicle, and slander's tool
To throw dark shadows over innocence,
And magnify misfortune into fault.
It often serpentinely creeps into
The sanctuary of domestic life,
And with the sacred key of confidence,
Draws out the secrets of the drawing room,
And puts them on the morning breeze afloat.

I hope I never shall commit a crime
Of such enormous magnitude, as to
Subject me to endure that frown of heav'n.
The torment of the Tattler's senseless tongue.

I'd rather live in solitude, amid
The deep impervious wilds, and listen to
The silent speech of Nature; and regale
My spirit with the music of the breeze.

As a final sampling of Eliza R. Snow's many poems, we turn
to one in which she outlines what she feels is the proper role for
a woman. Comfort, compassion, understanding, encouragement, wise

counsel, faith, fortitude—these are the special gifts that a woman can bestow on those she loves:

What Is, and What Is Not for Woman

'Tis not for her to plough the deep,
　And gather pearls from ocean's bed;
Or scale the rugged mountain's steep,
　For laurel wreaths to deck her head.
She gathers pearls of other name
　Than those the ocean's bosom yields—
Fair laurels never known to fame,
　She culls from wisdom's golden fields:

'Tis not for her to face the foe
　Amid the cannon's thund'ring blaze;
Or shudder at the winds that blow
　Tremendous gales in torrid seas.
But there are foes of other form—
　Of other aspect, she should quell;
And whisper music to the storm,
　When seas of passion rudely swell.

'Tis not for her to lead the van—
　To be ensconced in Chair of State,
To legislate 'twixt man and man—
　Nations and laws to regulate.
'Tis hers to fan the sacred fire
　Of manhood's true nobility—
The heart of nations to inspire
　With patriotism and liberty.

'Tis hers, with heav'nly influence
　To wield a mighty power divine—
To shield the path of innocence
　And virtue's sacred worth define.
'Tis hers to cultivate the germs
　Of all the faculties for good,
That constitute the Godlike forms
　Of perfect man and womanhood.

'Tis hers the sunbeam to sustain
　Amid misfortune's chilling breath—
To silence grief—to solace pain—
　To soothe and cheer the bed of death.

His pathway in the battle lies—
  He should not fear the raging flood;
Give man the breast-plate courage plies,
  But give to woman, *fortitude*.

Index of References to Authors

Index of Selections Quoted